REDEFINING PILGRIMA<

Compostela International Studies in Pilgrimage History and Culture

Series Editor: Antón M. Pazos

Instituto de Estudios Gallegos 'Padre Sarmiento',
CSIC (Spanish National Research Council),
Santiago de Compostela, Spain.

This series deals with the universal phenomenon of pilgrimage, understood in a wide sense, making available the latest research sponsored by the IEGPS (Spanish National Research Council, CSIC). It focuses on historical, cultural, political and religious aspects of the subject, prioritizing multidisciplinary and diverse approaches and analyses, with volumes covering historical periods from the medieval to the modern and a world-wide geographical range.

Redefining Pilgrimage

New Perspectives on Historical and Contemporary Pilgrimages

Edited by

ANTÓN M. PAZOS
Instituto de Estudios Gallegos 'Padre Sarmiento', CSIC, Spain

Routledge
Taylor & Francis Group

LONDON AND NEW YORK

First published 2014 by Ashgate Publishing

2 Park Square, Milton Park, Abingdon, Oxfordshire OX14 4RN
711 Third Avenue, New York, NY 10017

Routledge is an imprint of the Taylor & Francis Group, an informa business

First issued in paperback 2018

British Library Cataloguing in Publication Data
A catalogue record for this book is available from the British Library

The Library of Congress has cataloged the printed edition as follows:
Redefining pilgrimage : new perspectives on historical and contemporary pilgrimages / edited by Antón M. Pazos.
    pages cm. -- (Compostela international studies in pilgrimage history and culture)
 Includes bibliographical references and index.
 ISBN 978-1-4094-6823-3 (hardcover)
 1. Pilgrims and pilgrimages. I. Pazos, Antón M., editor.
 BL619.P5R43 2014
 203'.51--dc23

2014013550

ISBN 978-1-4094-6823-3 (hbk)
ISBN 978-1-138-54621-9 (pbk)

Printed in the United Kingdom
by Henry Ling Limited

Contents

List of Tables

To Professor José Andrés Gallego on his 70th birthday.

Notes on Contributors

Ellen Badone holds a PhD in Anthropology from the University of California Berkeley and is Professor in the Department of Anthropology and Department of Religious Studies, McMaster University, Hamilton, Ontario, Canada.

Linda Kay Davidson first walked the Camino de Santiago while preparing her doctorate at Indiana University (received in 1980). She has taught in a number of American universities and is the co-author of several books on pilgrimage.

Jackie Feldman holds a PhD in Religious Studies from the Hebrew University in Jerusalem and is Associate Professor of Anthropology in the Department of Sociology and Anthropology, Ben Gurion University of the Negev (Israel), and Head of the Esther and Sidney Rabb Center for Holocaust and Revival Studies.

David M. Gitlitz holds a PhD in Romance Languages from Harvard University and is Professor Emeritus of Hispanic Studies at the University of Rhode Island (United States).

George Greenia holds a PhD in Romance Languages from the University of Michigan. He is Professor of Hispanic Studies and Medieval and Renaissance Studies, and Founder of the Institute for Pilgrimage Studies at the College of William and Mary in Virginia (United States).

Paul Hollander, who was born in Budapest, Hungary, holds a PhD in Sociology from Princeton University. He is Professor Emeritus in the Department of Sociology, University of Massachusetts, Amherst and Associate of the Davis Center for Russian and Eurasian Studies at Harvard University. He is the author of *Political Pilgrims* (first published in 1981).

Brian Kolodiejchuk, MC holds an MA in Philosophy from the University of Manitoba, Canada, MDiv in Theology from St Joseph's Seminary, New York, and a PhD in Organizational Psychology from the Saybrook Institute, San

Francisco. He is Postulator of the Cause of Canonization of Mother Teresa of Kolkata and Superior General of the Missionaries of Charity Fathers.

Jeanne Kormina is Professor of Anthropology and Religious Studies in the Department of Sociology, Higher School of Economics in St Petersburg, Russia. Her books in Russian include *Rituals of Departure to Military Service in Late Imperial Russia* (2005) and *Dreams of the Mother of God*, co-edited with S. Shtyrkov and A. Panchenko (2006). She has also published chapters and articles in Russian and in English on such topics as Orthodox pilgrimage, veneration of new saints, social memory and charismatic Christianity in contemporary Russia.

Darius Liutikas holds a PhD in Sociology from the University of Vilnius and is an academic researcher at the Lithuanian Social Research Centre. His main research interests are pilgrimage, tourism and sacred spaces, and he is Chairman of the Community of Lithuanian Pilgrims.

Alfonsas Motuzas holds a PhD in Musicology and a Habilition in Ethnology. He is Professor at the Lithuanian University of Educational Sciences (Vilnius) and at Vytautas Magnus University (Kaunas). He is also a member of the Lithuanian Catholic Academy of Sciences.

Antón M. Pazos holds a PhD in History and a PhD in Theology from the University of Navarra. He is President of the CIHEC and Vice-director of the Instituto de Estudios Gallegos 'Padre Sarmiento' of the Spanish National Research Council (CSIC), in Santiago de Compostela.

Introduction

Antón M. Pazos

When we speak of today's panorama of pilgrimages, as we do in this book, it leads almost inevitably to a discussion of what is and what is not a pilgrimage, and to an awareness that today's world of pilgrimages is changing as much as the pilgrims themselves. Traditional pilgrimages have undergone a systematic process of change, as if they were in fact industrial products, to adapt to new times. Indeed, we can see that public planners treat them as an economic activity in the service sector. And, as with any product, they can be improved or adapted to the necessities of new users, always in search of a better return. In the first instance, the aim is usually greater economic profitability, which is also an aim of religious promoters at pilgrimage destinations. At other times, a more spiritual profitability is sought, and, in some cases, a pilgrimage may be adapted to find a connection with a new religious sensibility. For one reason or another, many of the old pilgrimage routes, like those recently established or re-established, have been under constant renovation and change for some decades.

There are very significant universal examples. Perhaps the most spectacular would be the Way of St James (el Camino de Santiago), especially meaningful here because this series is named after it. The Way has gone from being walked by few but active pilgrims (both culturally and religiously) in the first decades of the twentieth century, to today's hundreds of thousands of walkers – who are, in many cases, simply walkers. They do not see, they do not hear, they do not feel. They only walk from one shelter to another for the whole journey, trying to take each step as quickly as possible and resting for the entire journey in a shelter without ever seeing the incredibly significant works of art around them. The old adage about the traveller on the European circuit applies perfectly to them: if today is Tuesday, this is Belgium. For these pilgrims, the relationship to the land, artistic sensibility, and information that can intellectually enrich their pilgrimage are irrelevant. But everyone has to eat and so, albeit very modestly, the goal of revitalizing the small villages has been fulfilled. In any case, that would require an analysis more in tune with real profitability, incorporating into the inquiry the enormous cost that the promotion and maintenance of the Way itself entails.

Logically, the large increase in the number of pilgrims is also reflected in the pilgrimage itself: during Holy Years – when the Feast of St James falls on a Sunday – it is not unusual to see enormous queues at the cathedral in order that the faithful can give the traditional embrace to the image of the Apostle, while the grave – in theory, the true destination of the pilgrimage – attracts far fewer visitors.

Obviously, a change in the type of pilgrim also changes the pilgrimage itself, making it more touristy, more exotic or, possibly, more spiritual, but with a more contemporary and individualistic spirituality, with pilgrims in search of themselves and personal transformation. It is almost like therapy, a personal *metanoia* resulting from the difficulties and reflections which have arisen during the greatest journey on foot that they have ever undertaken in their lives.

The Jacobean model, moreover, has been replicated in faraway places, such as on the island of Shikoku, Japan, where the ancient pilgrimage to the 88 Buddhist temples has undergone a process of modernization – including the removal of images or votive offerings that could offend contemporary sensibility[1] – and which has revitalized the circuit while perhaps losing the richness it brought the primitive pilgrim who used to frequent them. In any case, the Shikoku pilgrimage has the advantage that the pilgrim must visit the temples. The Way of St James can be done with no obligation to visit anything, from beginning to end.

Certain long-since defunct routes have also been revived, such as the Via Francigena in Italy, from Canterbury to Rome – declared part of the European Institute of Cultural Routes[2] – or the pilgrimage to Trondheim,[3] restored in 1997, nearly five centuries after it was abandoned, and which today heads a thriving network of pilgrim circuits in a country with a Lutheran majority. At the same time, other pilgrimages have appeared or have been invented. Some are created to keep the memory of significant acts alive. Others, as in past centuries, are based around the grave of a revered body. Not all stand the test of time: some, despite their initial success, either spontaneous or forced, have failed. But

---

[1]　As expounded in one of the International Colloquia Compostela by Ian Reader, long-time Shikoku researcher, but not published in this volume.

[2]　The Via Francigena website highlights that it forms a part of the European Institute of Cultural Routes, 'like the Way of St James': http://www.viafrancigena.com/fra_fram.htm (accessed 22 February 2013).

[3]　And whose official web-page also places it in relation to the Way of St James: http://www.viafrancigena.com/fra_fram.htm (accessed 22 February 2013).

the important point is that this is a growing phenomenon involving more and more people, and one which can range from the very local to the universal.

In this book, as across the series, we have sought a variety of approaches, as we strongly believe that pilgrimages lend themselves well to multidisciplinary study. And we have focused on the two clearest types of changing pilgrimages: those by definition new, and the traditional, those undergoing a process of change. The combination allows us to get somewhat closer to what could be the redefinition of pilgrimage in the twenty-first century, and that itself deserves thorough examination. Notwithstanding the fact that each year there are more and more pilgrimages, we could be witnessing at the same time the end of what has always been understood by the term pilgrimage, a term that now runs the risk of losing its meaning. Of course, expanding the concept to include everything that involves a movement towards some transcendental objective in its basic sense, something distinct from the everyday, could confuse the possible study of the phenomenon. All the researchers in this volume have recognized this problem and attempt to provide more or less adequate responses, but have ended up considering as pilgrims all those who 'go' from one place to another. The term may yet need to be specified or defined further, though maybe not as much as the oft-cited definition by Dante, pointing out that the pilgrim is only someone who goes to or from Santiago. However, in the same text, the Florentine poet also accepts the more universal sense of the term: anyone going from one place to another in the thirteenth century can call themselves, and do indeed seem to have called themselves, pilgrims.[4]

One solution, apparent in several of the chapters collected here, is to invent new terms or hybrid words to describe the large stream of pilgrims who are also tourists or travellers or vice versa. In any case, a redefinition based on the motives of pilgrimage, or at least the principal motive, would prove enlightening. Today, both the new and the classical pilgrimages, and those who participate in them, have very diverse motives: religious, cultural, political or geo-mystical. Perhaps the only direct categories we can apply are ultimately conventional and non-conventional pilgrimage. At any rate, it is an irrefutable fact that both have

---

[4]   'E dissi "peregrini" secondo la larga significazione del vocabulo; ché peregrini si possono intendere in due modi, in uno largo e in uno stretto: in largo, in quanto è peregrino chiunque è fuori de la sua patria; in modo stretto non s'intende peregrino se non chi va verso la casa di sa' Iacopo o riede'. 'I say pilgrims according to the broadest sense of the term, as pilgrims can be understood in two ways, one general and the other strict. In the general sense, a pilgrim is anyone that is outside of their own land; in the strict sense a pilgrim is not understood to be a pilgrim unless he goes to or from the house of St James' (Dante Alighieri, *Vita Nuova*, XL, ed. M. Barbi, Firenze, 1931).

experienced phenomenal growth, as, in parallel, so too have the numerous studies, books and series dedicated to them. The approach in the following pages explores the births and rebirths of these new and old pilgrimages, from the general to the specific.

Ellen Badone opens the volume with a discussion in two distinct parts on the state of the question, supported by an excellent review of recent literature. In the first part, she proposes a theoretical framework for understanding sacred journeys. It is certainly a personal framework which can be shared and discussed, but it is useful in reflecting on the precise concept of pilgrimage. In the second part, she examines the main anthropological and sociological keys to interpreting the phenomenon which have been proposed in publications of the last 30 years concerning tourism and pilgrimages. Her chapter is a commendable effort at ordering and classifying the discussions of the last decades and will undoubtedly be of great value to those studying pilgrimages from a sociological or anthropological perspective.

A journey through the jungle of the new – and not so new – pilgrimages is represented by the work of David M. Gitlitz, author of a broad encyclopaedia of pilgrimages, published with a similar title in 2002.[5] The elements of pilgrimages have varied over the ages and across distinct cultures, usually with a strong religious component. Recently, religious territories have been flooded with pilgrims and any more or less significant circuit has come to be known as a pilgrimage. The analysis is based on a study of the fundamental elements found in any contemporary pilgrimage, namely, the place, the journey and its significance.

After these broad chapters, two studies address what we could call lines of pilgrimage; that is, diverse pilgrimages that are variations on the same concept. The first, by George Greenia, studies the emergence of epic or historical pilgrimage in the United States. A rediscovery of the roots of the nation has led to the creation of historical representations of events, relevant to different religious or ethnic groups. They reflect the participatory spirit of the American dream, as the historic circuits themselves are reconstructed.

The work of Paul Hollander, a respected specialist in political studies, returns to the mythological and transcendental perception of a 'new world', as experienced by intellectuals who visited Communist countries in the past century. The intellectual's amazement at Soviet achievements can be compared to a believer entering paradise. And it was, with propagandistic intention,

---

[5]   Together with Linda K. Davidson: L.K. Davidson and D.M. Gitlitz, *Pilgrimage: From the Ganges to Graceland: An Encyclopaedia* (Santa Barbara: ABC-CLIO, 2002).

certainly, but with the heightened responsibility of someone who has seen or touched a perfect reality, surpassing and transcending it.

The next two chapters analyse pilgrimages that we could also call political, but which have precise and defined objectives. Jackie Feldman, well known for his work on official Israeli pilgrimages to the Polish concentration camps,[6] introduces us to a different type of pilgrimage, those to 'negative sacred sites'. This classification applies quite well to the official expeditions that young Israelis make to Poland to finalize their media studies. The chapter analyses the objectives set by the State of Israel to strengthen the defensive patriotism of these young people, and the psychological and expository methods applied to these expeditions.

The work of Darius Liutikas and Alfonsas Motuzas also analyses a political pilgrimage, in this case, the resistance of the Lithuanian Catholics, initially towards Russian autocracy, and later to Soviet totalitarianism. Generation after generation of Lithuanian Catholics not only make pilgrimages to the Hill of Crosses but also replace those crosses that were destroyed time and again by the political enemy. It is a case in which the pilgrims themselves form not only part of the pilgrimage, but also transform the place to which they make their pilgrimage. Without the flood of pilgrims who, generation after generation, replanted crosses, the site itself would have disappeared. It is self-constructed by the pilgrim but it can also be destroyed if the contribution of the pilgrim is trivialized, as is beginning to happen. Leaving a cross on the hill can be transformed from a heroic testament into a mere touristic ritual, as suggested by the stalls selling crosses along the route.

Finally, two traditional pilgrimages are examined, both recent, although from two different religious backgrounds. Jeanne Kormina analyses the Russian tradition of the Living Saints, powerfully attractive personalities whose influence is reinforced many times by the miracles attributed to them by their devoted followers. Obviously this is not exclusive to the world of Russian Orthodoxy – for the Catholic world it is sufficient to mention Padre Pio of Pietrelcina – but it is characteristic of it.

Brian Kolodiejchuk takes a look at the story of Mother Teresa of Calcutta, showing us what we can consider the birth, today, of a traditional pilgrimage. The journey, the popular demonstrations, and the goal of this newly-born pilgrimage could be transposed perfectly to any one of the classical pilgrimages

---

[6] His essential work is *Above the Death Pits, Beneath the Flag: Youth Voyages to Poland and the Performance of Israeli National Identity* (New York: Berghahn Books, 2008).

centuries ago: faithful devotees marching towards a hallowed tomb surrounded by the aura of sanctity. The novelty is that the pilgrims come from all religions.

The book concludes with the work of Linda Kay Davidson on the evolution of the Way of St James in recent decades; a path whose transformation the author has followed not only theoretically but practically, having travelled the journey regularly during the years in question.

As can be seen, the theme and focus of the collected chapters is certainly varied but serve to cover the book's purpose and demonstrate the almost continuous reprocessing which is taking place in the world of today's pilgrimages.

Chapter 1

Conventional and Unconventional Pilgrimages: Conceptualizing Sacred Travel in the Twenty-First Century

Ellen Badone

This chapter represents a journey towards a new theoretical framework for understanding sacred travel, both historical and contemporary. At the point of departure is an outline of ideas about directions for that journey. Then follows some 'back-tracking' in order to review a number of the key anthropological and sociological works on pilgrimage and tourism published since the 1970s, before returning to my own framework as the destination at the end of the chapter.[1]

Human beings are more mobile at the beginning of the twenty-first century than at any other period in human history. Much of this mobility is involuntary, as in the case of the displacement of refugees, forced migrations, or travel arising from economic necessity. Nor does everyone have the luxury of being able to choose mobility. Depending on one's social class, gender and/ or ethnicity, opportunities for travel may be constrained. Nonetheless, travel is characteristic of contemporary society, and much of this travel *is* undertaken voluntarily. Why then do people travel by choice in the twenty-first century, and why did they do so in the past? There is no single, all-embracing answer to these questions, but a possible approach is to focus on one facet of an answer, by drawing attention to the ways in which social actors seek and construct meaning and value through connections with distant destinations. Here the meticulous scholarship and wide-ranging cross-cultural review of ethno-historical, archaeological and historical sources by Mary Helms shows that a fascination with distant places and the valorization of the things that come from them is not

[1] Special thanks to Sharon Roseman, and colleagues at the Centre for Ethnography, University of Toronto, Scarborough, for comments on earlier drafts of this chapter.

a new phenomenon, nor one restricted to any particular cultural tradition.[2] In *Ulysses' Sail*, Helms documents evidence for the ideological significance of space and geographic distance in non-industrial societies. She shows, for example, that esoteric knowledge was prized and sought out through travel by Australian aboriginal groups, indigenous peoples in South America, and Islamic scholars in West Africa. Likewise, in T'ang Dynasty China, sandalwood, exotic spices and precious stones from distant sources were prized by the imperial court, as were Buddhist scriptural texts and relics brought from holy places in India.[3] In these and countless other examples, objects perceived to be of heightened aesthetic value, or ideas perceived to be associated with heightened spiritual truth, were obtained from distant sources and 'brought home'.

A similar process underlies much voluntary travel, both today and in the past. Social actors, especially those with economic resources, travel to places where perceived 'goods' are believed to be located. These 'goods' may be tangible: fine food or wine, unique items of material culture, artistic or architectural treasures – or intangible: health, escape from stress, or religious enlightenment. Note the use of the qualifiers 'perceived' and 'believed'. Whether travellers actually obtain the 'goods' for which they set out on their journeys is a separate issue from the motivation for their travels.

Following this line of reasoning, both pilgrimage and tourism can be considered related forms of voluntary travel. Some sites of pilgrimage, such as Fatima or Mecca, are associated with established religions. Others, like Gettysburg[4] or Graceland,[5] are unconnected to formal religious institutions. The term pilgrimage is used here with reference to travel to both types of sites, 'conventional pilgrimage' being proposed for travel to sites connected with religious institutions, and 'unconventional pilgrimage' for travel to sites not associated with established religious traditions. Unconventional pilgrimage would, therefore, include many phenomena frequently subsumed under the category of tourism. Hence, not only Pre's Rock, the roadside memorial in

---

[2]   M.W. Helms, *Ulysses' Sail: An Ethnographic Odyssey of Power, Knowledge and Geographical Distance* (Princeton: Princeton University Press, 1988), p. 72.

[3]   Helms, *Ulysses' Sail*, pp. 124–5.

[4]   C.M. Cameron and J.B. Gatewood, 'Battlefield Pilgrims at Gettysburg National Military Park', *Ethnology*, 43/3 (2004), pp. 193–216.

[5]   E. Doss, 'Rock and Roll Pilgrims: Reflections on Ritual, Religiosity, and Race at Graceland', in P.J. Margry (ed.), *Shrines and Pilgrimage in the Modern World: New Itineraries into the Sacred* (Amsterdam: Amsterdam University Press, 2008), pp. 123–41; C. King, 'His Truth Goes Marching On: Elvis Presley and the Pilgrimage to Graceland', in I. Reader and T. Walter (eds), *Pilgrimage in Popular Culture* (London: Macmillan, 1993), pp. 92–112.

Oregon to long-distance runner Steve Prefontaine, falls into this category[6] but also places like Ground Zero[7] and even travel with a less overtly 'spiritual' dimension, such as a week spent relaxing and sunbathing at a Caribbean resort. In this chapter, religion is viewed through the lenses of Geertz and Durkheim: as a social and individual endeavour to interpret experience in ways that are perceived to be meaningful, and as an effort to overcome the isolation of the self through connections with persons, values and communities which possess the ability to transcend, elevate and empower the individual. Given this perspective, 'religion' is not restricted to the domain of the divine, the supernatural, or to any particular moral code. Moreover, the category 'religion' includes what some other researchers and many popular commentators call 'the spiritual'.

In this formulation, touristic journeys in search of recreation – the re-creation of the self by engaging in activities that are believed to promote health and/or relieve the drudgery of mundane labour – are both 'religious' and 'pilgrimages'. Perhaps the definitions of these terms will be perceived as excessively broad and inclusive. However, rigid distinctions between pilgrimage and tourism derive from an unreflective perception that tourism is a petty and hedonistic activity; that it is 'mere tourism' and that tourist destinations are 'kitschy' and fake rather than noble, intellectual and spiritually enlightening. We should recognize these critiques as situated in value judgments that define mass or popular pleasures as being less valuable than those of elites. Instead of engaging in such class-based distinctions of taste,[8] both pilgrimage and tourism are approached as products of ongoing processes of cultural construction that involve a dialectical interplay between the distant and the familiar through which travellers seek perceived meaning and value.

Any genealogy of anthropological approaches to pilgrimage must start with the work of Victor and Edith Turner, who saw pilgrimage as a 'characteristic type of liminality in cultures ideologically dominated by the "historical" or "salvation" religions'.[9] The Turners envisaged pilgrimage as comparable in some

---

[6]   D. Wojcik, 'Pre's Rock: Pilgrimage, Ritual and Runners: Traditions at the Roadside Shrine for Steve Prefontaine', in Margry, *Shrines and Pilgrimage*, pp. 201–37.

[7]   J. Selby, 'The Politics of Pilgrimage: The Social Construction of Ground Zero', in W.H. Swatos (ed.), *On the Road to Being There: Studies in Pilgrimage and Tourism in Late Modernity* (Leiden: Brill, 2006), pp. 159–85; M. Sturken, 'The Aesthetics of Absence: Rebuilding Ground Zero', *American Ethnologist*, 31/3 (2004), pp. 311–25.

[8]   P. Bourdieu, *Distinction: A Social Critique of the Judgement of Taste* (Cambridge, MA: Harvard University Press, 1984).

[9]   V. Turner and E.L.B. Turner, *Image and Pilgrimage in Christian Culture: Anthropological Perspectives* (New York: Columbia University Press, 1978), p. 3.

respects to the tribal rites of initiation they had studied in African contexts. Like rites of passage, the Turners claimed that pilgrimage involved:

> release from mundane structure; homogenization of status, simplicity of dress and behavior; *communitas*; ordeal; reflection on the meaning of basic religious and cultural values; ritualized enactment of correspondences between religious paradigms and shared human experiences ... movement from a mundane center toward a sacred periphery which suddenly, transiently, becomes central for the individual, an *axis mundi* of his faith; movement itself, a symbol of *communitas* ... as against *stasis*, which represents structure.[10]

However, the liminality of pilgrimage, according to the Turners, is assumed voluntarily, unlike the obligatory liminality of rites of passage, and if the pilgrim undergoes a type of initiation, it is 'to a deeper level of religious participation', rather than necessarily to an elevated social status.[11]

The second major landmark along the route of the anthropological study of pilgrimage came in the form of *Contesting the Sacred*, edited by John Eade and Michael Sallnow.[12] If indeed, prior to this publication of 1991, the anthropological study of pilgrimage was, as Eade and Sallnow have suggested, 'in its infancy', then *Contesting the Sacred* could be seen as inciting the field to adolescent rebellion.[13] Twenty years later, pilgrimage has emerged as a central, cross-cultural theme in anthropological research, both in terms of its contributions to theory and in numbers of ethnographic studies. Now indeed, we might say that the anthropological study of pilgrimage is in its prime, having weathered its fair share of mid-life crises.

In their introduction, Eade and Sallnow challenged the Turnerian paradigm of *communitas* and called for the recognition of pilgrimage as an arena for competing discourses and conflict.[14] In keeping with the postmodern, deconstructionist spirit of the crisis of representation of the period during which they wrote, Eade and Sallnow protested against the 'formulation of ever more inclusive, and consequently ever more vacuous, generalizations'.[15] Instead, they called for 'the examination of the specific peculiarities' of the construction of

---

[10]   Turner and Turner, *Image and Pilgrimage*, p. 34.

[11]   Turner and Turner, *Image and Pilgrimage*, pp. 14–15.

[12]   J. Eade and M.J. Sallnow (eds), *Contesting the Sacred: The Anthropology of Christian Pilgrimage* (London: Routledge, 1991).

[13]   Eade and Sallnow, *Contesting the Sacred*, p. 26.

[14]   Eade and Sallnow, *Contesting the Sacred*, p. 2.

[15]   Eade and Sallnow, *Contesting the Sacred*, p. 9.

individual pilgrimages in their historic and cultural contexts.[16] They also argued against the assumptions they identified as central to the Turnerian model, namely that the experience of pilgrims and the meaning of sacred centres are predetermined, homogeneous and universal. In a much quoted and disputed statement, which to some extent they later repudiated in the Introduction to the second edition of *Contesting the Sacred*,[17] Eade and Sallnow claimed that:

> the power of a shrine ... derives in large part from its character almost as a religious void, a ritual space capable of accommodating diverse meanings and practices ... a vessel into which pilgrims devoutly pour their hopes, prayers and aspirations.[18]

They also suggested that the coordinates of person, place and text could provide a useful framework for examining the particularities of specific pilgrimage destinations,[19] an approach skilfully illustrated by the papers in their volume, including those by McKevitt[20] on Padre Pio (person), Eade[21] on Lourdes (place), and Bowman[22] on Jerusalem (text). To this triad, anthropologist Simon Coleman and art historian John Elsner added a fourth term, movement, in their 1995 book, *Pilgrimage Past and Present in the World Religions*. As they argued, movement – both to and within sacred centres – distinguishes pilgrimage from other types of ritual.[23] Significantly, both *Contesting the Sacred* and Coleman and Elsner's volume had their origins in a 1988 interdisciplinary conference on pilgrimage held at Roehampton University in London. Whereas Eade and Sallnow restricted their volume to contributions dealing with Christian pilgrimage, Coleman and Elsner explicitly sought to be comparative,

---

[16]   Eade and Sallnow, *Contesting the Sacred*, p. 9.

[17]   J. Eade, 'Introduction to the Illinois Paperback', in J. Eade and M.J. Sallnow (eds), *Contesting the Sacred: The Anthropology of Christian Pilgrimage*, second edition (Urbana: University of Illinois Press, 2000), p. xiv.

[18]   Eade and Sallnow, *Contesting the Sacred*, p. 15.

[19]   Eade and Sallnow, *Contesting the Sacred*, p. 9.

[20]   C. McKevitt, 'San Giovanni Rotondo and the Shrine of Padre Pio', in Eade and Sallnow, *Contesting the Sacred*, pp. 77–97.

[21]   J. Eade, 'Order and Power at Lourdes: Lay Helpers and the Organization of a Pilgrimage Shrine', in Eade and Sallnow, *Contesting the Sacred*, pp. 51–76.

[22]   G. Bowman, 'Christian Ideology and the Image of a Holy Land: The Place of Jerusalem Pilgrimage in the Various Christianities', in Eade and Sallnow, *Contesting the Sacred*, pp. 98–121.

[23]   S. Coleman and J. Elsner, *Pilgrimage Past and Present in the World Religions* (Cambridge, MA: Harvard University Press, 1995), pp. 205–6.

highlighting the commonalities among pilgrimage traditions worldwide in order to prove the feasibility of interdisciplinary cross-cultural study in this domain.[24]

The *communitas* versus contestation debate dominated anthropological studies of pilgrimage from the end of the 1990s into the new millennium. Coleman and Elsner stressed that the focus on contestation encouraged by Eade and Sallnow has tended to divert attention from the way that differences between diverging religious discourses may actually be accommodated or reconciled at pilgrimage shrines.[25] Reflecting on their broad-ranging cross-cultural review of pilgrimage practices, Coleman and Elsner concluded that *communitas* emerges as an ideal in many pilgrimage traditions.[26] Yet they cautioned that '*communitas* is only an ideal', given the histories of conflict – both spiritual and political – that surround numerous pilgrimage centres such as Jerusalem or Amritsar.[27]

For Coleman and Elsner, therefore, pilgrimage held the potential for both *communitas* and contestation. A similar approach was apparent in the postmodern and reflexive study by Dubisch of the Greek Orthodox shrine of the Church of the Annunciation on the Aegean island of Tinos.[28] Dubisch proposed a useful modification of Turner's concepts of liminality and *communitas*, noting that in many cases, the significant social relationships of everyday life are maintained, not severed, during pilgrimage, as pilgrims tend to make their journeys in the company of friends or family members.[29] Moreover, pilgrims on Tinos generally perform their devotions individually, 'having little involvement with the hundreds of others who may be carrying out their own devotions concurrently, but separately'.[30] Nonetheless, Dubisch observed that on some occasions pilgrims to Tinos do identify with the sufferings of others, or join collectively in a common endeavour. The sense of *communitas* is heightened when pilgrims witness or participate in particularly dramatic performances of pain or suffering, as when women crawl up the steep hill to the shrine on their knees bearing afflicted children on their backs.[31] Such dramas, and the associated *communitas* between onlookers and performers, occur more frequently during major shrine

---

[24]   Coleman and Elsner, *Pilgrimage Past and Present*, p. 196.

[25]   Coleman and Elsner, *Pilgrimage Past and Present*, p. 208.

[26]   Coleman and Elsner, *Pilgrimage Past and Present*, p. 202.

[27]   Coleman and Elsner, *Pilgrimage Past and Present*, p. 202.

[28]   J. Dubisch, *In a Different Place: Pilgrimage, Gender, and Politics at a Greek Island Shrine* (Princeton: Princeton University Press, 1995).

[29]   Dubisch, *In a Different Place*, p. 95.

[30]   Dubisch, *In a Different Place*, p. 95.

[31]   Dubisch, *In a Different Place*, p. 96.

festivals, when especially large numbers of visitors come to Tinos.[32] In Dubisch's view, the experience of *communitas* thus varied according to occasion, and was also influenced by the social class of pilgrims. Like *communitas*, liminality from Dubisch's perspective was 'not an inherent feature of pilgrimage to Tinos, but [was] variable, situational and fluctuating'.[33] Dubisch's modification was therefore useful in outlining a flexible approach to the Turners' framework which would allow the anthropologist to draw upon the concepts of liminality and *communitas* when appropriate to particular ethnographic situations, without necessarily applying these ideas to all pilgrimage-related phenomena.

Likewise, in a 2002 article, Simon Coleman sought to move the field beyond the binary opposition between *communitas* and contestation, revalorizing the Turners' work and pointing out the potential for useful insights from both approaches.[34] Coleman also urged scholars to avoid getting trapped in a 'pilgrimage ghetto'.[35] Rather than engaging in dialogue only with other studies explicitly concerned with pilgrimage, Coleman encouraged anthropologists to broaden their 'theoretical and ethnographic horizons' in order to focus on the overlap between pilgrimage and 'tourism, trade, migration, expressions of nationalism, creations of diaspora, imagining communities'.[36] In Coleman's view, anthropologists should think of pilgrimage as a lens, through which the researcher can look outwards, 'making points about human behaviour *through* using "pilgrimage" as a case-study rather than focusing *on* the institution itself'.[37] Moreover, Coleman suggested that it is important for researchers to pay more attention to the ways in which pilgrimage is incorporated into an 'annual round of religious activity' instead of being 'divorced from the routines and habits of everyday life'.[38] In his own work, he has sought to accomplish this goal by interpreting the meanings of repeat visits to the Marian shrine at Walsingham in Norfolk, England.[39]

---

[32] Dubisch, *In a Different Place*, p. 96.
[33] Dubisch, *In a Different Place*, p. 97.
[34] S. Coleman, 'Do You Believe in Pilgrimage? *Communitas*, Contestation and Beyond', *Anthropological Theory*, 2/3 (2002), p. 361.
[35] Coleman, 'Do You Believe in Pilgrimage?', p. 363.
[36] Coleman, 'Do You Believe in Pilgrimage?', p. 363.
[37] Coleman, 'Do You Believe in Pilgrimage?', p. 363.
[38] Coleman, 'Do You Believe in Pilgrimage?', p. 364.
[39] S. Coleman, 'Pilgrimage to "England's Nazareth": Landscapes of Myth and Memory at Walsingham', in E. Badone and S. Roseman (eds), *Intersecting Journeys: The Anthropology of Pilgrimage and Tourism* (Urbana: University of Illinois Press, 2004), pp. 52–67.

The centrality of movement as a component of pilgrimage was reiterated by Coleman and Eade in the introduction to their 2004 volume, *Reframing Pilgrimage: Cultures in Motion*. Coleman and Eade coined the term 'kinetic rituals' to describe the pilgrimage experience.[40] Following work by Urry,[41] Clifford,[42] Appadurai[43] and others,[44] Coleman and Eade argued that the contemporary globalized world is one in which people 'dwell within mobilities'.[45] Not only does this constant state of movement make pilgrimage an interesting framework for thinking about postmodern displacements more generally, as Clifford suggests,[46] it calls into question earlier views of pilgrimage as an exceptional, liminal/oid activity.[47] Thus for social scientists studying pilgrimage the questions that need to be addressed concern how pilgrimage is perceived to relate to other types of mobilities, whether it is a voluntary or forced activity, whether it is carried out on a repeated or once-only basis, and whether it is marked by ritual formality or informality.[48]

Coleman and Eade advocated approaching movement in pilgrimage along four dimensions. First, movement can be viewed as performative action that constitutes social space. This modality is illustrated by Sallnow's examples of indigenous-Catholic pilgrimages in the Peruvian Andes which map out and symbolically reclaim sacred territory. Second, movement can be seen as embodied action. This perspective focuses on individual actors and their bodily experiences in pilgrimage, such as the women described by Dubisch[49] and Gemzöe[50] who undertake part of their journeys to the shrines at Tinos and

---

40   S. Coleman and J. Eade, 'Introduction: Reframing Pilgrimage', in S. Coleman and J. Eade (eds), *Reframing Pilgrimage: Cultures in Motion* (London: Routledge, 2004), p. 3.

41   J. Urry, 'Mobility and Proximity', *Sociology*, 36/2 (2002), pp. 255–74.

42   J. Clifford, *Routes: Travel and Translation in the Late Twentieth Century* (Cambridge, MA: Harvard University Press, 1997).

43   A. Appadurai, *Modernity at Large: Cultural Dimensions of Globalization* (Minneapolis: University of Minnesota Press, 1996).

44   Z. Bauman, 'From Pilgrim to Tourist – or a Short History of Identity', in S. Hall and P. Du Gay (eds), *Questions of Cultural Identity* (London: Sage, 1996), pp. 18–36; Z. Bauman, *Liquid Modernity* (Cambridge: Polity Press, 2000).

45   Urry, 'Mobility and Proximity', p. 258.

46   Clifford, *Routes*, p. 39.

47   Coleman and Eade, 'Introduction', p. 7.

48   Coleman and Eade, 'Introduction', p. 7.

49   Dubisch, *In a Different Place*, p. 77.

50   L. Gemzöe, 'Caring for Others: Mary, Death and the Feminization of Religion in Portugal', in A.K. Hermkens, W. Jansen and C. Notermans (eds), *Moved by Mary: The Power of Pilgrimage in the Modern World* (Farnham: Ashgate, 2009), p. 156.

Fatima crawling on their knees. Next, movement can be treated as a semantic field. From this vantage point, the significance of pilgrimage must be set in the context of local understandings of mobility, especially other types of movement that might be conceptually opposed to pilgrimage, or seen as an extension of it, like leisure travel or migration followed by return migration. Finally, movement can be understood as metaphor. In this conceptualization, pilgrimage constitutes a useful analogy for other activities or ideas that may not involve physical displacement, as in the Christian concept of pilgrimage as a metaphor for the journey of the soul.[51]

In contrast to Coleman and Eade's insistence on seeing pilgrimage as a kinetic ritual, which broadens the perspective of pilgrimage studies to encompass more than just what takes place at a specific sacred locale, Peter Jan Margry's 2008 paper 'Secular Pilgrimage: A Contradiction in Terms?', adamantly maintains that it is 'the presence of a cult object associated with a specific location' that provides the *raison d'être* of pilgrimage.[52] Thus, 'there is no justification for reducing the phenomenon primarily to the journey element'.[53] Margry proposes a new term, 'transit pilgrimage', to refer to long-distance pilgrimage such as those of the Camino de Santiago or the motorcycle pilgrimages to the Vietnam Veterans' Memorial in Washington described by Dubisch and Michalowski,[54] in which the journey itself almost eclipses the importance of arrival at its destination.[55] For Margry, however, transit pilgrimages are an aberrant sub-type of pilgrimage, a conclusion that as we shall shortly see, is called into question by the data of Ian Reader[56] and other non-Western examples of pilgrimage.

In a 2007 paper, Vida Bajc, with co-authors Simon Coleman and John Eade, borrows metaphors from complexity theory. Arguing that the idea of pilgrimage destinations as 'centres' remains important, Bajc et al. suggest that centres can be conceptualized as 'attractors' producing patterns of movement

---

[51]   Coleman and Eade, 'Introduction', p. 17.

[52]   J.P. Margry, 'Secular Pilgrimage: A Contradiction in Terms?', in Margry, *Shrines and Pilgrimage*, p. 24.

[53]   Margry, 'Secular Pilgrimage', p. 26.

[54]   J. Dubisch and R. Michalowski, *Run for the Wall: Remembering Vietnam on a Motorcycle Pilgrimage* (New Brunswick: Rutgers University Press, 2001).

[55]   Margry, 'Secular Pilgrimage', pp. 24–5. See E. Plasquy, 'El Camino Europeo del Rocío: A Pilgrimage Towards Europe?', *Journal of Religion in Europe*, 3 (2010), pp. 256–84, for discussion of a newly-created pilgrimage of this type.

[56]   I. Reader, *Making Pilgrimages: Meaning and Practice in Shikoku* (Honolulu: University of Hawaii Press, 2005).

out of random mobility.[57] At certain points in time, a process of bifurcation may occur, whereby the patterns generated by the attractors disperse and reappear in similar forms at new places, creating new attractors or fractals that exert their own centrifugal pull.[58] In this way, new pilgrimage destinations mirror and are inspired by earlier ones. This way of thinking is particularly applicable to recent research on Kerizinen, a Marian apparition site in north-western France dating from the 1940s, where motifs from Lourdes – messages, a healing spring – and Fatima – a strident anti-Communist discourse – are echoed.[59]

In his 2002 paper Coleman commented on the influence of the Western Christian context in which much anthropological theorizing about pilgrimage developed. He suggested that since 'religion' tends to be conceived of as 'an autonomous, isolated realm of human activity' in the Western worldview, so too have practices like pilgrimage, subsumed within the category of 'religion', been isolated from other aspects of behaviour.[60] This theme is also forcefully expressed by Ian Reader, on the basis of his extensive ethnographic research on the 1400 km long *henro* or pilgrimage route that encircles the island of Shikoku, Japan.[61] In this case-study of Buddhist pilgrimage, Reader shows how the *henro* is incorporated into participants' everyday lives, through practices such as repeating the route numerous times, joining local pilgrimage associations that promote devotional activities at home as well as organized trips on the Shikoku route, completing miniature versions of the *henro* with its 88 temples set up at local temples in other parts of Japan, becoming a priest or *sendatsu* (pilgrimage guide), and returning to the *henro* symbolically by writing about one's pilgrimage experience. He suggests that the tendency to become a 'permanent pilgrim' on the Shikoku route is reinforced by its circularity. Unlike the Camino or Way of Santiago and many Western pilgrimage routes, the *henro* has no definitive starting or ending points. Therefore, pilgrims who find the disjuncture between their experience on and off the *henro* alienating can simply avoid confronting the transition, by starting the route again.[62] Even for those who do not make the

---

[57]   V. Bajc, S. Coleman and J. Eade, 'Introduction: Mobility and Centring in Pilgrimage', *Mobilities*, 2/3 (2007), p. 322.

[58]   Bajc et al., ' Mobility and Centring', pp. 322–3, 325.

[59]   E. Badone, 'Echoes from Kerizinen: Pilgrimage, Narrative and the Construction of Sacred History at a Marian Shrine in Northwestern France', *Journal of the Royal Anthropological Institute*, 13 (2007), pp. 453–70.

[60]   Coleman, 'Do You Believe in Pilgrimage?', p. 363.

[61]   Reader, *Making Pilgrimages*, p. 252.

[62]   Reader, *Making Pilgrimages*, pp. 255–6.

henro their home, completing the circuit frequently marks more of a starting point than an end point in their lives.[63]

Reader cites other examples of Asian pilgrimages that have a long-term impact on the lives of their participants, including those of Rajasthani pilgrims studied by Ann Gold,[64] and pilgrimage to Benares (Kashi, Varanasi) studied by Diana Eck.[65] Interestingly, however, the study which to date best illustrates the incorporation of the pilgrimage experience into participants' ongoing lives comes from a Western context, namely Nancy Frey's ethnography of the revived walking pilgrimage to Santiago.[66] As Frey shows, the Camino can become a central organizing metaphor in the lives of pilgrims, many of whom – like those who walk the *henro* – repeat the route multiple times, join Friends of the Camino Associations to keep the experience alive 'at home', and see themselves as permanently transformed through the act of accomplishing the pilgrimage.[67] Perhaps it is not so much the case that Christian, or Western, pilgrimages are necessarily more compartmentalized from ordinary life than Asian pilgrimages, but simply that scholars of pilgrimage in the West have not been asking the right questions. The focus has been on pilgrims during their journeys to sacred sites and their experience on arrival, rather than on the aftermath.

Reader's work on the Shikoku *henro* underscores another tendency towards compartmentalization in some anthropological and popular thinking about pilgrimage: the attempt to make a categorical distinction between pilgrims and tourists. As he points out, 'praying and playing' are activities that frequently operate hand in hand both in Japan and elsewhere in Asia and Europe.[68] His research shows that all types of Shikoku pilgrims – those using motorized transport and those travelling on foot – were equally likely to engage in leisure activities such as visiting hot springs and other non-religious attractions along the route, and buying souvenirs.[69] Unlike some of the walking pilgrims on the Camino interviewed by Frey, who believe that only 'tourists' travel by car

[63] Reader, *Making Pilgrimages*, p. 250.

[64] A. Gold, *Fruitful Journeys: The Ways of Rajasthani Pilgrims* (Berkeley: University of California Press, 1988).

[65] D. Eck, *Banaras: City of Light* (London: Routledge and Kegan Paul, 1983).

[66] N.L. Frey, *Pilgrim Stories: On and Off the Road to Santiago* (Berkeley: University of California Press, 1998).

[67] See also D. Schrire, 'The Camino de Santiago: The Interplay of European Heritage and New Traditions', *Ethnologia Europaea*, 36/2 (2007), pp. 69–86.

[68] The same point was previously made in a publication by N.H.H. Graburn, '"To Pray, Pay and Play": The Cultural Structure of Japanese Domestic Tourism' (Aix-en-Provence: Centre des Hautes Études Touristiques, 1983).

[69] Reader, *Making Pilgrimages*, p. 37.

or take bus tours to Santiago, Reader found that bus tour participants on the *henro* usually spend longer at the temples than walkers 'who ... may engage only in cursory prayers'.[70] As a result, Reader concludes that it is 'methodologically problematic to separate out the "tourist" from the "pilgrim"'.[71] Here we see the ongoing relevance of the Turners' famous statement that 'a tourist is half a pilgrim, if a pilgrim is half a tourist'.[72]

Indeed, one of the most valuable and enduring contributions of the Turners' work is their insistence on the interpenetration of the ludic and sacred aspects of pilgrimage. In their view, under the influence of the Protestant ethic in Europe, religion has become an increasingly 'solemn' activity. The historians Delumeau[73] and Bossy[74] trace the same process in the purging of festive elements from Catholicism during the Counter-Reformation. As a result, in both popular and scholarly discourses, there is frequently a rejection of the possibility of inter-mixing between devotional and leisure activities and the binary opposition between pilgrimage and tourism is reified. This opposition is also reinforced by the perception that travel can only be authentically sacred if it is divorced from the realm of economic transactions.

Pilgrimage travel represents one of the key historical antecedents of tourism in the contemporary world.[75] In a 1992 paper sociologist Erik Cohen proposed that in traditional cultures, pilgrims were drawn towards the 'Centres' of their world, where spiritual and cosmological order prevail, while travellers or tourists were attracted to the 'Other' on the periphery.[76] Although analytically provocative, it is unclear that this distinction is actually supported by ethnographic and historical evidence. Furthermore, sociologists and anthropologists are divided in their interpretations of the connections between pilgrimage and tourism. For the 'culture critics', pilgrimage and tourism are qualitatively different; whereas pilgrimage and serious travel in earlier historical eras represented a deep spiritual

---

[70]   Reader, *Making Pilgrimages*.

[71]   Reader, *Making Pilgrimages*.

[72]   Turner and Turner, *Image and Pilgrimage*, p. 20.

[73]   J. Delumeau, *Catholicism between Luther and Voltaire* (Philadelphia: Westminster Press, 1977).

[74]   J. Bossy, 'The Counter-Reformation and the People of Catholic Europe', *Past and Present*, 47 (1970), pp. 51–70.

[75]   J. Adler, 'Travel as Performed Art', *The American Journal of Sociology*, 94/6 (1989), pp. 1366–91; E. Cohen, 'Pilgrimage and Tourism: Convergence and Divergence', in A. Morinis (ed.), *Sacred Journeys: The Anthropology of Pilgrimage* (Westport: Greenwood Press, 1992), p. 48.

[76]   Cohen, 'Pilgrimage and Tourism'.

quest, modern tourism is conceived of as superficial and frivolous.[77] Bauman echoes this distinction in his 1996 paper, which proposes the figure of the pilgrim as a metaphor for the 'modern man', who conceived of life as a directional project in a solid, unchanging world, where identity could be built in a continuous, orderly fashion.[78] In contrast, for Bauman, the figure of the tourist is a metaphor for the postmodern consumer, consciously seeking novel experiences, but only insofar as these experiences are superficial and domesticated, in a pliable world structured solely by aesthetic criteria.[79]

In contrast to this type of approach, an alternative framework was proposed in the 1970s, primarily in the work of sociologist Dean MacCannell and anthropologist Nelson Graburn. According to this argument, tourism performs many of the social functions of religion in the contemporary world, and touristic journeys are analogous to pilgrimage on a profound level.[80] MacCannell presented a complex sociological analysis of tourism that drew eclectically from many sources,[81] including among others, Durkheim, Marx, Erving Goffman, Lévi-Strauss, and Thorstein Veblen's *The Theory of the Leisure Class*.[82] Just as Durkheim argued that religion in so-called primitive societies mirrored the social order, MacCannell claimed that tourism in the contemporary world reflects the displacements and differentiations of modern society. Tourism and sightseeing were, for MacCannell, ritual activities that have as their goal transcendence of modern alienation. Through travel the tourist seeks to construct a meaningful cosmology that incorporates the diverse fragments of modern experience.[83] MacCannell argued that modernization, with its rapid pace of social and cultural change, has generated both instability and the notion that life in the modern world is inauthentic. Thus, 'for moderns, reality and authenticity are thought to be elsewhere: in other historical periods and other cultures, in purer, simpler lifestyles'.[84] It is the quest for authenticity and coherence that motivates touristic travel.[85]

---

[77]   D.J. Boorstin, *The Image: A Guide to Pseudo-Events in America* (New York: Harper & Row, 1964); Cohen, 'Pilgrimage and Tourism', p. 49.

[78]   Bauman, 'From Pilgrim to Tourist', pp. 22–3.

[79]   Bauman, 'From Pilgrim to Tourist', pp. 30–31.

[80]   Cohen, 'Pilgrimage and Tourism', p. 49.

[81]   D. MacCannell, *The Tourist: A New Theory of the Leisure Class* (New York: Schoken Books, 1976).

[82]   T. Veblen, *The Theory of the Leisure Class* (Harmondsworth: Penguin Books, [1899] 1979). Originally published in 1899.

[83]   MacCannell, *The Tourist*, p. 13.

[84]   MacCannell, *The Tourist*, p. 3.

[85]   MacCannell, *The Tourist*, pp. 3, 13.

Nelson Graburn advanced a parallel theoretical framework. Like MacCannell, Graburn too suggested that in contemporary society, authentic experience or 'real life' is thought to exist only apart from the context of quotidian routine.[86] The aim of tourism is renewal and recreation, interpreted to mean the re-creation of the self. According to Graburn:

> Tourism has a stated, or unstated but culturally determined, goal that has changed through the ages. For traditional societies the rewards of pilgrimages were accumulated grace and moral leadership in the home community. The rewards of modern tourism are phrased in terms of values we now hold up for worship: mental and physical health, social status, and diverse, exotic experiences.[87]

As early as the 1990s the usefulness of the concept of authenticity in tourism research was called into question. Following sociologist Erving Goffman,[88] MacCannell conceptualized tourist attractions as comprising 'front stage' and 'back stage' areas. The front stage represents the area where tourist spectacles are presented, whereas 'real' indigenous culture exists in the back stage. Progressively, the front stage permeates the back stage area, until there is no authentic culture left.[89] For this reason, some researchers claim that in the postmodern era, the quest for authenticity as a motive for travel is no longer relevant, partly because it is an accepted feature of postmodern mass culture that all supposedly 'real' back stage areas are fabrications. Moreover, ironic post-tourists are supposedly attracted by the very inauthenticity of tourist spectacles,[90] or at least are satisfied with 'good performances' regardless of their authentic value.[91] Other

[86]   N.H.H. Graburn, 'Tourism: The Sacred Journey', in V.L. Smith (ed.), *Hosts and Guests: The Anthropology of Tourism* (Philadelphia: University of Pennsylvania Press, 1977), pp. 17–31.

[87]   Graburn, 'Tourism', p. 24; See also N.H.H. Graburn, 'The Anthropology of Tourism', *Annals of Tourism Research*, 10/1 (1983), pp. 9–33 and 'Tourism, Modernity, Nostalgia', in A.S. Ahmed and C.N. Shore (eds), *The Future of Anthropology: Its Relevance to the Contemporary World* (London: Athlone, 1995), pp. 158–78.

[88]   E. Goffman, *The Presentation of Self in Everyday Life* (Garden City: Doubleday, 1959).

[89]   D. MacCannell, *Empty Meeting Grounds: The Tourist Papers* (London and New York: Routledge, 1992).

[90]   C. Rojek, 'Indexing, Dragging and the Social Construction of Tourist Sites', in C. Rojek and J. Urry (eds), *Touring Cultures: Transformations of Travel and Theory* (London and New York: Routledge, 1997), pp. 52–74; C. Lury, 'The Objects of Travel', in Rojek and Urry, *Touring Cultures*, pp. 75–95.

[91]   E.M. Bruner, 'Tourism in the Balinese Borderzone', in S. Lavie and T. Swedenburg (eds), *Displacement, Diaspora and Geographies of Identity* (Durham: Duke University Press, 1996), pp. 157–79.

approaches, however, have sought to reframe the notion of authenticity to avoid static models of cultural loss and disruption. Even as early as 1988, Erik Cohen suggested that '"authenticity" is a socially constructed concept and its social ... connotation is, therefore, not given, but negotiable'.[92] More recently, researchers such as Coleman and Crang[93] have argued for a dynamic, emergent approach that sees cultures as continually engaged in reconstructing themselves, partly through interaction with other groups through processes of mobility that include tourism.[94] They argue for a conceptualization of tourism as performance, that moves away from the idea that tourism produces superficial and 'inauthentic images that cloak and mask "real" world processes'.[95] Instead, they argue for 'the possibility of an "emergent authenticity" where, say, an artisan producing tourist art develops an aesthetic that satisfies the artisan's own cultural identity'.[96] In Coleman and Crang's view, rather than abandoning authenticity, it should be a term that is 'contested and used'.[97]

The term authenticity has also aroused considerable debate in the journal *Annals of Tourism Research*. Following sociologist Ning Wang,[98] contributors to this journal have proposed three types of authenticity in tourism experiences. Object authenticity refers to original objects, cultures or experiences which are objectively authentic. Constructive and existential authenticity are more subjective. Constructive authenticity refers to the beliefs and expectations of tourists and tourism promoters, while existential authenticity is a state of being that arises from tourism experiences and activities that are seen by participants as authentic.[99] While some of these researchers propose that the concept of object authenticity be dropped from the literature entirely, others suggest that as long

---

[92]   E. Cohen, 'Authenticity and Commoditization in Tourism', *Annals of Tourism Research*, 15 (1988), p. 374.

[93]   S. Coleman and M. Crang, 'Grounded Tourists, Travelling Theory', in S. Coleman and M. Crang (eds), *Tourism: Between Place and Performance* (New York and Oxford: Berghahn Books, 2002), pp. 1–17.

[94]   Coleman and Crang, 'Grounded Tourists', p. 10.

[95]   Coleman and Crang, 'Grounded Tourists', p. 9.

[96]   Coleman and Crang, 'Grounded Tourists', p. 10.

[97]   Coleman and Crang, 'Grounded Tourists', p. 7.

[98]   N. Wang, 'Rethinking Authenticity in Tourism Experience', *Annals of Tourism Research*, 26 (1999), pp. 349–70; N. Wang, *Tourism and Modernity: A Sociological Analysis* (Oxford: Pergamon, 2000).

[99]   Wang, 'Rethinking Authenticity', pp. 349–70; Wang, *Tourism and Modernity*; Y. Belhassen and K. Caton, 'Authenticity Matters', *Annals of Tourism Research*, 33/3 (2006), pp. 853–6; Y. Belhassen, K. Caton and W.P. Stewart, 'The Search for Authenticity in the Pilgrim Experience', *Annals of Tourism Research*, 35/3 (2008), pp. 668–89; A. Buchmann, K. Moore

as it remains an important concept for tourists, promoters and members of host communities, it cannot be ignored by academics.[100]

Elsewhere, I have suggested that authenticity should be seen not as an absolute or objective value, but rather as a culturally and historically situated ideal that is *perceived* to exist by people in specific social settings.[101] The desire to encounter 'the authentic' remains a key factor in motivating touristic travel, as do the 'mythologies of escape' described by David Chaney.[102] While the metaphor of escape 'cannot be literally true ... it brings out some of the privileged licence of a temporary phase when normality is "relaxed" by actors changing places'.[103] Similarly, authenticity in objective terms may not be encountered, but the perception remains that distant places provide privileged access to spiritual enlightenment, knowledge and the possibility of self-transformation including healing and recreation. It is this perception that provides the common ground underlying both pilgrimage and tourism. The tourist, no less than the pilgrim, seeks meaning, a coherent framework within which to interpret his or her reality, and spiritual as well as physical renewal. Moreover, these perceived 'goods' often are achieved phenomenologically as a result of pilgrimage or touristic travel, from the 'emic' or traveller's point of view.

At this point, the issue of commodification and economic transactions in tourism and pilgrimage comes into play. In an article on Irish traditional music 'sessions' performed for tourists in pubs in the town of Doolin in County Clare, Republic of Ireland, Adam Kaul distinguishes between commercialization, 'the introduction or intensification of monetary exchange *in relation* to the production and/or consumption of a thing', and commodification, which occurs when producers lose control of the production process, and objects or activities become valued solely in monetary terms.[104] Kaul suggests that commercialization without commodification has taken place in music sessions in Doolin pubs, since local musicians retain control over their performances, and although paid by pub-owners, the musicians do not receive direct payment from

and D. Fisher, 'Experiencing Film Tourism: Authenticity & Fellowship', *Annals of Tourism Research*, 37/1 (2010), pp. 229–48.

[100]   Belhassen and Caton, 'Authenticity Matters', p. 853.

[101]   E. Badone, 'Crossing Boundaries: Exploring the Borderlands of Ethnography, Tourism and Pilgrimage', in Badone and Roseman, *Intersecting Journeys*, p. 182

[102]   D. Chaney, 'The Power of Metaphors in Tourism Theory', in Coleman and Crang, *Between Place and Performance*, p. 195.

[103]   Chaney, 'Power of Metaphors', p. 194.

[104]   A.R. Kaul, 'The Limits of Commodification in Traditional Irish Music Sessions', *Journal of the Royal Anthropological Institute*, 13/3 (2007), pp. 706–7.

tourists. While the commercialization–commodification distinction may be a useful one, the implicit assumption must be questioned that only performances or objects that are, as Kaul states, 'off limits to the process of commodification' can be considered authentic. Following this line of reasoning, tourists *cannot* be considered pilgrims, because they pay for commoditized experiences, and are also the source of profits for tourism promoters. Likewise, tourists who accept commodified objects or performances are seen as people easily duped by 'fakes'. This perspective also underlies tourist fears of being 'exploited' by local people who want to charge high prices for inauthentic goods. For example, West describes how villagers from Maimafu in highland Papua New Guinea frequently give tourists gifts of garden produce, which they appreciate, praise and consume. However, villagers expect the tourists to reciprocate with gifts of Western goods.[105] 'If, in frustration, the person from Maimafu hints at what he or she might like in exchange, the tourist often becomes angry and begins to lecture about how village-based tourism will work only if residents do not bother tourists with requests for things such as flashlights, shoes and T-shirts.'[106] Here, the problem seems to be that the tourists perceive the gifts of food as 'off-limits' to commodification, and hence authentic. By asking for reciprocity, the Maimafu villagers are implicitly de-valuing the 'gifts' and rendering themselves 'inauthentic' in tourist eyes, all the more so since the items they desire in exchange for the garden produce are 'fallen' Western commodities. Similarly, Tucker describes tourism in the Turkish village of Göreme, located in Cappadocia, a region of volcanic landscape where people continue to inhabit dwellings carved out of the rock formations.[107] Backpackers travelling as individual tourists are often spontaneously invited by village women to 'come and look at a cave house'. This type of encounter is well-received by tourists, except when they are offered handicrafts to purchase during their visits to domestic space:

> For example, when the host presents a pile of head scarves for her visitor to buy
> at rather inflated prices, some tourists are disillusioned by the situation, which in
> their view, instantly becomes a tourist event and no longer one of true hospitality.
> According to a disillusioned tourist, the encounter "slides between being
> authentically real and what's done for tourists". Since tourists construe a strong
> dichotomy between friendships and market relationships, in situations like these

---

[105]   P. West, 'Tourism as Science and Science as Tourism: Environment, Society, Self and Other in Papua New Guinea', *Current Anthropology*, 49/4 (2008), pp. 597–626.

[106]   West, 'Tourism as Science', pp. 607–8.

[107]   H. Tucker, 'Tourists and Troglodytes: Negotiating for Sustainability', *Annals of Tourism Research*, 28/4 (2001), pp. 868–91.

where hospitality turns into an economic event, they feel duped because the two
seem irreconcilable.[108]

The paradox in both the New Guinea and Turkish examples is the same:
perception that an encounter with the Other can only be genuine and 'sacred' if
it is excluded from the realm of economic transactions. As anthropologists, we
need to challenge this dichotomous mode of thinking, and question the view that
economic transactions are necessarily polluting. Linked to the assumption that
pilgrimage must be separate from the economic sphere is another premise that
pilgrimage must also be ascetic travel. Neither is validated by the cross-cultural
and historical evidence linking pilgrimage sites to markets, fairs and leisure
activities. Nonetheless, such presuppositions continue to provide the basis for
dismissing tourism and unconventional pilgrimages as less valuable or spiritual
activities than pilgrimages connected with established religious institutions.

A growing area of research concerns precisely the type of travel that may
be categorized as unconventional pilgrimage. *Pilgrimage in Popular Culture* by
Reader and Walter (1993) drew attention to this kind of travel, with chapters on
visits to Graceland and First and Second World War battlefields and cemeteries
in Europe.[109] More recently, Peter Jan Margry's edited volume, *Shrines and
Pilgrimage in the Modern World*,[110] has continued the trend, with contributions
on New Age travel to Glastonbury, and visits to the grave of Jim Morrison, the
lead singer of The Doors, in Paris. Despite the use of the term 'pilgrimage' in
the titles of both of these volumes, there is a resistance to conceiving of this type
of travel as pilgrimage.[111] Margry, for example, cautions against broadening the
concept of pilgrimage to the point at which it becomes meaningless, or applying
the term in a metaphorical sense.[112] He also rejects the term 'secular pilgrimage'
arguing that it is an 'oxymoron or contradiction in terms'.[113]

Although his understanding of the religious is non-confessional, Margry's
definition of pilgrimage relies on the notion of journeys 'based on a religious
or spiritual inspiration', and the desire to 'seek a transcendental encounter with

---

[108]   Tucker, 'Tourists and Troglodytes', p. 878.
[109]   Reader and Walter, *Pilgrimage in Popular Culture*.
[110]   Margry, *Shrines and Pilgrimage*.
[111]   See, for example, T. Walter, 'War Grave Pilgrimage', in Reader and Walter, *Pilgrimage in
Popular Culture*, who argues that a clear distinction can be made between pilgrims and tourists
during travel to British cemeteries from the two world wars (pp. 63–91).
[112]   Margry, *Shrines and Pilgrimage*, pp. 14, 20.
[113]   Margry, *Shrines and Pilgrimage*, p. 14.

a specific cult object'.[114] In his view, visits and visitors to a single site may be distinguished as being either secular or religious: 'secular pilgrimages as such do not exist but ... within, or rather in addition to the secular practice of commemoration or worship around the graves of and memorials to a wide variety of individuals, religious pilgrimages may function to a great extent independently and should be distinguished as such'.[115] He suggests that owing to the 'religiosity and ritual' they exhibit, some visitors to such sites are 'pilgrims in the "classic" sense, and therefore their visits to these places are essentially different in function and meaning from those of others who go there for non-religious reasons'.[116] I agree with Margry that we should not restrict the use of the term 'religious' simply to those practices that fall within the purview of established religious institutions, and with his suggestion that we extend the use of the term 'pilgrimage' – without the modifier secular – to a broad range of travel. Yet it is problematic to draw rigid distinctions between pilgrims and other visitors at the same sites. How can we know, for example, that a 'secular' visitor will not have an entirely unanticipated emotionally moving or transcendental experience at a place like Graceland, thus turning into a pilgrim? And what is the value of maintaining such precise categorical distinctions unless we implicitly seek to elevate the religious domain over that of the secular or profane? This somewhat elitist approach is evident in Margry's statement regarding visitors to Morrison's grave: 'for a specific group of fans, the religious factor is in fact present and ... narratives employed by these fans during their visits are distinct from those of the *tourist masses*'[117] [emphasis mine].

We know that visitors to shrines connected to religious institutions often have unanticipated religious experiences, for example, the many stories at Kerizinen about the anticlerical or sceptical visitors who underwent emotional conversions as a result of the impact of being in the presence of the visionary or the statue of the Virgin at the shrine. Furthermore, how does one distinguish between 'secular commemoration or worship' and 'religiosity and ritual' at the same site? Margry formulates a definition of religion which involves ideas about 'experience of the sacred or the supernatural', yet the sacred is itself left undefined, unless we assume that it is equated with the supernatural.

To follow Durkheim in a loose sense, we should see the sacred as that which is perceived to transcend the individual and connect him/her to a larger reality

---

[114] Margry, *Shrines and Pilgrimage*, p. 36.
[115] Margry, *Shrines and Pilgrimage*, p. 327.
[116] Margry, *Shrines and Pilgrimage*, p. 327.
[117] Margry, *Shrines and Pilgrimage*, p. 29.

beyond the self. One element of the sacred could thus be the collectivities or imagined communities to which individuals belong. Another element could be the natural world in which individuals are embedded but which also extends beyond them. Margry claims that the 'main goals' of pilgrimage 'are the sacred, the religious, the *cultus* object', and that 'the beauty of the scenery, tourist aspects, the sociability of the collective journey' are only secondary motives.[118] Yet if we define the sacred as that which is perceived to transcend the individual, either in the social or natural realm, then both the beauty of the scenery and the collective journey become aspects of the sacred.

In the final analysis, it is necessary to recognize that 'the sacred' is always socially constructed. Objects of cult, elements of the natural world, people and places become sacred through the meanings projected onto them by specific communities and individuals. Katharina Schramm provides a moving vignette that illustrates this point in her article on travel to sites associated with the slave trade in Ghana by African-Americans.[119] She describes how an African-American professor visits the river Nnonkonsuo, identified as the place where captive slaves took their final bath before being loaded onto ships for the Middle Passage. Invited by the local guide to drink some of the river water, the African-American at first hesitates, mindful of 'all the warnings about unwholesome water and terrible diseases associated with it'. Then he reflects that

> maybe my great-great grandmother or ... grandfather took their last bath on African soil in that river ... so I reached down and got the water and drank it, so that always a part of me would be the last bath of my ancestors before they were taken away from Africa.[120]

As Schramm observes, this act repositions the man from 'an American tourist ... suspicious of the local water' to 'a worshipper' and makes the river sacred in his eyes. Schramm's vignette demonstrates the fluidity of the boundaries between tourist and pilgrim and the absence of anything inherently sacred in the locales they visit. Remaining on the subject of rivers and water that is constructed as sacred, it is worth noting the irony that the spiritually purifying waters of the Ganges are physically among the most polluted in India.

---

[118] Margry, *Shrines and Pilgrimage*, p. 29.
[119] K. Schramm, 'Coming Home to the Motherland: Pilgrimage Tourism in Ghana', in S. Coleman and J. Eade (eds), *Reframing Pilgrimage: Cultures in Motion* (London: Routledge, 2004), p. 146.
[120] Schramm, 'Coming Home to the Motherland', pp. 146–7.

As mentioned earlier, Margry claims that it is superficial to regard pilgrimage as a metaphor for other types of non-religious travel. Yet, as Lakoff and Johnson,[121] among others, have argued, metaphor structures and enables cognition. In his study of the Americans, Canadians, Australians and New Zealanders who travel to the Scottish Highlands to research their family origins, Basu shows that these 'roots' tourists' conceptualize their visits as pilgrimages, homecomings and quests. While many of these travellers have chosen to emphasize their Scottish background rather than other 'ethnic options' available to them, they deny the element of choice in favour of belief in an essentialized identity. Faced with the existential anxiety of late modernity – questions of 'What to do? How to act? Who to be?',[122] quoted in Basu,[123] – roots' tourists find answers and certainty through perceived physical and genetic links to an ancestral community localized in space. In Basu's view, the perceived sacredness of these journeys to the homeland derives from the fact that roots' tourists experience a transcendental discovery of themselves as part of a larger ethnic community, which is considered 'real'. Such a desire for authentic identity rooted in a distant homeland is particularly poignant for immigrant groups and diasporas living in 'new countries'.[124]

Like Schramm, Basu argues that 'it would be foolish to suggest that there is anything inherently "sacred" about these destinations outside the emotional, intellectual and physical journeys through which their sacredness is constructed'.[125] From the subjective experience of roots' tourists, however, the sacred does emanate from specific places and has the ability to generate self-transformation.[126] This argument does not apply only to roots' tourism but can be extended to all destinations deemed sacred, whether or not they are affiliated with religious institutions. The same reasoning can be applied to the concept of pilgrimage and tourism as quests for authenticity and self-transformation. Bruner[127] argues that despite the promises of self-transformation held out by advertising in the

---

121   R. Lakoff and M. Johnson, *Metaphors We Live By* (Chicago: University of Chicago Press, 1980).

122   A. Giddens, *Modernity and Self-Identity: Self and Society in the Late Modern Age* (Cambridge: Polity, 1991), p. 75.

123   P. Basu, 'Route Metaphors of "Roots-Tourism" in the Scottish Highland Diaspora', in Coleman and Eade, *Reframing Pilgrimage*, p. 166.

124   Basu, 'Route Metaphors', p. 151.

125   Basu, 'Route Metaphors', p. 169.

126   Basu, 'Route Metaphors', p. 169.

127   E.M. Bruner, 'Transformation of Self in Tourism', *Annals of Tourism Research*, 18 (1991), pp. 238–50.

tourist industry, in reality, tourists rarely experience personal change and it is more frequently the indigenous peoples living in tourist destinations that are transformed, through the negative impacts of 'development'. However, it is important to draw attention to the difference between the motivation for a journey and the fulfilment of the traveller's expectations. Moreover, following the negotiable and emergent view of authenticity advocated by Cohen,[128] Coleman and Crang,[129] Wang[130] and others, we see that travellers can achieve constructed, emergent or existentially authentic experiences in touristic settings. The sacred, or the authentic, is what individuals and communities perceive it to be and the desire for connection with this domain exists independently of its constructed character.

The work of British sociologist John Urry has generated an important impact on theoretical discussions of pilgrimage and tourism, starting with his 1990 book on the 'tourist gaze'.[131] More recently, he has proposed that in a world characterized by 'hypermobility' three bases of co-presence motivate travel: the need to be face-to-face with particular persons or groups of people (family members, work associates, professional colleagues); the need to face-the-place or put oneself in a specific environment, often for demanding physical activities such as rock-climbing or surfing that cannot be carried out elsewhere; and the need to face-the-moment, which involves travel to attend live artistic, political or sporting events.[132] Urry argues that even in a world where individuals are interconnected virtually through technology, the importance of embodied co-presence has not disappeared, which explains the heightened significance of travel in postmodernity. Since co-presence facilitates eye-contact and enables individuals to discern each other's degree of commitment or lack thereof to a common cause, what Urry terms 'intermittent moments of physical proximity' are critical to cultivating and maintaining long-term social relationships based on trust.[133] As a result, travel is essential for members of large multinational corporations, government bodies and special interest groups including academic and other professional organizations.

Urry's three bases of co-presence have been productively used by Marion Bowman in her ethnographic description of multi-faith pilgrimages to

---

[128]   Cohen, 'Authenticity'.

[129]   Coleman and Crang, 'Grounded Tourists'.

[130]   Wang, 'Rethinking Authenticity'.

[131]   J. Urry, *The Tourist Gaze: Leisure and Travel in Contemporary Societies* (London: Sage, 1990).

[132]   J. Urry, 'Mobility and Proximity', *Sociology*, 36/2 (2002), p. 262.

[133]   Urry, 'Mobility and Proximity', pp. 259–60.

Glastonbury. As she shows, members of both traditional religious institutions and New Age movements come to Glastonbury to be with those who share their respective beliefs. Others are motivated by the desire to face-the-place: Goddess devotees, for example, travel to Glastonbury because its landscape is perceived to embody symbols of the Goddess, with the Tor as her breast and the red iron-stained waters of the Chalice Well as her menstrual blood. Finally, occasions such as the Solar Eclipse of August 1999, and New Year's Eve 1999, when massive ritual celebrations were organized, attract pilgrims who come to face the moment.[134]

Urry's ideas about of co-presence can also be usefully applied to the computer software hacker conferences described by Gabriella Coleman,[135] although surprisingly she does not cite Urry's framework. Coleman describes the intense feelings of joy and connection experienced by hackers at conferences, particularly when they meet in person those with whom they have previously only interacted online. At the conferences, hackers work together on software problems, socialize all night, and celebrate with copious amounts of food and drink.[136] It is as if, during the period of the conference, hackers indulge in extremes of face-to-face sociability to compensate for the isolated character of their everyday work life in which the primary mode of communication is virtual. Coleman interprets the hacker conference as a ritual that condenses and celebrates a lifeworld, and acts as 'the basis for intense social solidarity that sustains relationships among people who are otherwise scattered across vast distances'.[137] For those who return to the same conferences every year, 'the hacker con takes on the particular ritual quality of pilgrimage'.[138] Coleman's analysis of the hacker conference applies equally well to academic conferences, such as the 2010 American Anthropological Association meetings which attracted 7,000 anthropological pilgrims to New Orleans, and closely parallels Urry's description of the intermittent co-presence which necessitates mobility:

> These moments of co-presence include festivals, conferences, holidays, camps, seminars and sites of protest ... Such intense moments of co-presence are necessary

---

[134] M. Bowman, 'Going with the Flow: Contemporary Pilgrimage in Glastonbury', in Margry, *Shrines and Pilgrimage*, pp. 241–80.
[135] G. Coleman, 'The Hacker Conference: A Ritual Condensation and Celebration of a Lifeworld', *Anthropological Quarterly*, 83/1 (2010), pp. 47–72.
[136] Coleman, 'The Hacker Conference', p. 50.
[137] Coleman, 'The Hacker Conference', p. 67.
[138] Coleman, 'The Hacker Conference', p. 63.

to sustain normal patterns of social life often organized on the basis of extensive time-space distanciation with lengthy periods of distance and solitude.[139]

Both Urry's and Coleman's formulations bear an uncanny resemblance to Durkheim's model of the Australian aboriginal oscillation between periods of dispersal when isolated small groups live on the land, and the collective effervescence of the corroboree, when clans reunite for feasting and celebration, and the norms of ordinary social life are temporarily suspended.[140] Of course, for Durkheim, it was this type of gathering that gave rise to the sacred, and the contrast between such heightened moments of sociability and the normal, more solitary routine was for him the source of the sacred–profane distinction. Likewise, Turner's *communitas* emerges in the anti-structural, betwixt and between occasions that bring people together in extraordinary circumstances, reinforcing social bonds. It is somewhat paradoxical, therefore, that Coleman and Eade use Urry's argument that mobility has become the norm in the globalized world to de-emphasize the exceptional character of pilgrimage, since Urry simultaneously makes the claim that the heightened mobility of postmodernity enables the creation and sustenance of social ties that transcend distance through exceptional and intermittent periods of sociability. As Coleman and Eade hypothesize, and ethnographies by Bowman and others document, 'pilgrimages have the potential to provide excellent examples of such "intermittent co-presence"'.[141] Yet, does this observation not return us to our points of departure: the Turners' emphasis on the *communitas* that is generated in liminal situations, and Durkheim's insight that the sense of the sacred arises from the perception of belonging to a community that extends beyond and empowers the self?

Many observers have drawn attention to the renaissance of pilgrimages around the globe in the latter part of the twentieth century and the first decade of the third millennium. From the Kumbh Mela and Shikoko *henro* to the Hajj, Lourdes and Santiago de Compostela, pilgrimages in all the major world religions have enjoyed an exponential growth in popularity and numbers of pilgrims. At least for European Catholicism, this revitalization of pilgrimage has occurred in the context of dramatic declines in regular religious practice. We could speculate that as *communitas* becomes de-localized and individuals

---

[139]   Urry, 'Mobility and Proximity', p. 261.

[140]   E. Durkheim, *The Elementary Forms of the Religious Life*, trans. K.E. Fields (New York: The Free Press, 1995 [1915]).

[141]   Coleman and Eade, 'Introduction', p. 7.

are detached from specific geographic bases of identification, routine attendance at local religious services becomes less meaningful. Concomitantly, sporadic or intermittent participation in larger-scale, more extra-ordinary ritual events that require long-distance mobility and unite like-minded individuals from far-flung territories may be more compelling in the contemporary globalized world.

Technologies of transport have simultaneously led to de-localization, and provided the means for the creation of new broader-based communities that find their ritual expression in pilgrimages, both conventional, like Lourdes, and unconventional like Coleman's hacker conferences, the Star Trek conventions described by Jennifer Porter,[142] or the Burning Man festival in Nevada's Black Rock desert studied by Lee Gilmore.[143] Whereas Margry[144] would claim that the similarities between these types of travel are based only on superficial analogies, it can be argued that their common roots become evident if we employ flexible, inclusive understandings of pilgrimage, tourism and religion. We need this type of broad interpretive framework to encompass the wide range of travel activities in the twenty-first century that seek to construct meaning and self-transcendence through connections with distant places where these ideals are perceived to be attainable.

---

[142]   J. Porter, 'Pilgrimage and the IDIC Ethic: Exploring Star Trek Convention Attendance as Pilgrimage', in Badone and Roseman, *Intersecting Journeys*, pp. 160–79.

[143]   L. Gilmore, 'Embers, Dust and Ashes: Pilgrimage and Healing at the Burning Man Festival', in J. Dubisch and M. Winkelman (eds), *Pilgrimage and Healing* (Tucson: University of Arizona Press, 2005), pp. 155–77, and L. Gilmore, *Theater in a Crowded Fire: Ritual and Spirituality at Burning Man* (Berkeley: University of California Press, 2010).

[144]   Margry, *Shrines and Pilgrimage*, p. 20.

Chapter 2

Old Pilgrimages, New Meanings; New Pilgrimages, Old Forms: From the Ganges to Graceland

David M. Gitlitz

Pilgrimage is not always about going somewhere to visit God, at least not in these days when new pilgrims take it upon themselves to define the forms, purposes and meanings of the journey that they hold to be a pilgrimage. Until fairly recent times – perhaps in the last 200 years or so[1] – pilgrimage has been largely the province of religion, not just in Catholic Europe but worldwide. At its core lie three concepts:

- That the deity is universal, but the divine entity is especially accessible to human beings in a particular place or places, and often at a particular time or times.[2]
- That visits to holy places, in other words, pilgrimages, weigh in on the side of good when the deity evaluates the merit of human beings.
- That pilgrimage in some metaphysical way involves transaction. Pilgrims offer their devotion, ritual and sacrifices and in return hope for rewards, both temporal (such as health, life, fertility) and transcendental.

---

[1]   C.K. Zacher, *Curiosity and Pilgrimage: The Literature of Discovery in Fourteenth-Century England* (Baltimore: Johns Hopkins University Press, 1976), p. 47, where Zacher points out that although the secularization of pilgrimage intensified in the Romantic period, by the Renaissance pilgrimage for some people had devolved into an excuse for educational travel.

[2]   T. Russell (ed.), *The Works of the English Reformers: William Tyndale and John Frith* (3 vols, London: Ebenezer Palmer, 1831), p. 66. Philosophers have often drawn attention to the paradox at the heart of this belief. William Tyndale, writing in the early sixteenth century, argued that 'to believe that God will be sought more in one place than in another, or that God will hear thee more in one place than in another, or more where the image is than where it is not, is a false faith'.

These three principles infuse the traditional pilgrimages of people in most religions, namely Jews who visit the Western Wall of the Temple Mount in Jerusalem, Jains at Sravana Belagola in India who climb up to the statue of Bahubali Gommateshvara, Tibetan Buddhists who circle Mount Kailash, and Muslims who circumambulate the Ka'ba in Mecca.

As an aspect of the province of religion, these pilgrimages have been endorsed and validated by religious tradition and also, when they exist, by the religions' authorizing mechanisms. The authorities' motives have not always been exclusively religious. Perhaps the earliest documentation of multiple motives involves the three annual Jewish pilgrimages to Jerusalem. The evidence is scattered in the historic and prophetic books of the Jewish Bible. They tell how kings David and Solomon refocused the three traditional harvest festivals of the tribes of Israel – Passover, Shavu'ot and Sukkot – into pilgrimages to Jerusalem to pay homage to and receive a spiritual boost from the *shechinah*, the ineffable essence of God, who was proclaimed to inhabit the Holy Temple on Mount Moriah. By creating a single, national, shrine at Jerusalem, the monarchs also effectively reduced to secondary, subservient, status the tribal shrines at Beersheba, Bethel, Schechem and Shiloh, thus asserting centralized authority and helping to create a sense of national identity for the Israelite people. The Jerusalem pilgrimages also proved an effective vehicle for collecting annual taxes.[3]

In pre-modern agrarian societies most people did not travel very much. There were, of course, exceptions: soldiers, merchants and diplomats, people whose professions required travel. But if a peasant in rural Aragon, a serf in medieval France or England, or a potter in the Punjab, felt the urge to take to the road, there were few legitimate reasons for him to do so. Most people were bound to the land by the agricultural cycle, the needs of their families, and in many places by the legal restrictions of serfdom. Travel for its own sake was not widely endorsed in the pre-modern world. There was no word yet for tourism. The concept of the vacation lay far in the future.

In most pre-modern societies, for most people, at most times, the primary socially legitimizing excuse for travel was pilgrimage.[4] Even if religion was the

---

3   It was only later, in Babylonia during the period of exile, when it was no longer feasible for Jews to make the three annual pilgrimages to Jerusalem, that the exilic prophets gave the festivals symbolic and memorializing content: Passover (the exodus from Egypt), Shavu'ot (the giving of the law at Sinai) and Sukkot (the 40 years of wandering in the desert). See D.M. Gitlitz and L.K. Davidson, *Pilgrimage and the Jews* (Westport: Praeger, 2006), ch. 3.

4   Pilgrimage had, of course, its detractors. See G. Constable, 'Opposition to Pilgrimage in the Middle Ages', *Studia Gratiana*, 19 (1979), pp. 123–46. For example, St John Chrysostom (fourth century), decried pilgrimage travel: 'Let each of us at home invoke God earnestly' (cited in

ostensible motive for their journey, there must have been some who were drawn principally by the urge to travel, to see new things, to escape for a while the deadening numbness of routine.[5] The pilgrim to a national or international holy site could be assured of a few days or months away from the plough, the squalling children, the mother-in-law. Support systems – financed by political and religious entities and private contributions – helped defray the costs.[6] The safe conduct generally extended to pilgrims provided a measure of security.[7] Most importantly, travel was legitimized under the protective umbrella of religious devotion, sanctioned by authority, buttressed by tradition, and wholly, comfortably, incorporated within the devotional repertoire of that particular religion. Pilgrimage was not only legitimate, it was meritorious. In pilgrimage the individual ego, never absent, but never completely trusted in tradition-bound, religiously cohesive, pre-modern societies, was channelled into an activity that almost all parties could respect and honour.

Pilgrimages are made to special places. They require a journey. And both the journey and the destination have spiritual significance for the voyager. The pilgrims' performance during the journey and at the special place – the rituals, if you will – confirm the pilgrimage's significance. In earlier times all

---

'Pilgrimages', *Catholic Encyclopedia Online*, http://oce.catholic.com/index.php?title=Pilgrimages (accessed 10 January 2014). St Boniface (747) warned that women on pilgrimage were likely to become prostitutes (Boniface, *S. Bonifatii et Lulli*. MGH Epistolae 3, ed. E. Dümmler (Berlin: Weidmann, 1892), pp. 354–5). The opposition of Reformation clerics like Luther, Calvin and Zwingli is well known. Nanak, founder of Sikhism in the fifteenth century, wrote: 'One gains but a seed's weight of merit through pilgrimages', cited in S. Coleman and J. Elsner, *Pilgrimage: Past and Present in the World Religions* (Cambridge, MA: Harvard University Press, 1995), p. 162. The fifteenth-century Muslim philosopher, Kabir, considered that: 'Going on endless pilgrimage, the world died' (cited in D. Eck, *Benares, City of Light* (New York: Knopf, 1982), p. 86).

[5]   For example, Jacques de Vitry, writing around 1220, noted that 'some light-minded and inquisitive persons go on pilgrimages not out of devotion, but out of mere curiosity and love of novelty' (cited in J. Sumption, *Pilgrimage: An Image of Medieval Religion* (Totowa: Rowman and Littlefield, 1975), p. 257).

[6]   The vast infrastructure of pilgrimage – roads and bridges, caravanserai and hospices, medical and security services – was supported by local and regional governments, religious institutions, voluntary associations and individuals.

[7]   Ancient Greece: M. Dillon, *Pilgrims and Pilgrimage in Ancient Greece* (London: Routledge, 1997), p. 56. Islam: M.T. Houtsma et al., *First Encyclopaedia of Islam* (Leiden: Brill, 1993), p. 651. Pre-Columbian Pachacamac and Cholula: G. Kubler, 'Pre-Columbian Pilgrimages in Mesoamerica', *Diogenes*, 125 (1984), pp. 11–23. C. Martínez Marín, 'Santuarios y peregrinaciones en el México prehispánico', in J. Litvak and N. Castillo (eds), *Religión en Mesoamérica* (México: Universidad de las Américas, 1972), pp. 161–79.

these concepts were defined by religion and confined within the parameters of religious doctrines and practices.

And then came the Renaissance, when for many people pilgrimage became an excuse – one of many – for educational travel,[8] and the Enlightenment, which, ultimately, weakened the ties between temporal and religious authority, and then Romanticism, whose proponents wore their egos on their sleeves and brought to the fore a philosophy of *me*, doing *my* things, for *my* reasons and *my* pleasure. The Romantics were, with the perspective of two centuries now, only a flamboyant few, but they planted seeds that are still bearing fruit and, many would say, their offspring now dominate the orchard. Today the concept of pilgrimage has taken on new meanings and has accepted new forms, sites and modes of travel. This shift has also influenced in significant ways the structures and meanings of traditional pilgrimage.

The essence of what for the purposes of this chapter may be called the 'new pilgrimages' is that to a large extent each individual feels empowered to tweak the definitions and set the boundaries of each of the core concepts. New pilgrims – like me in 1974 when I devised an academic programme to re-enact the medieval pilgrimage to Compostela – perform pilgrimage as they see fit, for their own idiosyncratic purposes. Although new pilgrims often emulate old forms with the intent of making them meaningful in what they believe to be traditional ways, the important difference is that they appropriate to themselves the right to do so. This shift has broadened the range of special places to which pilgrimages are made, changed the nature of the journey, and vastly expanded the meanings given to the experience. In essence, our age has shifted the focus of pilgrimage from the deity to the individual pilgrim.

Special Places

Traditionally the targets of pilgrimage, the places deemed special, have a kind of magic aura about them. That aura, which religions in their diverse ways term 'holiness', derives from the belief that there are forces larger than ourselves – gods, spirits, sources of energy – and that these forces are preferentially accessible at certain places. Our remote ancestors posited that since these forces cannot be directly perceived in the visible environment, they must reside far above or far below us. Mountaintops could be their abode; caves could be the entrances to their world below our world. Springs and rivers channelled their life-giving

---

[8]   Zacher, *Curiosity*, pp. 58–9.

essence to the world of human beings. Such places were portals, contact points between the human and the divine; that was what made them holy. Many of them still are, mountains like Japan's Mount Fuji and watercourses like the Ganges River, and the *cenotes* at Mexico's Chichén Itzá.

Somewhat less remote in time are places made holy by historic or mythical spiritual figures, places like the forest in India near Vrindaban where Krishna seduced the milkmaids and the Middle Eastern hilltop where God stopped Abraham from sacrificing Isaac and later allowed Jesus to be crucified and Muhammad to ascend to heaven on his night journey. Also special are places frequented by the exemplary disciples of religions: sages and exegetes, Christian apostles and saints, Jewish *tzadiqim*, the early imams of Islam, the diverse deities of Hinduism. Places touched by or associated with such figures retain a residual aura. Any physical remnants of these special people – a garment, a lock of hair, and especially, a body or a bone, things we often term relics[9] – can render a site holy, allowing us in their presence to feel the tingle of the divine.

These traditional ways of being special are still valid for many people. But today we have expanded the range of conditions that create special status and have broadened the categories of people whose aura favours a special place. The tombs of a handful of political figures such as Lenin and Ghandi became pilgrimage destinations.[10] It is notoriously hard to predict which leaders, even which martyred leaders, will inspire a major pilgrimage cult. To date John Kennedy has not and neither has England's Lady Diana, despite the efforts of her family to create a shrine on their estate at Althorp in Northamptonshire. Spain's Francisco Franco, who clearly planned that his tomb at the Valle de los Caídos near Madrid would become a major pilgrimage destination, would be disappointed to see the relatively modest numbers of the Falangist devout who visit the site today.[11]

---

[9] For the importance of relics in motivating medieval Christian pilgrimage, see Sumption, *Pilgrimage*, pp. 22–53. Islam: B. Wheeler, *Mecca and Eden: Ritual, Relics, and Territory in Islam* (Chicago: University of Chicago Press, 2006). Buddhism: K. Trainor, *Relics, Ritual, and Representation in Buddhism: Rematerializing the Sri Lankan Theravada Tradition* (Cambridge: Cambridge University Press, 1997); R.H. Sharf, 'On the Allure of Buddhist Relics', *Representations*, 66 (1999), pp. 75–99. On Jains, see P. Flügel, 'The Jaina Cult of Relic Stupas', *Numen*, 57 (2010), pp. 389–504.

[10] Some of the themes in following paragraphs are treated in Coleman and Elsner, *Pilgrimage*, pp. 213–20.

[11] The massive cross and basilica appear deliberately ambiguous, combining a Benedictine monastery, a monument to victims of the Spanish Civil War that Franco termed a 'national act of atonement', and which would in time also be a tomb–shrine to the deceased dictator. By 2009, when it was closed by the Zapatero government for repairs, it had become the third most visited

The tombs of a handful of luminaries of popular culture have likewise achieved pilgrim destination status. Graceland, the home and burial site of Elvis Presley in Memphis, Tennessee, which draws over a million pilgrim-visitors each year, is perhaps the most famous. It is noteworthy that traditional pilgrimage ritual behaviours can adhere to sites like these. Pilgrims enter a 'sacred' precinct set apart from the world by a wall. They go through a portal, are instructed in the ritual behaviours expected at the site, and are directed to begin a journey retracing in the holy place several key events in the life of the site's protagonist. The route through Graceland is not exactly a Via Crucis, but it leads the pilgrim by several stations, themes, and events in Elvis's life, and past cases displaying relics of his experiences and achievements. The journey culminates at his gravesite in a memorial garden. Davidson and I have witnessed pilgrims clustering there, their hands folded, their faces sombre, as they quietly mumble prayers. Many of them light candles from an Eternal Torch next to his grave. Graffiti on the estate's brick boundary walls express pleas for help and thanks for favours granted through Elvis's intervention. On special days, particularly for the anniversaries of Elvis's birth and death, thousands of pilgrims gather at Graceland for all-night vigils. Just outside the sacred precinct are gift shops that offer to the pilgrims mementos of their journey.[12]

Elvis's estate is not the only such place. As with political figures, it is hard to fathom which pop star graves will become pilgrimage destinations. The graves of Marilyn Monroe and Frank Sinatra are not. The most powerful current magnet is the grave of Jim Morrison, the lead singer of The Doors, in Paris's Père Lachaise Cemetery.[13] Pilgrims approach Morrison's grave, kneel or sit on the ground,

---

monument under the sway of Spain's Patrimonio Nacional. For a time flag-carrying Falangist sympathizers continued to gather at the memorial for an outdoor mass, despite the government's attempt to prevent what it termed a political celebration of the Francoist ideology – which is banned under the Law of Historical Memory – rather than a religious demonstration.

[12]   See Coleman and Elsner, *Pilgrimage*, pp. 214–16; J.W. Davidson, A. Hecht and H.A. Whitney, 'The Pilgrimage to Graceland', in G. Rinschede and S.M. Bhardwaj (eds), *Catholic Pilgrimage in the United States* (Berlin: Dietrich Reimer, 1990), pp. 229–52; C. King, 'His Truth Goes Marching On: Elvis Presley and the Pilgrimage to Graceland', in I. Reader and T. Walter (eds), *Pilgrimage in Popular Culture* (Basingstoke: Macmillan, 1993), pp. 92–104; K.A. Marling, *Graceland: Going Home with Elvis* (Cambridge, MA: Harvard University Press, 1997).

[13]   Père Lachaise Cemetery was an economic disaster when it first opened around 1800, but it became a pilgrimage site when its clever owner re-interred de la Fontaine, Molière, and the legendary medieval lovers, Abélard and Heloïse, within its grounds. Crowds of pilgrims increased when the musical genius, Frédéric Chopin, was buried there in 1849, and Balzac in the following year. More recently, the graves of Edith Piaf, Gertrude Stein and Alice B. Toklas, too, regularly attract homage.

light a candle or – more commonly – a joint, plug in their headphones and sing quietly along to their favourite Morrison tune. They almost always touch his grave marker with their hands. Phil Cousineau described his visit to the tomb in the late 1980s this way:

> I was standing next to ... Jim Morrison's Grave ... [when] a swarthy young man approached me ...

> "I have been here ... thirty-three times now". He paused and looked back at the rainbow of colors painted onto Morrison's bust atop the grave. "The first time I came I *walked*".

> "Why have you come so far?" I asked him with astonishment.

> "He understood".

> "Understood what?" I asked.

> "How to break on through ... how to get to the other side".[14]

There are other people whose star status is so great, whose message is so appealing, and whose charisma is so attractive that pilgrims follow them around during their lifetimes. Both the Buddha and Jesus possessed this magnetism, and silver-tongued preachers like St Francis of Assisi and St Vincent Ferrer were accompanied by crowds from city to city as they preached their message. A few such people exist today, namely the Dalai Lama and numerous Hindu gurus whose devotees follow them from place to place.

A handful of popular culture figures have also had this power. Perhaps the best known were the Grateful Dead, revered both for their powerful, innovative music and their over-indulgence in mind-altering drugs. The so-called Deadheads, the masses of peripatetic groupies who followed the band, sometimes for years, often spoke of their journeying in terms of pilgrimage. They caravanned from venue to venue, camping like gypsies on the outskirts of each town, emulating the dress, the attitude and the psychedelic tripping of their idols. Jerry García's biographer Blair Jackson wrote: 'If the shows were the sacrament for Deadheads – rich and full of blissful, transcendent musical

---

[14]   The phrase references a famous interview with Morrison. P. Cousineau, *The Art of Pilgrimage: The Seeker's Guide to Making Travel Sacred* (New York: MJF Books, 1998), p. 142.

moments that moved the body and enriched the soul – then getting to the shows, buying tickets, finding a place to crash and people to hang out with was part of the pilgrimage.'[15] Even today, long after the breakup of the band, these pilgrims of the road trip wear T-shirts chronicling their tour with the band, the succession of venues and dates resembling the stamps in a pilgrim's passport.

Some sites marking contemporary events possess this aura too. The bridge in Selma, Alabama, from where, in 1965, Reverend Martin Luther King led civil rights marchers into the batons and German shepherd dogs of southern segregationists in Montgomery, is such a place. Every year school and church groups, civil rights groups, and individuals re-enact this key event in the struggle to extend equal rights and opportunities to American citizens of colour. Organizers term the walk from the Selma bridge to Montgomery the Freedom March Pilgrimage. Ron Daniels describes his 2001 experience this way: 'I made the pilgrimage ... this year to feel the spirit of the ancestors, to hear the heroic accounts of those among us who marched on that day, facing death so that we might take the struggle to the next level.'[16]

People are often drawn to make pilgrimage to another sort of historic site, too. Disaster sites and memorials to disasters can also become places of pilgrimage. Currently in the United States the Vietnam War Memorial in Washington is the most powerful site.[17] For Jews, the extermination camps of the Holocaust attract diaspora and Israeli youth groups, Israeli army recruits, and associations of survivors who routinely make pilgrimages to such places.[18] Wounded Knee, the

---

[15]   B. Jackson, *Garcia, An American Life* (London: Penguin, 2000), p. 219. See also J. Rocco and B. Rocco (eds), *Dead Reckoning: The Life and Times of the Grateful Dead* (New York: Schirmer Books, 1999).

[16]   R. Daniels, 'The Meaning of the Pilgrimage to Selma', at www.tbwt.com/content/article.asp?articleid=288 (accessed 24 March 2002).

[17]   L. Palmer, *Shrapnel in the Heart: Letters and Remembrances from the Vietnam Veterans Memorial* (New York: Random House/Vintage: 1987); T.B. Allen, *Offerings at the Wall: Artifacts from the Vietnam Veterans Memorial Collection* (New York: Turner, 1995).

[18]   J. Feldman, '"It is my brothers whom I am seeking": Israeli Youths' Pilgrimages to Poland of the Shoah', *Jewish Folklore and Ethnology Review*, 17/1–2 (1995), pp. 33–7. J.E. Young, *The Texture of Memory: Holocaust Memorials and Meaning* (New Haven: Yale University Press, 1993). Gitlitz and Davidson, *Pilgrimage and the Jews*, pp. 156–88. The staying power of such places as pilgrimage destinations seems to be a generation or two after the germinal event. This is particularly true of battlefields and the cemeteries and monuments that are their aftermath. Gettysburg, the site of an 1863 key battle in the American Civil War, was a pilgrimage destination through the 1940s. Now that the last Civil War veteran has died, it has become a National Park, more of a tourist site than a pilgrimage destination. See L.K. Davidson and D.M. Gitlitz, *Pilgrimage: From the Ganges to Graceland: An Encyclopedia* (Santa Barbara: ABC-CLIO, 2002), pp. 582–4. In 2000 Davidson and I visited the memorial wall at Sainte-Anne-d'Auray in Bretagne with its 240,000 inscribed

North Dakota battlefield, is such a place for the Lakota Sioux and for indigenous Americans in general.[19] Wounded Knee, like Masada in Israel and the slave forts in Ghana, is an identity site, where pilgrims go to affirm their sense of who they are. In fact, all of Israel can be an identity site for modern Jews, even the most secular. Stuart Berman was asked by one of his friends, 'If you go to Israel, what do you do there?' He answered, 'Do? You don't do anything. You walk around Jerusalem, you sit in a café and you figure out who you are'.[20]

No brief survey of new pilgrimage destinations can omit those of the New Age religions. The term is applied to a number of decentralized movements, born in the 1970s and come to full flower in the mid-1980s. New Age adherents tend to put emphasis on individual healing and transformation, on living in tune with natural forces, and the belief that certain natural energies can effect individual change, leading to an interest in such things as crystals, pyramids and certain privileged natural geographic features, and that ancient cultures possessed valuable knowledge that must be recovered. New Agers often express an interest in Delphic, Druidic, Mayan and Celtic mysteries, shamans and vision quests. It is not uncommon for traditional pilgrimage routes to be imbued with the signs, symbols and meaning of ancient cults, real or imagined.[21] An example close to home is the linkage of the Camino de Santiago by some pilgrims to both Druidic and Templar mysteries.[22]

---

names of Bretons who lost their lives in the First World War. In the three hours we wandered through the grounds we were the only visitors.

[19]   P.C. Smith and R.A. Warrior, *Like a Hurricane: The Indian Movement from Alcatraz to Wounded Knee* (New York: New Press, 1996). M. González and E. Cook-Lynn, *The Politics of Hallowed Ground: Wounded Knee and the Struggle for Indian Sovereignty* (Champaign-Urbana: University of Illinois Press, 1999). See also O. Baruch Stier and J. Shawn Landresp, *Religion, Violence, Memory, and Place* (Bloomington: Indiana University Press, 2006), p. 84.

[20]   S. Berman, 'A Reform Jew's Perspective in Israel' (2 August 1997), at www.bluethread. com/imagecredits.html (accessed 20 January 2005).

[21]   P.J. Margry, 'Secular Pilgrimage: A Contradiction in Terms?', in P.J. Margry (ed.), *Shrines and Pilgrimage in the Modern World: New Itineraries into the Sacred* (Amsterdam: Amsterdam University Press, 2008), p. 42; E. Doss, 'Rock and Roll Pilgrims: Reflections on Ritual, Religiosity, and Race at Graceland', in Margry, *Shrines and Pilgrimage*, p. 130; M. Bowman, 'Going with the Flow: Contemporary Pilgrimage in Glastonbury', in Margry, *Shrines and Pilgrimage*, p. 268. D. Kemp and J.R. Lewis, *Handbook of New Age* (Wallingford: CABI, 2007), p. 274.

[22]   E. Aviva, *Following the Milky Way* (Boulder: Pilgrim's Press, 2001), pp. 12–13; C.C. Davidson, P.D. Eisenman, K.W. Forster et al., *Codex: The City of Culture of Galicia* (New York: Monacelli Press, 2005), p. 33; K.A. Codd, *To the Field of Stars: A Pilgrim's Journey to Santiago de Compostela* (Grand Rapids: William B. Eerdman's, 2008), p. 191; O. Olsen (ed.), *The Templar Papers: Ancient Mysteries, Secret Societies, and the Holy Grail* (Pompton Planes: New Page Books, 2006), p. 89.

These sorts of associations are rife on the web. 'I invite you to join me on the Autumn 2010 Pilgrimage of the Seven Sisters on the Celtic Camino ... from Santiago de Compostela ... to Léon along the well known and travelled path of the [*sic*] El Camino de Santiago. As we walk, we will ... infuse ... the entire pilgrimage with the loving power of the Divine Feminine.'[23] For New Age writers like Shirley MacLaine, the Santiago pilgrimage is more than merely Christian: 'The Camino lies directly under the Milky Way and follows the ley lines that reflect the energy from those star systems above it.'[24] Jesús Jato's famous mystical *queimadas* at the Ave Fénix hostal in Villafranca del Bierzo, Tomás Martínez de Paz's recasting of Manjarín as a Templar stronghold, and the calendrical functions attributed to the Annunciation capital at San Juan de Ortega all attest to New Age significance being grafted onto a traditional pilgrimage.

Frequently New Age pilgrims concoct new rituals to layer meanings onto their pilgrimages. The neo-Druidic dances at Britain's Glastonbury Tor are an example. Santiago pilgrims burning their clothes at Finisterre might be considered another.

The Journey

New pilgrimages have changed the concept of journey in two paradoxical ways: they have either eliminated it, or they have made it their primary focus.

On a journey to Lourdes or Mecca one will meet pilgrims from a dozen different countries. But none of them is likely to have walked there. Their journeys took them hours, or at most, a day or two. They travelled by plane, automobile and train. At the shrine these modern pilgrims enact traditional religious rituals. They perform ablutions, they pray, they visit a number of ritual stations in a prescribed order, they acquire religious souvenirs – some tangible bits of holiness to take with them – and they return home by motorized transport as they came.

It was not so long ago that most pilgrimage journeys took a long time and tended to be made on foot. What new pilgrims eliminate is the lengthy, arduous, uncomfortable and sometimes risky journey of traditional pre-modern pilgrimage. The long days of walking, the solitude of empty pathways that invite introspection, the creation of a temporary community of fellow traveller-

---

[23]   http://weavingyourdreams.com/celtic-camino (accessed 27 September 2010).

[24]   http://www.shirleymaclaine.com/shirley/books-camino-intro.php (accessed 27 September 2010).

pilgrims, the constellation of experiences that lead to what some scholars, following the insights of the anthropologist Victor Turner, call liminality, a state of in-between-ness.[25] Modern religious pilgrims whose focus is on *being* at the holy site, rather than on the *process of reaching* the holy site, strip pilgrimage of the emotional, physical and social transition that had for centuries been one of its most important components.

On the other hand, for many new walking pilgrims the centre of focus seems to have shifted back to the journey, not the destination. Almost every Compostela veteran talks not of having made a pilgrimage but of having 'done the Camino'.[26] They start out eager to reach Compostela. But the nearer they get to Galicia the more they value the pleasures of being on the Road and the more they regret – even before it is over – the fact that their experience on the Road is coming to an end. Getting to Compostela puts an end to doing the Camino. This shift of focus to the going, rather than the getting there, can be seen in the numbers of pilgrims – me among them – who have felt compelled to do the Camino multiple times.[27]

There is another way in which modern walking pilgrimages differ from traditional ones. Many tens of thousands have walked the approximately 800 kilometres from southern France to Compostela. They have all walked *into* Compostela, but few have walked *out of* Compostela. For most walking pilgrims, new pilgrimage is uni-directional. Elimination of the lengthy return journey truncates the opportunity to process, gradually, iteratively, the spiritual effects of the visit to the holy place, and to allow those insights to evolve, with time and distance, in an environment still free of the constraining familiarities of home.

---

[25]   V. Turner, 'Betwixt and Between: The Liminal Period in Rites de Passage', in V. Turner, *The Forest of Symbols* (Ithaca: Cornell University Press, 1967), pp. 93–111. Turner later distinguished *liminal* experiences (integral to society, often part of established religious or social ritual) from *liminoid* experiences (which are optional, essentially secular, and often break, sometimes playfully, with established norms) in V. Turner, 'Liminal to Liminoid in Play, Flow, and Ritual: An Essay in Comparative Symbology', in E. Norbeck (ed.), *The Anthropological Study of Human Play* (Houston: Rice University Press, 1974), pp. 53–92.

[26]   An August 2011 Google search of the phrase 'doing the camino' produced 42,300 hits. See N.L. Frey, *Pilgrim Stories: On and Off the Road to Santiago* (Berkeley: University of California Press, 1998).

[27]   Carmen Pugliese documents numerous repeaters in the nineteenth century and before, but the data hints that although their primary focus was probably religious, the experience of being on the road may also have been a motivating factor. C. Pugliese, *El Camino de Santiago en el siglo XIX* (Santiago de Compostela: Xunta de Galicia, 1998), pp. 317–19.

Significance

It should be clear from the preceding that one important difference between new and traditional pilgrimages hinges on the significance of the act. Pre-modern pilgrimages were ostensibly framed by religion, and the individual pilgrim's stated goals were whatever spiritual rewards his particular religion offered and had prepared him to encounter. Traditional pilgrimage enhanced worthiness. In traditional pilgrimage the accrual of merit gave significance to the act.

New pilgrimages do not displace these traditional modes; they add new ones, focusing them not on the contract between the human soul and the divine, but on the ego, the individual pilgrim's temporal wants and desires. New pilgrimages are not transactional in the way that traditional pilgrimages were. For example, inheriting from the Romantics the belief that prolonged experience of our natural environment is cleansing, many modern pilgrims have embraced long-distance hiking as a way of refreshing their spirit while escaping the workaday world. Any long-distance hike will fulfil this purpose, as the summer crowds in the Alps, the Hindu Kush, and on the Appalachian Trail make clear. The Camino de Santiago, the circuit of Shikoku Island in Japan, the English roads to Canterbury and Walsingham – all invest the long-distance hike with the prestige of historic precedent, and enliven it with a string of interesting artistic monuments along the way. They validate the extended vacation by portraying it as something useful, spiritual, sanctioned by tradition.

For the new walking pilgrim, as for the old, the vast spaces of pilgrimage invite introspection. Free of the impedimenta of daily life, the spirit has room to expand. But it tends to focus on itself, not the Divine. Barbara Wilson, writing of her pilgrimage to a rock-climbing site in California's Mojave Desert, characterized her experience this way: 'my old, constructed stories fell away and ... I was only desert wind on bare skin. I was the moon and stars, a new heart emerging from a hardened cactus, a wash that was a path, a white path through a valley choked with old boulders.'[28]

To the modern individual, almost any place can be hallowed as a pilgrimage destination. In our contemporary world, people tend to believe that they are empowered to decide for themselves which things, people and places are meaningful to *them*. Significance emanates not only from external authority – a church, a state, a religious tradition – but also from each individual. Are they devotees of the Old Masters? If so, they may make pilgrimages to the Uffizi

---

[28]   B. Wilson, 'Joshua Tree', in B. Bouldrey (ed.), *Traveling Souls: Contemporary Pilgrimage Stories* (San Francisco: Whereabouts Press, 1999), p. 105.

or the Prado. Are they golfers? Their pilgrimages may take them to Scotland's St Andrews. For opera lovers: perhaps La Scala. For country music fans: Nashville's Grand Old Opry. For avid readers: Shakespeare's Stratford on Avon, or Cervantes' El Toboso. If people are so inclined, they may make pilgrimages to festivals: Rio in March, Pamplona in July, Munich in October, Pátzcuaro on 1 November. For that matter, a pilgrimage destination can be the village where one's mother was born, one's grandfather's farm, or the restaurant where a man proposed to his wife. Any of these can be simultaneously an ordinary place, a tourist attraction and a pilgrimage destination, depending on the intent of the visitor.

It should be obvious, then, that the lines between pilgrimage and tourism can be fuzzy. With my colleague Linda Davidson I have journeyed to the Mount of the Beatitudes and Lourdes, to Madrid's monument to the Atocha victims, to the grave of Lala Sol ha-Tzadikah in Fez, to Dachau, Varanasi, the oracular centres of Pachacamac and Delphi, Jim Morrison's grave in Paris and, of course, Graceland. Did we go as tourists? As pilgrims? As anthropologists? Or perhaps with some combination of these motivations to validate our commitment of time and resources to satisfy our curiosity and bring a very-difficult-to-define *something* to our spirit?

What makes a journey a pilgrimage in our times is what each individual brings to it. If a person yearns to visit a place because it is – for some reason that he may or may not be able to articulate – important to him, meaningful, special, then for him the journey is a pilgrimage.

One last point needs to be made, and that is that in traditional pilgrimages the defining parameters are generally known beforehand: why the place is special, what the journey entails, why it will prove significant. A Hindu walks to Allahabad to bathe in the *sangam*, the confluence of the Yamuna and Ganges rivers, because it will cleanse his soul and help him attain a favourable reincarnation. An orthodox Jew who goes to Jerusalem may write his prayer on a scrap of paper and slip it into a fissure in the Western Wall of the Temple, because he believes the essence of the *shechinah* hovers nearby and his prayer will more easily reach the divine ears. An Australian aborigine walks with his people each year to Uluru rock because the spirits and memories of their aboriginal ancestors will speak to them there.

In contrast, modern, non-traditional pilgrims often undertake their journeys without an overtly religious motive and devoid of any expectation of spiritual content. Indeed, they may undertake a journey without labelling it for themselves a pilgrimage. And even if they explicitly hold themselves to be pilgrims, when they embark on their journey they may not be wholly clear of what their motives are, or what exactly they expect to get from the experience. And even if they think they are clear, it may turn out that they are mistaken. Parameters turn out to be fluid: they may change once the pilgrims find themselves on the road. The meanings of pilgrimage can be stealthy, and the results, the after-effects, can be surprising. For the new pilgrim, form, substance, meaning and effect are imparted in the main not by traditional religious schema or the institutions that transmit them – although they may be influenced by them – but by the individual pilgrim's interpretation of his or her personal experience.

Chapter 3

Pilgrimage and the American Myth

George Greenia

I set out to look for America in the spring of 1990. The decade had turned ...
Love of country was back in fashion, replacing love of money, and so was patriotic
travel. American families began to hit the road, going in search of the founding
ideals they felt the country had lost during the '80s. I like the idea of pilgrimages,
and I liked reading about the new pilgrims.[1]

Despite nearly constant references to their routine travel circuits as 'pilgrimages',
Americans are relatively unaccustomed to announcing either short or long
distance trips as quests for transformative, let alone sacred, experiences. We
commonly borrow the term to acknowledge some repetitive treks densely   *NB*
embedded in personal or social custom. There is the weekly 'pilgrimage' to the
shopping mall, soccer meet or swimming pool, the annual trek to the lake or
family reunion. Sometimes the goal suggests a weightier purpose such as periodic
visits to elderly relatives or cemeteries, treks that are solemnized by assignment
to the vague category of pilgrimage. Much of what we dub pilgrimage would
not earn that name according to traditional religious criteria, yet many other
activities Americans commit themselves to clearly fall within critical assessments
of pilgrim behaviour, customs, aspirations and processes.

Truer to the spirit of traditional religious pilgrimages are the non-routine
and, for many individuals and families, defining journeys undertaken to
admire and take in national landmarks, historic sites and natural wonders.
By the twentieth century, tourism – especially in the United States – eclipsed
the grand tour of Europe usually reserved for the moneyed elite, and became
massively democratized and re-channelled in the celebration of one's own
present nationalism rather than submissiveness to foreign cultures or the past.
The American middle class came to form the vast majority of domestic tourists
supported by whole agencies of the federal government, such as the National
Park Service or the Bureau of Land Management, or state and local cultural

[1]   W.K. Zinsser, *American Places: A Writer's Pilgrimage to 16 of this Country's Most Visited
and Cherished Sites* (New York: HarperCollins, 1992), p. 1.

authorities, entrusted with the preservation and interpretation of sites declared by popular assent national treasures. The homes of presidents, battlefields of the Civil War, trails of exploration, and memorials to key moments and movements in US history swelled the list of potential sites of solemn visitation as well as recreation. The 'mere' tourist is often the covert identity of the patriotic pilgrim who seeks to enlighten and educate himself while paying homage to a heritage landscape which anchors his identity as citizen and cultural heir.[2] Within a 20-mile radius of my own home in Williamsburg, Virginia, is the largest living museum of America's colonial period, the pristine parks that enshrine the first permanent English settlement in Jamestown, and the battlefields of the final British defeat in the Revolutionary War at Yorktown. Even private entrepreneurial concoctions like the local Presidents Park with its cartoonishly oversized (and hollow) heads of US presidents garner respectful visitors willing to overlook the questionable taste of the display out of deference to its patriotic aspirations.[3]

Deprived of a single unitary religious myth but galvanized by a 400-year history of endless lurching into a vast, nearly endless continental expanse, Americans derive their collective consciousness through perpetual displacement from early coastal settlements like Jamestown (1607) and Plymouth Rock (1620), to their first incursions into the thickly forested Midwest, to the celebrated explorations of Lewis and Clark (1804–6) that took these wayfarers all the way to the shores of the Pacific. To this we add the scarred battlefields where some 620,000 US citizens died in internecine bloodshed between North and South (1861–4), a conflict which forever marked our landscape with solemn memory. Taylor notes the long history of this confluence of land and identity whose greatest mythic expression in the Western imaginary inaugurated itself in the Sinai desert with the birth of the Jewish nation in its Exodus Event in the course of which 'which G-d manifests Himself in awesomely direct forms. The myth establishes the sacred, chosen character of the Hebrew people, but also serves to inscribe them in a landscape in such a way as to make them, in

---

[2]   The National Park Service, the Bureau of Land Management, the US Forest Service, the Fish & Wildlife Service and other agencies administer a vast treasury of honoured sites including 58 Natural Features and Wonders (Yellowstone was the first, in 1872), 2,354 National Historic Landmarks (Woodlawn Cemetery, Bronx, NY; Medicine Mountain, Wyoming; Andrew Wyeth's various homes), 45 National Historic Parks (Appomattox, Jamestown, Yorktown, Lewis and Clark Trail, etc.), 89 National Historic Sites (Brown v. Board of Education National Historic Site, Topeka, Kansas), and 100 National Monuments (Statue of Liberty; Devil's Tower, Wyoming).

[3]   During its six years of operation in Williamsburg, Presidents Park drew some 350,000 visitors. It closed in September 2010.

a powerful if special sense of the term, indigenous'.[4] The merger of people and land through travel allows Americans too to feel truly indigenous despite their newcomer status and despite the variety of countries their ancestors once came from. Even those just arriving on these shores from Mexico, Pakistan or Kenya can eventually acquire a sense of belonging by collecting American experiences, performing their new tribal and national identity on the road. Pilgrimage defines the highways to citizenship.[5]

English-speaking Europeans arrived in a New World that had – for them – no sacred places. All sites were equally secular, unlike Spanish explorers who encountered numerous durable monuments to locations visibly regarded as holy by indigenous cultures from central Mexico through the high Andes. But the blank North American landscape rapidly became inscribed by newcomers seeking to establish utopian villages, 'New Jerusalems' in the making, that would validate their founders' beliefs and reinforce their faith with a sense of physical place. Pilgrimage seems therefore the somewhat inevitable expression of religious sentiment in the United States. It helped forge the imaginative impulses that led to the founding of most of the Protestant utopian communities of the nineteenth century from Plymouth Rock – whose pioneers most blatantly called themselves 'Pilgrims' – to more subtle founders of the many semi-sacred settlements of the New World, untroubled by the fact they were the descendants of Anglicans, Puritans, Calvinists, Quakers, Lutherans, Mennonites, Baptists, members of the Dutch Reform Church, and others who all thought to reject old style Roman Catholic practices including pilgrimage.

Their first foundations, almost unwittingly, themselves became sites of pilgrimage, new spiritual homelands to which later settlements looked back with longing and deference. American Protestants trying to opt out of the secular world lived pilgrimage as their guiding concept when they left Europe for the New World and plunged into the heartland of the continent to build idealized Christian collectives like the Shaker foundations, also called the

---

4   L.J. Taylor, 'Centre and Edge: Pilgrimage and the Moral Geography of the US/Mexico Border', *Mobilities*, 2/3 (2007), p. 385.

5   '[D]issenting Puritans, Calvinist Boers or Mormons … saw the movement to the edge (their own or that of their forebears) as itself the definitive pilgrimage, a journey once again to a place where a new destiny and identity, always with great difficulty and many trials, could be inscribed in the landscape. As with the ancient Hebrews, there was an ideology of self-transformation possible within these pilgrimages but also a collective rebirth in the form of a construction of indigenousness accomplished in the course of these movements through the landscape: a fundamental encounter with the land that was mutually transforming. The people and land become one another' (Taylor, 'Centre and Edge', p. 386).

Millennial Church, brought to the United States in 1774 and among the most successful in maintaining an internal culture that spread to take its place in the American mythology of new beginnings and self-reliance. Other foundations include the likes of New Harmony, a socialist community in south-west Indiana founded by Robert Owen in 1825, and the Amana Church Society, founded in Germany in 1843 and transplanted to Iowa in 1855 where its villages have flourished as cooperative corporations since 1932. Ephrata Cloister near Lancaster, Pennsylvania, a foundation of Conrad Beissel for his German Baptist brethren (1732–1814) stands in this heritage line as well. Steeped in Old World trappings, emigration morphing into pilgrimage is a gesture common to almost all the religious traditions currently in vogue in the United States, from conservative Catholicism, to all varieties of Protestantism, to Buddhism, and on to New Age wandering and the call of the open road.

I would argue that the enactment of travel for transcendence has been a major factor in American history since the earliest colonial settlements, marking our national landscape and collective mental maps and as such it forms part of a nationalist narrative, akin to that of the Camino de Santiago supposedly marching in step with the Spanish Reconquest of Christian lands held under the military control of Muslim invaders.[6] There are vast stretches of American history in the nineteenth and twentieth centuries that we must elide in this treatment, but essential elements will likely persist in most analyses.[7] What Americans rarely do is either adopt a self-conscious identity as 'pilgrims' or recognize that status in others. Even more decidedly there is a near total disregard of historical displacements within our continent as instances of pilgrimage travel. But the omission of the word does not belie that enduring practice. The American myth, as a shared experience sought by means of travel along certain routes and to specific places, intersects with traditional pilgrimage in immersing the individual self in the collective enterprise of an imagined community that spans generations. What was a blank expanse when we arrived is now richly populated

---

[6] The myth of the glorious Reconquista, so much a part of the nationalist narrative of Iberia, is by now fairly disassembled. The nearly 800 years that Muslims lived, and yes, fought in Spain was marked by long periods of negotiated co-existence and an undulating frontier that swung north and south as military strength and political fortunes grew and faltered. The interpenetration of Moorish and Christian culture saw more influences flowing north to the roughshod and poorly-educated Christians than Christian influences colouring the elegant court culture of Andalusian Spain.

[7] For an example from early in the twentieth century, see D. Shiffman, 'Ethnographic Pilgrimage in Depression-Era America', *Pilgrimage. A Special issue of Mosaic. A Journal for the Interdisciplinary Study of Literature*, 36/4 (2003), pp. 155–69.

with sites and trajectories that confer membership in a vital community and allure travellers with the promise of transcendence.

Because pilgrimage journeys have to be voluntarily embraced for higher purposes, this discussion excludes immigrant groups using remembered pilgrimages as a part of their legitimate attempts to sustain traditions in a new and perhaps unwelcoming environment, or forced migrations except as transformed by solemn re-enactments or 'ritual historicizing'[8] as in the case of the native Americans who reanimate the Trail of Tears, African Americans who venerate the Underground Railroad, or the Future Generations Ride of the Lakota Sioux to Wounded Knee, South Dakota, all of which are important and very deliberate manifestations of collective will to make travel reverent, restorative and even sacred. Pilgrimage may be obedient to a tradition, community or belief system, but there is a required element of agency even in one's abandonment to the odd fortunes of the road. Even believing in providentialism is a choice. And while acknowledging that tourism has frequently overshadowed, eclipsed or been the socially acceptable pretext for more direct expressions of the desire for transformative travel, I will not address the specific tensions between tourism and pilgrimage well studied by anthropologists of tourism as Graburn,[9] Coleman and Elsner,[10] Coleman and Eade,[11] Swatos,[12] Swatos and Tomasi,[13] York[14] or Badone and Roseman,[15] and which go back to the earliest days of Christianity

---

[8]   C.V. Prorok, 'Transplanting Pilgrimage Traditions in the Americas', *The Geographical Review*, 93/3 (2003), p. 283, at http://www.jstor.org/stable/30033919 (accessed 5 March 2013).

[9]   N.H.N. Graburn, 'Tourism: The Sacred Journey', in V.L. Smith (ed.), *Hosts and Guests: The Anthropology of Tourism* (Philadelphia: University of Pennsylvania Press, 1977), pp. 17–31.

[10]   S. Coleman and J. Elsner, *Pilgrimage Past and Present in the World Religions* (Cambridge, MA: Harvard University Press, 1995).

[11]   S. Coleman and J. Eade, 'Introduction: Reframing Pilgrimage', in S. Coleman and J. Eade (eds), *Reframing Pilgrimage: Cultures in Motion* (London: Routledge, 2004), pp. 1–25.

[12]   W.H. Swatos, 'Homo Viator: From Pilgrimage to Religious Tourism via the Journey', in W.H. Swatos and L. Tomasi (eds), *From Medieval Pilgrimage to Religious Tourism: The Social and Cultural Economics of Piety* (Westport and London: Praeger, 2002), pp. 1–24.

[13]   Swatos and Tomasi, *From Medieval Pilgrimage*, pp. 1–24.

[14]   M. York, 'Contemporary Pagan Pilgrimages', in Swatos and Tomasi, *From Medieval Pilgrimage*, pp. 137–58.

[15]   E. Badone and S. Roseman, 'Approaches to the Anthropology of Pilgrimage and Tourism', in E. Badone and S. Roseman (eds), *Intersecting Journeys: The Anthropology of Pilgrimage and Tourism* (Urbana: University of Illinois Press, 2004), pp. 1–23.

and its popularization of religious sightseeing in Syria and Palestine, as Adler,[16] Cohen[17] or Olsen.[18]

We need not obscure the fact that this nascent field is resistant to neat packaging. Pilgrimage studies, by their very nature, examine a troop on the move. Getting pilgrims to stand still to analyse their moving parts is the job of researchers who are also sometimes participants, if only to keep up with the surging tide of 'true believers'.[19] Art historians freeze-frame gestures, mostly high ideals, while anthropologists provide snapshots of behaviours both singular and borrowed from other moments in life. Scholars in religious studies take spiritual sketches of travellers' yearning for the transcendent, while sociologists capture glimpses of mixed motives and intrusions of the definitely non-sacred. Even tourism studies help us see past the picture postcard images of the exotic and wondrous and show us vacationers, trekkers, sceptics, seekers and spenders flowing in and out of the channels of belief.

Taxonomies of Pilgrimage

Diverse forms of travel are undertaken for goals greater than sightseeing or commerce. Many sojourners alternate among their interior identities as pilgrim, tourist or merchant, or use one to disguise or justify another. Even those who set out on consecrated and well-defined religious journeys admit that in the end it is easier to be a gawker who is never a pilgrim than a pilgrim who is never a gawker. Although they tend to overlook important differences between travelling pilgrimages and mere site visits, several researchers have proposed configurations of ritualized or solemn travel among Americans and other contemporary groups.

---

[16]   J. Adler, 'The Holy Man as Traveler and Travel Attraction: Early Christian Asceticism and the Moral Problematic of Modernity', in Swatos and Tomasi, *From Medieval Pilgrimage*, pp. 25–50.

[17]   E. Cohen, 'Pilgrimage and Tourism: Convergence and Divergence', in A. Morinis (ed.), *Sacred Journeys: The Anthropology of Pilgrimage* (Westport: Greenwood Press, 1992), pp. 47–61.

[18]   D.H. Olsen and D.J. Timothy, 'Tourism and Religious Journeys', in D.H. Olsen and D.J. Timothy (eds), *Tourism, Religion and Spiritual Journeys* (Abingdon: Routledge, 2006), pp. 1–21.

[19]   M. Tate, 'Tourism and Holy Week in León, Spain', in Badone and Roseman, *Intersecting Journeys*, pp. 110–24; C. Turnbull, 'Postscript: Anthropology as Pilgrimage, Anthropologist as Pilgrim', in Morinis, *Sacred Journeys*, pp. 257–74.

Juan Eduardo Campo[20] employs a simple tripartite division for modern pilgrimage expressions in this country: pilgrimages of organized religion, treks expressing 'civil religion', and others encoding 'cultural religion'. The first embraces mostly avatars of Catholic practices transposed into the New World by immigrant populations. By his own acknowledgement, the examples Campo offers of domestic Hindu pilgrimage are limited and confined to constructed shrine sites and never sacralized landscape features, while Muslim pilgrimage is non-existent within the United States.

Campo's two other categories are given the tag of 'religion' but are probably better understood as convergent values systems and national sentiment. His pilgrimages of civil religion promote patriotic values and enjoy the backing of large government agencies as custodians and interpreters of these prestige sites such as Lexington and Concord, Massachusetts; Civil War battle sites like Gettysburg; Mount Rushmore in the Black Hills of South Dakota; Pearl Harbor and the sunk battleship *Arizona* in Hawaii; Yellowstone National Park in Wyoming, etc. Each of these receives countless millions of visitors every year. We might add several sites which rapidly became focal points of national identity, even a profound sense of national mourning, such as Ground Zero in New York after the terrorist attacks of 11 September 2001 and before then the sites of the assassinations of John F. Kennedy and Martin Luther King, Jr.

Sellars and Walter (1993) anticipate Campo in their exploration of civil religion but emphasize, for the memorials of heroes and historical personages, the contingent nature of a tomb acquiring the status of sites of sober visitation: a 'shrine's development is by no means a certainty';[21] 'in some instances ... a memorial to the deceased is built or the place of death preserved, and then come the pilgrims ... In others, the pilgrims come regardless, the place becomes sacred, and a memorial has to be erected in response'.[22]

Pilgrimage of cultural or 'implicit' religion forms a 'third group [which] comprises pilgrimages that in a significant way incorporate elements deriving from the sphere of cultural values and practices but that are distinct from those identified with organized religions and civil religion'.[23] Americans who wish to feel themselves full participants of their cultural world seek

---

[20]   J.E. Campo, 'American Pilgrimage Landscapes', *The Annals of the American Academy of Political and Social Science*, 558/1 (1998), pp. 40–56.

[21]   R.W. Sellars and T. Walter, 'From Custer to Kent State: Heroes, Martyrs and the Evolution of Popular Shrines in the USA', in I. Reader and T. Walter (eds), *Pilgrimage in Popular Culture* (Basingstoke: Macmillan, 1993), p. 180.

[22]   Sellars and Walter, 'From Custer to Kent State', pp. 179–80.

[23]   Campo, 'American Pilgrimage Landscapes', p. 44.

distinctly American venues to take the pulse of popular landmarks in time and space. Graceland, Elvis Presley's home near Memphis, Tennessee, Las Vegas, Disneyland in California and Walt Disney World in Florida all qualify. Such sites are uniquely American and experienced by so many that their blatant commercial aspects do not prevent visitors from feeling that they are acquiring a repertoire of essential touchstones. Those who never leave home to be drenched in the mists of Niagara Falls or to take in the view from the top of the Washington Monument are in some sense diminished citizens of the nation.

Finally, Campo recognizes that with the increased fluidity of communication and travel pilgrimage has become a global phenomenon. Americans readily leave the United States to participate or at least become observers at fully religious places like Rome, Jerusalem, Seville during Semana Santa, and Mecca, or in terms of patriotic pilgrimage they travel to the cemeteries of Normandy in France or to the Hiroshima Peace Memorial in Japan. Cultural pilgrimages would include any return to the ancestral homeland of a more or less well defined minority group of immigrants to the United States, whether they be Poles, Italians, Indians or any other group in diaspora. A special case can be made for a 'reverse pilgrimage' not named by Campo, the growing traffic of black citizens of the United States who seek to visits the slave forts of Ghana and other locales on the West African coast to pay homage at the sites of embarkation of their ancestors condemned to foreign servitude.

Like Campo, Carolyn V. Prorok[24] emphasizes the role immigration has played in overlaying 'old country' practices onto a new landscape by replicating traditional pilgrimages in new sites or with fondly remembered ones recreated here, sometimes in miniature.[25] She identifies the principal mechanisms for immigrants as 'co-opting sacred sites of host communities, maintaining links to their homeland, or re-creating sacred sites ... through replication, (re)cognition,

---

[24]   Prorok, 'Transplanting Pilgrimage', pp. 283–307.

[25]   The nostalgic memorial in miniature is first immortalized in Western literature in Aeneas's discovery of a colony of fellow Trojans in exile who have built a scale model replica of their now lost city and its outlying rivers and hills (*Vergil's Aeneid* Books I–IV, ed. C. Pharr (Boston: D.C. Head & Company, 1964), pp. 294–351). The threat of slipping into kitsch is real, and Charles Witke, the great classicist of the University of Michigan, used to joke with his students that this episode was one of Virgil's few true lapses in taste, envisioning a layout that we would now attribute to a putt-putt golf course. Miniature Lourdes (12 US locations) and Fatima shrines (8 US locations) are among the most numerous manifestations of pious miniaturization among American Catholics (see L.K. Davidson and D. Gitlitz, 'Replica Pilgrimages', in *Pilgrimage: From the Ganges to Graceland: An Encyclopedia* (2 vols, Santa Barbara: ABC-CLIO, 2002), vol. 2, pp. 519–22, which includes examples from Jewish, Hindu and other faith communities but whose replica shrines are all outside the United States).

creating movable rituals, celebrating sites of sacred embodiment, and ritual historicizing'.[26] She underscores the precarious nature of trying to reassemble pilgrimage traditions in new, sometimes hostile environments but finds that the energy to pull it off arises from a need to anchor our temporal, individual selves in a 'collective selfhood'. She points out that most cultures are rooted in an essentially nomadic past which generated identity through the spaces people traversed, spaces which became sacred through repetition and ritualization. The result was the consecration of unique but constantly evolving pilgrimage circulation systems as a standing feature of a given culture, and such systems are evident in many modern religions whether viewed as a unitary system (all Muslims direct their steps and worship wherever they find themselves toward Mecca) or as a highly diversified system in which territories are mentally mapped as a complex of holy points and paths (Hindu and Christian landscapes). Prorok recognizes that the glance backward towards an ancestral homeland can transform any return there into a pilgrimage to one's origins, a mother country 'made sacred by its role in the diasporic imagination'.[27]

Linda Kay Davidson and David Gitlitz are among the pioneering researchers and adventurers on the Camino de Santiago and have published the best guide to that Catholic sacred journey, *The Pilgrimage Road to Santiago: The Complete Cultural Handbook*,[28] and the invaluable *Pilgrimage and the Jews*.[29] In their two-volume *Pilgrimage: From the Ganges to Graceland: An Encyclopedia*,[30] they provide extensive coverage of world pilgrimage including 38 sites in the United States. There are excellent general essays on 'Activities During Pilgrimage', 'Criticism of Pilgrimage', 'Life as Pilgrimage', 'Literature and Pilgrimage', 'Motives for Pilgrimage', 'Sacred Space', 'Secular Pilgrimage', 'Tourism as Pilgrimage', and so on. Their more capacious taxonomy recognizes and discusses overlapping pilgrimages – sites, journeys and periodic events – that they recognize as religious, secular popular (Grateful Dead concerts; visits to the grave of Jim Morrison in Père Lachaise Cemetery, Paris), secular political (the Alamo in San Antonio, Texas; the Hiroshima Peace Memorial in Japan; the D-Day landings sites on the beaches of Normandy), and those of secular identity (the Ghana

---

[26]   Prorok, 'Transplanting Pilgrimage', p. 283.

[27]   Prorok, 'Transplanting Pilgrimage', p. 289.

[28]   L.K. Davidson and D. Gitlitz, *The Pilgrimage Road to Santiago: The Complete Cultural Handbook* (New York: St Martin's Griffin, 2000).

[29]   D. Gitlitz and L.K. Davidson, *Pilgrimage and the Jews* (Westport: Praeger Publishers, 2006).

[30]   Davidson and Gitlitz, *Pilgrimage: From the Ganges to Graceland* (Santa Barbara: ABC-CLIO, 2002).

Slave Forts in western Africa; the Stonewall Inn where the American gay rights movement started; and Wounded Knee).

American Indian Religions and Pilgrimage

Of special importance for understanding contemporary American myth and its pilgrimage sites are the head article of Davidson and Gitlitz and the 13 place entries on Native American Religions (Bear Butte, South Dakota; Mount Shasta, California;[31] Sedona, Arizona, etc.), in essence pagan sites in that they hold in common 'certain overarching principles' which repeatedly centre on the unity of the spirit and physical worlds and humankind's role in maintaining their balance and living in harmony with elemental components like the weather, the cardinal directions, and companion species such as horses, birds and buffalo. In calling these religious traditions and their pilgrimages 'pagan', I certainly do not mean to slight them, but only to identify some of their key features implicit but relatively unexplored in Davidson and Gitlitz. Pagan belief systems, in classical antiquity, within traditional indigenous populations, or among modern Euro-American or Euro-Oceanic peoples routinely manifest an 'intense locality in [their] ... perception of and encounter with deity' and their 'this-worldly orientations' without a 'fundamental interest in soteriology or afterlife affairs'. Pagans feel that 'the godhead is immanent within the world rather than ... radically and transcendentally other ... both personal and impersonal as well as male and female', and that 'supernatural reality is considered neither good nor evil but potentially a mixture of the positive and negative'. In examining a pagan's reasons for undertaking a pilgrimage journey 'the magical act of contact with a sacred site or object ... is crucial and leads to the acquisition of fortune, power, or healing usually ... in tangible terms'.[32] There are some 500 tribal groupings scattered within the 50 American states, many of whom were forcibly relocated when colonizing European settlers seized their lands and slaughtered their defenders. Their creation myths, healing rituals, rites of ethnic identity and vision quests[33] are not just woven into the mythology of the modern American consciousness – and a rebuke to the nation's historical misdeeds – but are part of the fabric of the more ecologically sensitive leading edge of American aspirations.

---

[31]   L. Huntsinger and M. Fernández-Giménez, 'Spiritual Pilgrims at Mount Shasta, California', *Geographical Review*, 90 (2000), pp. 536–58.

[32]   York, 'Contemporary Pagan Pilgrimages', pp. 141–2.

[33]   Davidson and Gitlitz, *Pilgrimage: From the Ganges to Graceland*, vol. 2, pp. 431–4.

Taylor, exploring the vast migration of Mexicans and other Hispanics through the Sonoran Desert to seek employment or political asylum, notes the continuity of ancient native traditions in this annual surge of vulnerable travellers:

> Native Americans, the Tohono and Hia C-ed O'odham, moved transhumantly or nomadically among seasonal camps and villages through a territory that encompassed thousands of square miles on both sides of what became the border between the US and Mexico. But they also moved on pilgrimage, first to acquire salt and rain from the sea, and, beginning in the earlier decades of the nineteenth century, on their own version of a Catholic pilgrimage to the shrine of San Francisco Xavier in Magdalena de Kino, Sonora ... Also on a "spiritual mission" are many devotees of "Wilderness" who come alone or in groups to walk through such official and "authentic wilderness" as can be found in the national lands along the border, including Organ Pipe National Monument and the Cabeza Prieta National Wildlife Refuge [both in Arizona]. While ostensibly concerned with other goals, these movements, like those of the anti and pro-immigrant groups, can also be understood as pilgrimages that narrate, perform and geographically inscribe versions of America.[34]

Eade and Sallnow[35] proposed a tripartite analysis of pilgrimage through its *persons*, *places* and *texts*. S. Coleman and J. Elsner[36] expanded this list by adding *movement* as a key feature that operates as a configuring force in a given pilgrimage. Native American pilgrimages – those of the Lakota Sioux, the Pueblo Indians of New Mexico, and elsewhere – show their unique character on the American landscape for being habitually 'closed' rather than 'open' expeditions: members of these tribes are the sole *persons* who may enact their rituals and non-native Americans may not join in no matter how sympathetic or supportive they may feel. The *place* is the original landscape of their traditional rites, even though interstate highways, public and private lands now overlay its sacred circuits, spanning streams, prairies and hillsides. The *movement* may also be highly choreographed, such as for the Lakota who execute their commemorative Bigfoot Memorial Ride, more recently evocatively renamed the Future Generations Ride, on horseback. And in terms of *text*, the Lakota are also exemplary, having bequeathed to American lore a work of deep mystical insight,

---

[34]   Taylor, 'Centre and Edge', p. 384.
[35]   J. Eade and M.J. Sallnow (eds), *Contesting the Sacred: The Anthropology of Pilgrimage* (Urbana and Chicago: University of Illinois Press, 2000).
[36]   Coleman and Elsner, *Pilgrimage Past and Present*, pp. 196–220.

Black Elk Speaks,[37] revered by scholars of many traditions worldwide and now embraced by nearly every native tribe in the United States, many of whose oral traditions have been lost over time along with the extinction of their languages. Taylor brings these features together in an insightful contribution to what he calls 'moral geography':

> the cultural practice of ascribing symbolic significance and moral valence to particular landscapes. In the case of nationalism [i.e., for native American nations] there are of course countless examples, including "ancient homelands", or "where our dead are buried". Such places are never simply given or remembered; rather they are created and sustained through the cultural work of specific actions and narratives. In the category of actions comes movement through the landscape, a particularly potent form of which we often call pilgrimage.[38]

One factor elided by all four of the preceding scholars,[39] is a distinction between pilgrimages which are more precisely identified as site visits and those which include – and may be essentially qualified as – travelling pilgrimage for which the journey is an indelible component. The completion of the trek is always presumed, even in cases like the modern Camino de Santiago which Spanish pilgrims in particular may assemble over the course of several years by doing short stretches as vacation time and means allow. Following the routes to Santiago is the primordial experience, and many who perform this multipurpose rite for personal or cultural reasons – or who feel disaffected from the Catholic Church or religion in general – never enter the cathedral at all nor collect the certificate of completion which is offered either as a formal Latin proclamation issued by the Church or as a simple Spanish diploma with no implied religious significance.

Religious Pilgrimages in the United States

There are abundant sites of religious pilgrimage in the United States. For American Catholics there is the Shrine of the Immaculate Conception in Washington, DC and St Patrick's Cathedral in New York, both of which stand

---

[37]   J. Neihardt, *Black Elk Speaks: Being the Life Story of a Holy Man of the Oglala Sioux* (Albany: SUNY Press, 2008).

[38]   Taylor, 'Centre and Edge', p. 384.

[39]   Campo, 'American Pilgrimage Landscapes'; Prorok, 'Transplanting Pilgrimage'; Davidson and Gitlitz, *Pilgrimage: From the Ganges to Graceland*.

in as 'head churches'. Other sites may draw visitors from around the nation but are still basically local devotions managed by a given parish church or religious order, places which may have little more to boast than a congregation or an unusual building (St John's Abbey Church, Collegeville, Minnesota), statue or cross (The Cross in the Woods, Cheboygan, Michigan).[40]

There are only a few cases of Catholic shrines where a walking pilgrimage is an essential component and greater than a procession conducted in the course of a specific liturgical service, or access to a more or less elaborate outdoor Way of the Cross, itself a medieval devotional invention meant to reproduce in miniature a trek to the Holy Land. The Spanish colonial era Mission of Chimayó north of Santa Fe, New Mexico, is a distinctive walking pilgrimage: its Good Friday crowds carry crosses to the humble chapel from miles away. The California Mission Trail embraces an extensive string of venerable Franciscan churches like San Juan Capistrano and Santa Bárbara, but plans for relinking them for walking pilgrims are complicated by the California highway system which lies atop the old mission roads and now blocks many land routes from one to the next. Across the border to the north, the Canadian pilgrimage shrines of Sainte-Anne-de-Beaupré and St Joseph's Oratory, both in Québec, are informally linked by an 18-day walking path being developed in imitation of the Camino de Santiago.[41]

Among American Protestants, only the pilgrimage practices of the Church of Latter Day Saints (Mormons) are fully 'nativized': the original foundational trek happened in the United States in the 1830s and 1840s and from the beginning was interpreted from within that community as a divinely choreographed re-enactment of biblical journeys with Brigham Young styled as a new Joshua for his people. The Mormons undertook a mass exodus from their Sacred Grove in upstate New York, suffered a massacre of their leaders by mobs in Nauvoo, Illinois, and finally took up residence next to the remote Salt Lake in Utah to

---

[40] On American Catholicism, see studies by V. Baker, 'Breaking Bread with Prisca: Catholic Women, Pilgrimage, and Identity Politics and Theology', *Theatre Annual. A Journal of Performance Studies*, 63 (2010), pp. 1–26 and L. Russell, 'The Pilgrim Paths', *Theatre Annual. A Journal of Performance Studies*, 58 (2005), pp. 1–65 and D.A. Menchaca, 'Performing Identities', *Theatre Annual. A Journal of Performance Studies*, 58 (2005), pp. 67–121. M.J. Chiat's *The Spiritual Traveler. Chicago and Illinois. A Guide to Sacred Sites and Peaceful Places* (Mahwah: Hidden Spring [Paulist Press], 2004) announced as the first volume of a 50-state project, mostly covers significant Christian churches and shrines but also Muslim, Hindu and Buddhist holy places, and sites of historical and cultural interest.

[41] Personal communication from Austin Cooke, president of the Canadian Company of Pilgrims.

escape persecution for their unorthodox beliefs and practice of polygamy. This trajectory spanned the settled continent of their historical moment and only stopped when they reached the furthest edge of their known world, a rather unplanned pilgrimage that achieved biblical proportions, real martyrdoms, and an epic sweep. It is important to add that this Church has in recent decades staged re-creations of their historic pilgrimage in period costumes and wagons. Deployed as a transgenerational rite of passage and catechetical tool, the popular and theatrical nature of the costuming finds echoes in the evocative wardrobes seen in the Passion Play of Oberammergau (Bavaria, Germany) or even among those who choose to walk the Camino de Santiago in playful re-creations of medieval garb. The Mormon practice is halfway between the German staging, with its fully biblical narrative and dramatic arc but (in common with the Lakota) a similarly closed rite to which outsiders cannot volunteer themselves as participants, and the Camino stylings which are un-scripted historical approximations that recall a primordial community's experience. Pilgrims in Spain are not acting out a transgenerational educational practice among living believers so their outfits are entirely personalized. The Mormon re-enactments are especially notable for making the travel component the essential element whether it takes place along some of the still rutted wagon trails that marked their first passage out West in the 1840s or on any random stretch of woods and fields within reach of their local Stake (comparable to a diocese).[42] The Mormon treks, especially those accompanying Pioneers Day, 24 July, which is an official holiday in the state of Utah, are deeply imbued with religious overtones. The youth taking part pause for organized prayers, and perform traditional songs and dances.

Secular Pilgrimages in the United States

The journeys that explicitly entail trekking a distance within the United States are all instances of cultural pilgrimage intimately tied to esteemed natural settings. A 'Triple Crown' of distance hiking trails in the continental United States include the Continental Divide Trail, the Pacific Crest Trail and the celebrated Appalachian Trail. The 'AT' is a route of over 2,000 miles of frequently strenuous and nearly always isolated terrain stretching from northern Georgia to northern Maine, a trek which lingers in the background imagination of many

---

[42]   L. McCoy, 'A Pioneer's Journey', *The Daily Press* [Hampton Roads, Virginia], Good Life section (1 August 2010), pp. 1, 9.

Americans who view it as an epic achievement even when done in stages let alone accomplished in a single season from early spring to early fall. There are no significant cultural monuments to visit along the way and no history other than its founding and growth in infrastructure and popularity.[43]

There are a growing number of historic trails that retrace the paths of major events in American history. Although often maintained by national or local government authorities, they are not patriotic in any normative sense and some constitute 'dark pilgrimages' in that they are journeys of remembrance and even reparation. The Lewis and Clark Trail exists as a well-documented route by the explorers commissioned by Thomas Jefferson to locate a passage to the Pacific coast. Only some sections, such as those near Columbia, Missouri, are marked and readily accessible.[44]

Sites of secular pilgrimage, rather than travelling adventures, embrace innumerable gatherings throughout the United States which draw enthusiasts who, in part, may be celebrating their whimsy rather than any transcendent value or aspiration. High Pointers take as their sites of cultural pilgrimage the highest points in each of the 50 states. Some of the ascents are extremely easy while others require advanced mountaineering skills. In addition to an online community and annual convention of enthusiasts, the national organization sponsors a newsletter, publishes guides for the more challenging summits, and cultivates friendly relations with owners of high points on private property. The annual Harley Davidson motorcycle rallies are festive events that indulge in loud concerts, outrageous leather costumes and casual tourism. They occur in Daytona Beach, Florida, Laconia, New Hampshire, and Sturgis, South Dakota, where for two weeks each August participants and vendors double the population of that state.[45] Among the event sites of secular pilgrimage, one could point to those who travel to rendezvous with other fans for concerts by bands such as the Grateful Dead, whose devotees are known as Deadheads, and by Jimmy Buffett, whose followers are called Parrotheads, after the Hawaiian shirts and parrot headgear worn by many of them. The Burning Man event in the Black Rock Desert, Nevada, is a free-spirited, deliberately counter-cultural celebration of self-reliance (mostly surviving the fierce desert heat for a week), art

---

[43] For a personalized and popular – and rather witty – account of walking the Appalachian Trail, see B. Bryson, *A Walk in the Woods* (New York: Broadway Books, 1998).

[44] T. Schmidt, *National Geographic Guide to the Lewis & Clark Trail* (Washington, DC: National Geographic, 2002).

[45] Jill Dubisch examines 'motorcycle pilgrimage' as a uniquely American expression (J. Dubisch, '"Heartland of America": Memory, Motion and the (Re)Construction of History on a Motorcycle Pilgrimage', in Coleman and Eade, *Reframing Pilgrimage*, pp. 105–32).

and free expression (temporary displays of outlandish and ingenious concepts), a rigorously inclusive sense of community, and environmentalism.[46] The sprawling Star Trek conventions held around the world deserve mention as well for their mass appeal at home and abroad.

Many of these events are quirky extensions of American culture and camp pilgrimages, but in their own way respectful encounters with displays of hospitality, goodwill and, in the Turners' classic formulation, *communitas*.[47]

Pilgrimage and Narratives of the United States

From antiquity pilgrimage has bequeathed a legacy of writing about natural history and cultures in conflict and encounter. It is, arguably, the root source of all subsequent travel writing as a genre, and more importantly seems to have been the medieval forge where modern autobiography and other kinds of life writing draw their nascent forms. Among writers in English, fifteenth-century Margery Kempe – a difficult travelling companion even by her own admission – chronicles her life through a series of pilgrimage trips, while fourteenth-century Geoffrey Chaucer created an international literary monument by using an expedition to a martyr's shrine as the setting for his *Canterbury Tales*. Other non first-person English travel writing emerged and flourished over the centuries, like the historical novel invented by Walter Scott (*Ivanhoe* 1819 and the Waverley Novels) and the maritime novel launched by James Fenimore Cooper (*The Pilot* 1823). The nineteenth century was an age of intensified exploration and exploitation of colonial lands and resources and a Romantic personalization of nationalist sentiments as individuals sought to refine their identity in contrast with their country's history and perceive character. Many European writers still returned to 'colonize' their more remote, preferably medieval, past where they felt the authentic roots of their ethnic or national experience lay preserved. Others like Benito Pérez Galdós celebrated more recent formative events like the French invasion and Spanish war of independence from the Battle of Trafalgar

---

[46]   See Taylor on 'wilderness cults' which seek to venture into endangered natural landscapes. He gives special consideration to groups which feel somehow threatened and which 'are worried about the profanation of sacred ground and seek to preserve, protect and experience (in a religious/spiritual transformative way) the wild authentic landscapes crucial to both individual and national redemption' (Taylor, 'Centre and Edge', p. 391).

[47]   V. Turner and E. Turner, *Image and Pilgrimage in Christian Culture: Anthropological Perspectives* (Oxford and New York: Basil Blackwell and Columbia University Press, 1978).

(1805) to the restoration of the Bourbon monarchy (1875) in the 46 novels in his wildly successful series of *Episodios nacionales* (1873–1912).

The literary legacy of the United States has been enriched by foreign travellers who described the United States they encountered and their own pilgrimages through this country, figures like the Argentine educator Facundo Sarmiento, the Cuban poet José Martí, and most indelibly of all the Frenchman Alexis de Tocqueville whose *Democracy in America* (1835 and 1840) was prescient in its understanding of the American psychological profile. De Tocqueville came to New York City in 1831 and spent nine months ostensibly touring prisons but also taking shrewd notes on social *mores* and the dynamics of political life, an obsession with material goods, the vitality of private enterprise, the negotiation of labour and the contested ownership of its fruits, Russo-American rivalries, and the impending crisis over slavery which would lead to the United States' near dissolution during its bloody Civil War.

The twentieth century saw an efflorescence of travel writing worldwide including pilgrimage narratives. Authors of scant literary merit, like Paulo Coelho[48] and Paul Cousineau,[49] still seize the imagination of their countrymen and inspire countless seekers to set out on travels that have already been scripted for them in comforting visions. Part of motivation for travel is a longing to reconnect with a simpler, more authentic time. Many contemporary pilgrimage narratives display both a belief in the journey's power faithfully to recreate the experience of those who went before on the same trails and a concomitant 'distrust of modernity': yarns of solemn adventuring are the armature 'whereby travel is narrated as a nostalgic encounter with a past made desirable by the crippling effects of modernity'.[50] Americans who write of their expeditions for other Americans – and Americans never write with foreign readers in mind – are in search of authenticity, their historic and heroic past, an American myth they can believe in, and as part of a flight from the uniformity of strip mall marketing

---

[48]   A *New Yorker* magazine biography of Paulo Coelho observes that 'Coelho writes in Portuguese; some literary critics in Brazil joke among themselves that translation must improve his prose. "He writes in a non-literary style, with a message that confirms common sense", Manuel da Costa Pinto, a columnist for Folha de S. Paulo, said. "He gives readers a recipe for happiness" ... Most "Brazilian critics ... reflexively dismiss Coelho"' (D. Goodyear, 'The Magus: The Astonishing Appeal of Paulo Coelho', *The New Yorker* (7 May 2007), p. 39). The essay portrays Coelho, for all his wealth and popular acclaim, as an amused charlatan and a flake.

[49]   P. Cousineau, *The Art of Pilgrimage: The Seeker's Guide to Making Travel Sacred* (Berkeley: Conari Press, 1998).

[50]   P. Genoni, 'The Pilgrim's Progress Across Time: Medievalism and Modernity on the Road to Santiago', *Studies in Travel Writing*, 15/2 (2011), p. 157.

and mass media towards a Golden Age of lost innocence.[51] Part of the allure of sometimes arduous travel is the opportunity to become part of the experience of others, like those who trek to the Vietnam Memorial in Washington to tell their war stories for the benefit of willing listeners. Hearing from a veteran who lost friends and fellow soldiers, and his youth, in the jungles of south-east Asia is for many 'mere tourists' a transformative encounter with authentic witness and holy man in one.

Travel freighted with special meanings has become so thoroughly laced throughout American culture that it has spawned literary classics like Jack Kerouac's *On the Road*,[52] the obvious model for the Jack Hitt[53] first-person pilgrimage narrative, *Off the Road*, which did so much to popularize the Spanish trek to Santiago de Compostela among English language readers. Other noted American writers include John Steinbeck[54] whose *Travels with Charlie* inspired Charles Kurault's 'On the Road',[55] broadcast segments starting in 1967, over 20 years' of sentimental and often quirky mini travel documentaries for CBS television, and William Zinsser's beloved *American Places*.[56]

---

[51] Travel and the search for authenticity are themes explored by D. MacCannell, *The Tourist: A New Theory of the Leisure Class* (New York: Schoken Books, 1976); Badone and Roseman, 'Approaches', p. 14; E. Badone, 'Crossing Boundaries: Exploring the Borderlands of Ethnography, Tourism, and Pilgrimage', in Badone and Roseman, *Intersecting Journeys*, p. 182; and Genoni, 'The Pilgrim's Progress', pp. 167–9, 174, n. 34. Conrad notes that 'A pilgrim is not a tourist. You have a deeper experience precisely because you are not an observer in the traditional sense ... The locals look to you as a special experience, as authentic. Despite the distance, you are a participator, an authenticator, even more than the locals themselves' (R. Conrad, *Pilgrimage to the End of the World* (Chicago: Chicago University Press, 2004), p. 34; also cited by Genoni, 'The Pilgrim's Progress', p. 167). In examining the American myth Taylor concurs that 'The frontiersman was at the same time both the enemy of wild nature and its embodiment ... This was a ... transformation ... that stripped off "the veneer" of civilisation and left "essential man"' (Taylor, 'Centre and Edge', p. 388). The quest for 'genuine' experiences may not need ironic comeuppance, but see A. Potter, *The Authenticity Hoax: Why the 'Real' Things We Seek Don't Make Us Happy* (New York: Harper Perennial, 2010).

[52] For the durable appeal of this travel narrative see Jennifer Schuessler's and David L. Ulin's report on how it became the 'top-grossing book' app for the iPad; D.L. Ulin, 'Jack Kerouac on the App Road', *Los Angeles Times* (22 June 2011), at http://latimesblogs.latimes.com/jacketcopy/2011/06/jack-kerouac-on-the-app-road.html (accessed 5 March 2013).

[53] J. Hitt, *Off the Road: A Modern-Day Walk Down the Pilgrim Route into Spain* (New York: Simon & Schuster, 1994) [Rpt. 2005].

[54] J. Steinbeck, *Travels with Charlie: In Search of America* (New York: Viking, 1962).

[55] C. Kuralt, 'On the Road', CBS Evening News (1967).

[56] Zinsser, *American Places*.

While Kerouac, Steinbeck and Kerault dedicate themselves to the telling vignette in miniature, Zinsser opts for iconic and monumental sites like Mount Vernon, Niagara Falls and Pearl Harbor: 'I had looked for America long enough in its microcosmic places. This time I was going after the big ones.'[57] Although he was clearly engaged in serial site pilgrimage rather a journey from place to place, Zinsser felt that he partook in the motivation held in common by fellow arrivals at each place: 'What I also saw was why we all go. I don't mean that I know the story behind every family trip; people bring different needs to sacred places and take different things away. It is also true that these places are not static; they keep being reshaped by new events and social currents ... on a deeper level all of us are on the same quest. We are looking for continuity.'[58] Repeat visitors to Yellowstone or Rockefeller Plaza felt that they were reconnecting with 'a family possession', that they 'had been brought there as children and were now back with children of their own, pilgrims to the memory of what they once did with their parents. Old Faithful and the Skating Rink were twins in their ability to link the past and the present and the future across the generations and to reaffirm the pleasure of bringing up a family in America.'[59]

Zinsser's patriotic credulity leads him and his reader to a willing trust in the power of place, especially locales long reverenced by American visitors. His very occasional ironic detachment is reported with a certain humility, something he has to acknowledge and keep under control, like his mistrust of sanitized and 'Disneyfied' American history, an accusation levelled (unfairly) at Colonial Williamsburg, the largest and most carefully planned living museum of colonial America and Virginia's role in the Revolutionary Era. Other writers with even greater mass appeal than Zinsser do indulge to the full their private notions, such as the reincarnation imaginings of Shirley MacLaine[60] and the sardonic humour of German comic Hape Kerkling.[61]

Movies about Travel are not Pilgrimages

Fictionalizations of travel claim their own popular movie genre, but one disqualified as a form of virtual pilgrimage because it focuses on individual

---

[57]   Zinsser, *American Places*, p. 2.
[58]   Zinsser, *American Places*, p. 187.
[59]   Zinsser, *American Places*, p. 188.
[60]   S. MacLaine, *The Camino: A Journey of the Spirit* (New York: Pocket Books, 2000).
[61]   H. Kerkeling [Hans Peter], *I'm Off Then: Losing and Finding Myself on the Camino de Santiago* (New York: Free Press, 2006).

experiences, characters and a unique narrative, and not on the enduring power of places in themselves. Film inevitably privileges the visual and aural. The viewer's passivity and the loss of a sense of space and place detach movies from lived pilgrimage. The dislocation and estrangement of pilgrimage are interiorized and privatized, never participating in a communal experience that spans generations and builds communal membership. Films are obviously durable cultural treasures with the power to entrance and unite decades of viewers. Endless holiday replays of *Wizard of Oz* (1939, heartland Kansas and a fantasy land), *It's a Wonderful Life* (1946, small town America) or *Miracle on 34th Street* (1946, quintessential New York City) attest to the power of iconic art forms, but do not constitute leaving one's home turf. The overwhelmingly popular British trilogy on the printed page and silver screen, *The Lord of the Rings* (2001, 2002, 2003), is essentially a peripatetic quest narrative of conflict between the fictionalized tribes representing good and evil, but still not a pilgrimage.

Sharing beloved movies is all about feeling centred, not volunteering oneself to be uncentred by a voyage to foreign territories or to seek a high plane, a touch of the transcendent. The spell of movies is strong and may express profound truths shared by a nation or culture, but it is technologically sophisticated, collaborative to the point of artistic anonymity (*pace* our reverence to the director's controlling vision), a form consumed but never produced by the recipient, and endlessly repeatable in an identical way – just the opposite of what actual pilgrims experience as they make a path through their own weather and emotional warren.

There are countless classic American road trip movies, well represented by *It Happened One Night* (1934), *Easy Rider* (1969), *Rain Man* (1988), *Thelma and Louise* (1991), *Sideways* (2004) and *Into the Wild* (2007), and movies that both celebrate and parody the form like *The Muppet Movie* (1979), *National Lampoon's Vacation* (1983), *Planes, Trains and Automobiles* (1987) and *Little Miss Sunshine* (2006). David Denby has observed that 'Things happen on trips; that's why the road-movie genre, with its radical concentration of means, never seems to tire. An opening to landscape, movement, adventure, and the eternal American desire to drop everything and light out for the territories, the form is both inherently dramatic and supremely flexible'.[62] We even interpret the lives of non-Americans through the lens of formative, often youthful, treks,

62   Denby goes on to note that the genre 'has served as the basis for crime thrillers ("They Live by Night", "Bonnie and Clyde"), for violent explorations of the limits of freedom ("Easy Rider", "Thelma and Louise"), for bruising tests of love and friendship ("Two for the Road", "Scarecrow")' (D. Denby, 'Drinking and Driving', *The New Yorker* (25 October 2004), p. 96).

such as *The Motorcycle Diaries* (2004) about the Argentine revolutionary Che Guevara.[63] But in almost every case the actual routes chosen are circumstantial, random, barely reported in the script and merely shown on the screen as a series of landscape backdrops, essential to the mood but fairly irrelevant to the interaction of the characters.

The latest addition to this genre is a telling example. *The Way* (2010), starring Martin Sheen and written, directed by and co-starring his son, Emilio Estévez, displays all the *bona fides* one could hope for in inducing, if not reproducing, a pilgrimage experience. The movie is set on the Spanish Camino de Santiago heading towards Galicia, home of the shrine and relics of the Apostle St James the Elder in Compostela. Both Sheen and Estévez are of Galician descent, and decided to make the film as a tribute to their fondly recalled touristic trip along portions of the Santiago route from the Pyrenees through northern Spain. They even subjected themselves to filming the movie in dramatic sequence as they travelled the modern trail westward, relying on real pilgrims as extras. The son, played movingly by Estévez, sternly rejects his father's conservative values and his own barely started doctorate in anthropology at the University of California-Berkeley, and resolves to live the world, not just read about it. He makes for St Jean Pied-de-Port in south-west France and the trail head of the Camino only to die on his first day in the mountains, caught in a freak snowstorm. The father flies to France to identify the body and decides in his grief and regret to carry his son's backpack and ashes to complete the pilgrimage in his place. The fictional father and son who suffered a generational divide are healed through a pilgrimage they make together, with the son appearing to his father as a silent companion invisible to others.

This may be an enticing inducement to undertake pilgrimage and the highly accessible modern Spanish version of it. But *The Way*, while a dramatic and artistic success and a faithful depiction of the motives and camaraderie of modern Jacobean pilgrims journeying to Santiago, is a story of people using a malleable emotional landscape, not characters made pliant by the grandeur and authority they have granted to the mythic journey they undertake. The tensions are inherently eternal: impassive nature is the screen onto which humans project their aspirations, while at the same time the lens and physical reality which guides travellers' interpretation of the meaning of their trek. In movies about

---

[63] The film *Diarios de motocicleta/Motorcycle Diaries* was filmed in Spanish by Brazilian director Walter Salles and was a co-production of companies in Argentina, the United States, Germany, the United Kingdom, Chile, Peru and France with executive producers Robert Redford, Paul Webster and others.

journeys, land and air and water are most often mere backdrop, stage props for actors who tell the story. For live pilgrims, land and air and water *are* the story and the only path towards their journey's resolution.

Movies about travel may not be surrogates for actual pilgrimages but they may well help consecrate sites accepted in the national mythology as focal points of the national experience. *North by Northwest* (1959) helped enshrine the monumental countenances on Mount Rushmore as symbols of a nation's heroes, and countless films rely on Rockefeller Plaza, the Lincoln Memorial, the Grand Canyon, the Great Plains and the giant redwoods of California as backdrops which function as concrete extensions of a people, as do manmade structures like the Twin Towers of New York City and the Pentagon. To attack them, as happened on 11 September 2001, defaces the nation itself and leaves a vacuum in real space but more importantly in the national imaginary. To touch them, as pilgrims inevitably do at the memorials for the Vietnam War (in Washington, DC) or the Civil Rights Movement (in Montgomery, Alabama), both designed by architect Maya Lin, is to touch one's own body politic and confirm its solidity and permanence.

American Motives for Pilgrimage

Medieval motives for making a pilgrimage could be holy or unholy, but the latter always included at least a veneer of righteousness and an inevitable susceptibility to realignment of one's life while undertaking commerce, tourism or war. Medieval pilgrims set out hoping to approach something greater than themselves and they travelled under the presumption that they would come closer to the divine or transcendent. Putting oneself in contact or proximity with a saint or figure of renown and to some extent participating in that person's world, ideology or community of believers helps justify an individual's existence. There was also pilgrimage to fulfil a promise or pledge either out of gratitude for a favour already granted or in token of spiritual fealty when asking for some benefit, like a cure, a miracle, or help for a loved one. On the far side of the scale, so to speak, one can also undertake a pilgrimage to do penance for a crime or sin, or to set right a transgression against the belief system which the sacred place or person represents. Traditional religious pilgrimage often entails a degree of abandonment to the will of God expressed through the uncontrollable circumstances of one's trip. The inscrutable divine will expose the person to danger, perhaps to death, and the pilgrim submits himself to that judgement out of humility or for the sake of the revelations it may bring.

American citizens feel little need to use patriotic or cultural pilgrimage to negotiate with higher powers, to travel for reparation, gratitude, personal reform, seeking benefits or favours. It is not commonly a quest for conversion, a self-imposed change of life that can alter a personal direction and spirituality by means of meditative stretches of solitude and exertion, or through service to others. Submitting to a higher will and risking deprivation or death are likewise perfectly unexpected. Melding with their ideological community is, however, part of the ethos that puts Americans on the road to visit battlefields, the homes of presidents and national historic monuments. They already feel themselves full members of the national community and they lay claim by right to everything within the borders of their nation – a somewhat presumptive stance that can put them at odds with those who feel that traditional sites are being exploited for mere tourism or recreation. Mount Shasta in California, Devil's Tower in Wyoming and Bear Butte in South Dakota are all sites where vacationing hikers and rock climbers – and devotees of New Age practices – demand access to places held sacred by indigenous communities.

The transgenerational is enacted in a unique way by each traveller even if thousands or millions have preceded him or her on this path or in coming to this site, and repeat pilgrims are fully aware of the differences among each of their treks and arrivals, and savour that qualified glimpse of spiritual solidarity. American exceptionalism regularly exempts itself from traditional 'Old World' modes of self expression and rarely undertakes the travelling pilgrimages so heavily inscribed on the local, historical landscapes of medieval Europe. Yet Americans took what they perceived as a blank canvass to sketch a history of their mythic travel across new territories and eagerly established what they only dimly intended as future sites of pilgrimage, utopian foundations for religious goals. Later generations of Americans recognized that their shared landscapes provided them with wondrous portals to Nature as a non-sectarian stand-in for God. Lincoln's Gettysburg Address, arguably the most famous speech in American history, is in essence the inauguration and consecration of a site ready made for pilgrimage.

Pilgrimage both sacred and secular is deeply ingrained in the American myth, on the contemporary landscape, and in cultural practices as varied as visits to cemeteries and amusement parks. In Washington, DC our shrines of democracy crowd each other for space on the National Mall and many of those sites announce their sacred character in the most obvious of ways: arguably, the most blatantly temple-like structure in Washington is not the National Cathedral but the National Archives where the Constitution and Declaration of Independence are honoured as relics of living power which justify the city-reliquary which shelters them. Despite being something of newcomers to examining their history as one of interwoven pilgrimages, both religious and secular, travel for transformation – and for affirmation of a self-renewing national identity – contributes one of the most frequent cultural practices that allow American citizens to immerse themselves in their national myth.

Chapter 4

Heaven on Earth:
Political Pilgrimages and the Pursuit of
Meaning and Self-Transcendence

Paul Hollander

It is the point of departure of this chapter – as it was of my earlier writings on the same subject – that political pilgrimages resemble in some significant ways the traditional pilgrimages of religious inspiration and origin. The most obvious similarity is that both types of pilgrims are motivated by a desire to venerate certain symbols of their beliefs found at various specific and often distant locations and both expect spiritual benefits of some kind as a result.[1]

In my previous writings I did not address explicitly the similarities and differences between the two types of pilgrimages, although I recognized that the political pilgrimages cannot be properly understood without reference to their predecessors, the religious ones.[2] My use of the word 'pilgrimage' indicated

---

[1] It is far from self-evident why deeply religious human beings believed, and still believe, that visiting certain physical locations has great spiritual or redemptive meaning and significance and that such visits yield great spiritual, psychological or even bodily, or physical, benefits. Not having studied religious pilgrimages I can only make impressionistic observations about religious pilgrimage sites and the likely criteria for their selection. Most of these sites were associated with particular individuals who lived and died in those locations and were distinguished by their conduct and contributions to the religious faith in question. Burial sites are pre-eminent destinations of the pilgrimages. Other sites had been the chosen because of miraculous events of divine origin which took place there. Religious pilgrimages have two objectives: to venerate an outstanding individual who personifies religious virtues or to venerate some physical object (a church or chapel, a spring, maybe a tree, a rock) that had some spiritual-religious significance or association. The second goal of the pilgrimages was spiritual or physical rejuvenation or recovery from specific illness or bodily infirmity – as for example at Lourdes.

[2] I realize that generalizations should be qualified by distinguishing between different kinds of religious pilgrims, as for example Christian, Muslim, Buddhist and others. I cannot do this here given the limitations of time and because addressing these differences would have required a comparative study of religious pilgrimages.

that I attributed some similarity to the two phenomena but the nature of this connection, or the similarities between them were not fully explored and they require further reflection. I welcome the opportunity to do so here.

Let me first provide some factual information on the political pilgrimages which I have studied and written about. My major study of the phenomenon[3] was based on the travel writings of Western intellectuals (let us not be detained here by definitions of who is an intellectual) who visited the Soviet Union between 1928 and 1978 – China under Mao, and Cuba under Castro, as well as some smaller communist states. In the later editions of this book I updated and extended the pilgrimages into the 1990s. I also wrote at some length about the pilgrimage to Sandinista Nicaragua during the 1980s in my book on anti-Americanism.[4] In my more recent book, a collection of essays,[5] there are further scattered references to the phenomenon and its current far more limited manifestations.

The pilgrimages, regardless of time and destination, were highly patterned as regards the motivation of the participants, the perceived attractions of the countries they visited and the treatment they received in these countries.

There is a close and significant connection between the political pilgrimages and certain characteristics of Western intellectuals – in fact the two help to understand one another. It would be difficult to discuss political pilgrimages without reference to intellectuals since they were the most typical participants in these pilgrimages. At the same time their participation in and accounts of these pilgrimages shed new light on intellectuals and suggest reasons for rethinking conventional conceptions of their defining characteristics. Why these intellectuals seemed to display a greater need for sustaining beliefs and communal bonds, and why they were more deeply estranged from their societies than the rest of the population is another intriguing question I cannot pursue here but address in the books mentioned earlier as well as other writings.

It is of some significance that only communist (or state socialist) societies stimulated and attracted political pilgrimages. This was probably the case because these were the only social systems which embarked on the pursuit of what might be called 'heaven on earth', to be brought about by sweeping social transformations, by means of large-scale, ambitious social engineering projects

---

[3]   P. Hollander, *Political Pilgrims: Travels of Western Intellectuals to the Soviet Union, China and Cuba* (New York: Oxford University Press, 1981). Several editions followed in 1983, 1990 and 1998. There were also translations into Spanish, Italian, Hungarian and Russian.

[4]   P. Hollander, *Anti-Americanism: Critiques at Home and Abroad* (New York: Oxford University Press, 1992).

[5]   P. Hollander, *The Only Super Power* (Lanham: Lexington Books, 2009).

and mass mobilization. These systems promised nothing less than a change in the human condition as it has been known throughout history. These were secular religious systems and the political pilgrims were motivated by secular religious beliefs – the most obvious reason for comparing them to their religious counterparts. The concept of secular religion will be discussed more fully below.

Let us start with an interesting paradox. A closer look at the political pilgrimages makes clear that these ostensibly secular pilgrimages had a strong, underlying non-political, spiritual or quasi-religious dimension. Most of these pilgrims were not merely interested in political and revolutionary change, or social reform, or the more equitable distribution of goods and services, or higher standards of living for the poor, but they also yearned for what can only be described as spiritual uplift, rejuvenation and self-transcendence.

Four ideas help to connect religious and political pilgrimages: utopia-seeking (heaven on earth), self-transcendence (related to the pursuit of community), secular religion and the concept of the true believer. Secular religious beliefs – such as the political pilgrims held – have several features they share with the religious ones. Both offer a comprehensive belief system that claims to provide guidance for leading a meaningful life; both have a sacred or quasi-sacred doctrinal basis which incorporates these teachings and instructions. The secular religious doctrines (or ideologies) are authoritatively interpreted by a deified leader. Both religious and secular religious doctrines provide highly polarized, sharply differentiated conceptions of good and evil (except Buddhism). Both provide communal rituals which are linked to displays of religious or secular religious sentiments and are designed to strengthen them. Both de-emphasize the importance of the individual compared to the community and both are future-oriented. Both designate entities that should guide or inspire the believer; the secular one, the deified supreme leader, as the major authority figure inspiring devotion and obedience. These leaders are portrayed as possessing qualities which in the past were attributed to divinity or to saints; these leaders, like deities, demanded unconditional veneration. Needless to say secular religions have no divine underpinnings and have nothing to say about life after death.[6]

The political pilgrims shared with their religious counterparts a strong desire to find a morally superior, spiritually enriched world, and a strong desire to make life more meaningful by visiting certain locations of great moral significance. These places were associated with ways of life, and values seen as superior to those which the travellers were familiar with in their own society. The political

---

[6]   I do not know who introduced the concept of secular religion but it has been used for decades and it used to be associated with the totalitarian systems and beliefs of the past century.

pilgrims believed that the communist societies were promised lands of social justice, constituted a vibrant community and emanated sense of purpose – as opposed to the conditions supposedly prevalent in the societies these pilgrims came from. The political pilgrims were favourably predisposed towards these countries and their socio-political systems and hoped to learn more about them during their visits; they also wished to apply what they learned to their own societies. They did not expect miraculous physical rejuvenation, as did many religious pilgrims, but expected and found temporary spiritual rejuvenation.[7]

Political pilgrims sought redeeming utopian social arrangements and fulfilment here and now; the religious ones in the afterlife. The holy places of the political pilgrims were sometimes literal parallels to those visited by their religious counterparts, such as the birthplace of Stalin, the mausoleum of Lenin in the former Soviet Union and that of Mao in China. There were many other sites to be admired and revered and shown to these visitors: new factories, model farms, model prisons, schools, kindergarten – anything that symbolized the accomplishments of the system and the fulfilment of the hopes of the visitors.

There are further reasons for applying the word 'pilgrimage' to the journeys of these Western travellers to communist countries, most of whom were not religious, at any rate not in the ordinary sense of the word, and examine more closely what their trips had in common with religious pilgrimages. Some of these travellers actually saw themselves as pilgrims. Jonathan Kozol, a well-known American social critic, wrote: 'Each of my two visits to Cuba was a pilgrimage and an adventure.'[8] John Brentlinger, an American professor, went to Sandinista Nicaragua motivated by the desire to be 'part of something larger and redeeming'.[9] He also averred: 'There was a vision there I wanted to hold on to, to bring back and transplant.' He thought Nicaraguans 'rejected the inhumane order based on individual greed … they re-ignited the hope for a new order, a nurturant community'. The two types of pilgrims have in common the expectation that it is desirable and possible to radically alter and improve one's way of life and the social environment in which one lives and that a pilgrimage could significantly contribute to such improvements. Many deeply religious

---

[7]   P. Berger, *Pyramids of Sacrifice* (Garden City: Anchor, 1976), p. 17, writes about the appeal of the Third World which often overlapped with the appeal of communist countries located in the Third World: 'Perhaps what is at work here is an archaic mythic motif, that of simpler and purer lands far away, from which some healing secret might be learned.'

[8]   J. Kozol, *Children of the Revolution: A Yankee Teacher in the Cuban Schools* (New York: Delacorte Press, 1978), p. xx.

[9]   J. Brentlinger, *The Best of What We Are: Reflections on the Nicaraguan Revolution* (Amherst: University of Massachusetts Press, 1995), pp. 2–4.

human beings, including those who go on religious pilgrimages, also share with the political pilgrims a degree of estrangement from their own society and an acute awareness of its moral-spiritual shortcomings and depravities. Religious beliefs often nurtured by such an awareness.

The alienation of the political pilgrims was rooted primarily in their rejection of materialism, capitalism, social injustices (especially inequality) and the unsatisfactory quality of life and social bonds in modern Western societies (exemplified by the cash nexus). It would be difficult to propose a similar generalization about the motivation of religious pilgrims – especially for someone who has not studied religious pilgrimages. It would be doubtful to suggest that they too were motivated by a discomfort with modernity, since most religious pilgrimages took place in pre-modern times; hence the issue of accepting or rejecting modernity is irrelevant. On the other hand the recent resurgence of Islamic religious beliefs is very closely connected to the hatred of, or ambivalence towards, modernity and the moral depravities it supposedly creates and nurtures.

Many political pilgrims were favourably impressed not only by the supposedly superior social, political and economic accomplishments of the communist countries they visited, but also by their surviving traditional, non-industrial aspects which the visitors associated with simplicity and authenticity, notwithstanding the fact that these countries were furiously industrializing. Thus Pablo Neruda admired what he considered a combination of socialist modernization with the preservation of traditional ways of life:

> I loved the Soviet land at first sight and I realized that not only does it offer a moral lesson for every corner of the globe ... but I sensed that an extraordinary flight would begin from this land ... The entire human race knows what a colossal truth is being worked out here ...

> I was in the middle of a forest where thousands of peasants in traditional festive costumes were listening to Pushkin's poems. Everything hummed with life ... Nature seemed to form a triumphant union with man.[10]

Waldo Frank, an American writer, was moved by the forms of traditional life he discerned in the 1930s in the Russian countryside: 'I stood in the village mud and sensed the organic rhythm of this telluric world – the pulse of earth and beast and man together.' Elsewhere he wrote: 'the immediate human, the want

---

[10]   P. Neruda, *Memoirs* (New York: Farrar, Straus and Giroux, 1977), p. 194.

of stereotype, that makes Russia so exciting. There are no separate persons ... Therefore he is vital ... Here was the deepest proof – music and folk dance do not lie – that the Communist Revolution is Russian.'[11] Harrison Salisbury, the American journalist on his visit to China was impressed by 'the world in which men and women laboured with their own hands, with a few animals, a few primitive implements – experiencing a life so simple, so integrated with the land, the weather and the plants that its symmetry seemed almost magical'.[12]

These travellers often conflated not only the attractions of traditional ways of life with the virtues of a new social system, but even managed to find validation for their enthusiasm in the physical beauty of the landscape. Thus Felix Greene, a British journalist, wrote of Mao's China: 'The view from the train window was like a scene from a Sung painting ... Old clustered villages with their curved roofs among the terraced rice fields. Tiny silver waterfalls sparkled ... Peasants in the fields in their wide cone hats ... everything green and lush.'[13] It did not seem to occur to him that the view from the train would have been the same before the communist seizure of power and the same idyllic scenes could also have been associated with, and used to legitimate, a feudal or capitalist society.

Lewis Lapham, an American writer and journalist, after visiting the military headquarters of Ho Chi Minh in North Vietnam scornfully commented on what he considered the essential difference between traditional authenticity and American style hollow modernity: 'On one side [the Vietnamese] a few small men, poor and thinly clothed, seated among flowering trees; on the other side the technological splendour of the Pentagon and ... generals decorated with gold braid ... in an air-conditioned room.'[14] The contrast between flowering trees and air conditioning encapsulates the observer's reverence for tradition and disdain for modernity and technology.

The pursuit of utopia, or utopian fulfilment, is a major conceptual bridge between the attitudes associated with religious and political pilgrimages. The belief in and search for utopia (religious or political) also conjures up the image of the 'true believer'[15] who may be religious, or secular religious, that is, a political true believer. The true believers among the political pilgrims were

---

[11]   W. Frank, *Dawn in Russia* (London: C. Scribner's Sons, 1932), pp. 98–9, 111–13, 121.

[12]   H.E. Salisbury, *To Peking and Beyond: A Report on the New Asia* (New York: Quadrangle, 1973), pp. 73–4.

[13]   F. Greene, *Awakened China: The Country Americans are not Allowed to Know* (Garden City: Doubleday, 1961), pp. 21–2.

[14]   L. Lapham, 'Notebook: Vietnam Diary', *Harpers* (May 1999), p. 13.

[15]   The term was introduced by Eric Hoffer, *The True Believer: Thoughts on the Nature of Mass Movements* (New York: Harpers, 1950).

looking for and were predisposed to find a perfected socio-political system, some approximation of 'heaven on earth'. The key to this perfection was the impending or ongoing dissolution of the endemic conflict between personal and social, or private and public interest. Other attributes of such a social system included the absence of social conflict, and the progressive disappearance of scarcities, both material and psychic, the latter referring to the expansion of the capacity to love. Social pathologies – poverty, crime, delinquency, prostitution, alcoholism, drug addiction, family disintegration – were also expected to disappear or were supposedly already vanishing in these societies. Especially important was the belief that these political systems changed, or were in the process of changing, human nature itself, creating vastly improved human beings no longer selfish, aggressive and narrow-minded but generous, altruistic and communal.

Religious believers seek ultimate fulfilment in a blissful, other-worldly existence that would result from having led exemplary lives determined by the commandments of their religion. Undertaking pilgrimages confirmed and highlighted their religious beliefs. Religious pilgrimages were and are an important expression of religious beliefs but it is difficult to know to what degree the experience of the pilgrimage altered attitudes and behaviour in its aftermath. By contrast the secular-political pilgrims sought fulfilment here and now.

Todd Gitlin, former 1960s radical, captured the motivation of people who were likely to become political pilgrims: 'they were hungry to believe that somewhere out there, preferably on the dusky side of the globe where people looked exotic, some decency was under construction.'[16] Doris Lessing wrote about a similar predisposition: 'these attitudes ... can only come out of some belief, one so deep it is out of sight, that a promise of some kind had been made and betrayed.'[17] Malcolm Cowley, an American writer, thought that 'Communism ... seemed capable of supplying the moral qualities that writers missed in bourgeois society: the comradeship in struggle, the self-imposed discipline, the ultimate purpose ... the opportunity for heroism and the human dignity.'[18]

For these travellers the political pilgrimage was an exhilarating, liberating experience. Lion Feuchtwanger, the German novelist, wrote in the 1930s:

> I came to the Soviet Union from countries ... whose inhabitants, discontented with both their physical and spiritual condition, crave change ... The air which

---

[16] T. Gitlin, 'Lost Cause: Why Intellectuals of the Left Miss Communism', *Los Angeles Times* (14 January 1996), p. M3.

[17] D. Lessing, *Under My Skin* (New York: HarperCollins, 1994), p. 15.

[18] Quoted in G. Hicks, *Where We Came Out* (New York: The Viking Press, 1954), pp. 35–6.

one breathes in the West is stale and foul. In the Western civilization there is no longer clarity and resolution ... One breathes again ... in the invigorating atmosphere of the Soviet Union.[19]

John Strachey, the English writer, had similar responses to his visit: 'there is perceptible an exhilaration of living which finds no parallel in the world. To travel from the capitalist world into Soviet territory is to pass from death to birth.'[20]

Self-transcendence is the other concept that links religious and political pilgrimages. The desire for secular self-transcendence often overlapped with the desire for 'wholeness' especially prominent among the political pilgrims of the 1960s generation but also present earlier. Waldo Frank found, in the Soviet Union, 'happy workers, because they are whole men and women'.[21] Self-transcendence, it was often felt, could be attained in an emotionally sustaining community, and the subordination of the individual to some group, or collective. Self-sacrifice for communal or social purpose, or cause, was another path to self-transcendence. Joseph Freeman, an American author, wrote:

Here [in Soviet society] the individual was supposed to subordinate himself to the general interest of society ... he actually expanded by virtue of being part of something greater than himself. Except for the remnants of the former privileged classes, everyone acted as though the general good was his personal good, as though his personal difficulties could be solved by conquering the common difficulties ... Here the "average" man felt himself master of everything.[22]

Paul Sweezy, an American Marxist economist, projected similar hopes and wishes upon the Cubans, supposedly transformed by the new political system:

To be with these people, to see with your own eyes how they are rehabilitating and transforming a whole nation, to share their dreams of the great tasks and achievements that lie ahead – these are purifying and liberating experiences. You come away with your faith in the human race restored.[23]

---

[19]   L. Feuchtwanger, *Moscow 1937* (New York: The Viking Press, 1937), pp. 3, 149–50.
[20]   J. Strachey, *The Coming Struggle for Power* (New York: The Modern Library, 1935), p. 360.
[21]   Frank, *Dawn in Russia*, p. 135.
[22]   J. Freeman, *An American Testament* (New York: Octagon Books, 1973), p. 461 (first published 1936).
[23]   Quoted in P. Clecak, *Radical Paradoxes* (New York: Harper & Row, 1973), p. 152.

There are also explicitly religious themes and undertones in the writings of the political pilgrims, many of whom commented on the seeming paradox of ostensibly atheistic (communist) societies realizing the values and goals of Christianity. Hewlett Johnson, Dean of Canterbury at the time, wrote:

> From this capitalist world of storm and stress, where ancient pillars of society collapse, where morals are outraged ... and poverty unchecked, we turn at last to the Soviet world ...
>
> Here was something wholly new. Here was something laid down ... by men at the head of affairs in a great nation, which we Christians had been told by our own men of affairs ... was wholly impracticable in the world as it is today ... this Soviet programme regards men as persons and plans for them as brothers. There is something singularly Christian and civilized in this intention ...
>
> Russia is the most moral land I know.[24]

John Dewey, the American philosopher, following his visit to the Soviet Union felt, 'as if for the first time I might have some inkling of what may have been the moving spirit and force of primitive Christianity'.[25] D.F. Buxton, an English Quaker, wrote:

> what impressed me most in Russia was a sense of moral advance represented in the new order of society which the Communists are trying to establish ...
>
> In the emphasis they place on the spirit of service, the Communists take to heart some of the most important maxims of the New Testament ...
>
> The Communists repudiate ... the language of religion, but their actions are so much more important than their words ...

---

[24]   H. Johnson, *The Soviet Power* (New York: Modern Age Books, 1940), pp. 45, 63; and H. Johnson, *Soviet Russia Since the War* (New York: Boni and Gaer, 1947), p. 89.

[25]   J. Dewey, *John Dewey's Impressions of Soviet Russia and the Revolutionary World* (New York: New Republic, 1929), p. 122.

> The Communists have, in fact, revived and applied what are ... essentially
> Christian ideas and applied them ... to society and our moral duties ... in spite of
> all their irreligious jargon their society is more Christian than ours.[26]

Pilgrims to China included theologians similarly impressed by the moral lessons imparted by their visits: 'If the reports [of these theologians] had a common theme it was that Christianity had much to learn from the social transformation in China ... China has come to exert some particular impact on our understanding and experience of God's saving love.'[27] Hewlett Johnson projected on China the same qualities he had earlier discerned in the Soviet Union: 'China, I feel, is performing an essentially religious act, entirely parallel with this Christian abhorrence of covetousness ... freeing men from the bondage of the acquisitive instinct and paving the way for a new organization of life on a higher level of existence.'[28] Anna Louis Strong, an American journalist who first admired the Soviet Union under Stalin and later China under Mao and lived in both for extended periods, also sensed a welcome affinity between the policies of the Chinese communist regime and the true principles of Christianity.[29]

A conversion experience (similar to religious ones) sometimes preceded the political pilgrimage. Angela Davis, 1960s radical, subsequently professor of philosophy at the University of California, pilgrim to the Soviet Union, recalled:

> The *Communist Manifesto* hit me like a bolt of lightning. I read it avidly, finding
> in it answers to many seemingly unanswerable dilemmas which had plagued me ...
> Like an expert surgeon this document cut away cataracts from my eyes ... it all
> fell into place ... The final words of the Manifesto moved me to an overwhelming
> desire to throw myself into the communist movement.[30]

The political pilgrimages, like the religious ones, often became transformative experiences. Carol Tavris, an American psychologist, wrote about her visit to China:

> When you enter China you walk through the looking glass into a world that
> reflects a reality antithetical to yours. You leave Watergate, the energy crisis,

---

26   D.F. Buxton, *The Challenge of Bolshevism: A New Social Ideal* (London, George Allen & Unwin, 1928), pp. 7, 27, 81–2, 85.

27   'Churchmen Find a Lesson in China', *New York Times* (19 September 1974), p. 13.

28   H. Johnson, *The Upsurge of China* (Peking: New World Press, 1961), p. 368.

29   A.L. Strong, *Letters from China*, numbers 21–30 (Peking, 1965), p. 172.

30   A. Davis, *An Autobiography* (New York: Random House, 1974), pp. 110–111.

crime, privacy, dirty movies, cynicism and sex at the border and step across into safety. Stability, enthusiasm, clean streets, clean talk and positive thinking ... you leave diversity and controversy, the hallmarks of America, to be wrapped in a uniformity of belief and single-mindedness of purpose.[31]

Shirley MacLaine, the famous American actress, had similar feelings entering China: 'There were no hawkers selling goods, no frenzied bargaining. Nobody was buying and nobody was selling ... There were no billboards screaming out their false promises, no slums ... Serene, I said to myself. That is the word. Serene.' She even succeeded in determining that Chinese 'women had little need, or even desire for such superficial things as frilly clothes and makeup, children loved work and were self-reliant. Relationships seemed free of jealousy and infidelity'.[32] MacLaine's transformation had physical aspects as well: she stopped smoking on the second day of her visit, and stopped picking her fingers and biting her nails. She 'began enjoying sunsets and trees and food instead of rushing through each day because time meant money'. Maria Macciocchi, an Italian journalist, found the Chinese people 'emanating purity ... men without sin'.[33]

In North Vietnam Susan Sontag discovered that 'The phenomenon of existential agony, of alienation just don't appear among the Vietnamese [they] are "whole" human beings, not "split" as we are'. Daniel Berrigan, a Catholic priest and 1960s activist, found 'a naive faith in human goodness powerfully operative in North Vietnamese society'.[34] Similar projections characterize the observations of Tom Hayden and Staughton Lynd, two 1960s radicals: 'We knew too what the Vietnamese contribution to a human socialism would be; it was evident in the unembarrassed handclasps among men, the poetry and song at the center of man-woman relationships, the freedom to weep ... Here we began to understand the possibilities for a socialism of the heart.'[35] In such writings communist Vietnam emerges as a wishful combination of the Berkeley campus of the University of California in the 1960s and an American psychotherapy group.

The transformed perceptions of many visitors were also reflected in their different evaluation of the same phenomena depending on their context, that is

---

[31] C. Tavris, 'Field Report: Women in China', *Psychology Today* (May 1974), p. 43.

[32] S. MacLaine, *You Can Get There from Here* (New York: Norton, 1975), pp. 126–7, 183, 245.

[33] M.A. Macciocchi, *Daily Life in Revolutionary China* (New York: Monthly Review Press, 1972), p. 106.

[34] S. Sontag, *Trip to Hanoi* (New York: Farrar Strauss and Giroux, 1968), pp. 69, 77; D. Berrigan, *Night Flight to Hanoi* (New York: Macmillan, 1969), p. 79.

[35] S. Lynd and T. Hayden, *The Other Side* (New York: New American Library, 1966), pp. 58, 62.

to say, whether they were observed in their own society or in the idealized country they visited. For example in Cuba the spectacle of people standing in lines, an obvious reflection of scarcities and a physically tiring experience, did not dismay Jonathan Kozol. He wrote: 'The long lines ... the ration cards and other forms of deprivation do not seem to dampen the high spirits of most people.'[36] We cannot tell what led him to this conclusion but we can be certain that food lines in the United States would have elicited a different interpretation. Likewise for Felix Greene, poverty in communist China had a totally different meaning than, say, in England. Signs of poverty on the streets of a Chinese city he observed were not 'a sullen or apathetic poverty ... Here in spite of squalid surroundings, [there is] a general atmosphere of vitality ... Children playing lustily everywhere.'[37] For Greene, as for other pilgrims, poverty was transformed by its context, by the expectation and promise that it will disappear. They were also certain that poor people were cheerful about their condition. There is little doubt that similar phenomena in a capitalist city – including children 'lustily' playing on the street – would have elicited different comments and interpretations.

Such impressions and assessments suggest that these travellers were in a state of mind resembling an altered state of consciousness – their critical faculties suspended, ready and eager to attribute traits to communist societies and their citizens they could not possibly have experienced or verified. They engaged in a veritable orgy of projections, they endowed these societies with qualities they longed for in their own society and considered essential attributes of a perfect society, or one approaching perfection.

The transformative experiences of the political pilgrimage were further stimulated by the revolutionary ethos of the societies visited. A revolutionary society was highly appealing for reasons which Raymond Aron specified half a century ago; his observations help further to define the nature of secular religious beliefs:

> The myth of the Revolution ... fosters the expectation of *a break with the normal trend of human affairs* ... A revolution seems capable of changing everything ... [*the*] *Revolution* provides a welcome break with the everyday course of events and *encourages the belief that all things are possible* ... The myth of the Revolution serves as a refuge for utopian intellectuals; it becomes the mysterious, unpredictable intercessor between the real and the ideal.[38] (My emphases)

---

[36]   Kozol, *Children of the Revolution*, p. 102.
[37]   Greene, *Awakened China*, p. 23.
[38]   R. Aron, *The Opium of the Intellectuals* (London: Secker & Warburg, 1957), pp. 35, 43, 65.

Thus the pursuit of utopia (heaven on earth), the promise of all-encompassing, imaginary revolutionary transformations of both the individual and society and self-transcendence came together in the expectations and imagination of the political pilgrims.

The pilgrims' perceptions of the supreme leaders of the communist states they admired also had a religious dimension and were influenced by the official cults of these leaders endowed with superhuman qualities by the propaganda machinery. Pablo Neruda was struck by the continued '*presence*' (my emphasis) of Lenin, as he watched the parade on the anniversary of the October Revolution in Moscow: 'They [the marchers] were being observed by the sharp eyes of a man dead many years, the founder of this security, this joy, this strength: Vladimir Ilyich Ulyanov, immortal Lenin.'[39] Graham Greene, an admirer of both the Soviet Union and Cuba, was said to be 'always trying to discover sainthood in secular figures; he prized in others simplicity and an innocence he had been denied and his later works are a kind of pilgrimage in search of a different kind of faith'.[40] Orville Schell, an American journalist, wrote of Mao: 'I was struck in a very forceful way by the fact that even prior to his death Mao had transcended his own personality ... the thought of Chairman Mao became inculcated in almost every Chinese. The word almost literally became flesh ... he had almost become transubstantiated in his people.'[41] Elizabeth Sutherland, a British journalist, was under the impression that 'when he [Castro] speaks, it is as if his own dedication and energy were being directly transfused into his listeners with an almost physical force'.[42]

Like many saints, the leaders of communist states were also seen by the political pilgrims as charismatic heroes. Norman Mailer, the famous American writer, felt that Fidel Castro 'gave all of us who are alone in this country ... some sense that there were heroes in the world'.[43] Sartre had a similarly exalted vision of Castro and Che Guevara, veritable supermen for whom 'sleeping doesn't seem like a natural need, just a routine of which they more or less freed themselves ... Of all these night watchmen, Castro is the most awake. Of all these fasting people, Castro can eat the most and fast the longest ... [these leaders] exercise a veritable dictatorship over their own needs ... they roll back the limits of the possible'.[44]

---

[39] Neruda, *Memoirs*, p. 250.

[40] M. Korda, 'The Third Man', *New Yorker* (25 March 1996), p. 50. Korda was Greene's editor.

[41] O. Schell, *In the People's Republic* (New York: Random House, 1977), pp. VII–VIII.

[42] E. Sutherland, 'Cubans' Faith in Castro', *Manchester Guardian Weekly* (7 December 1961).

[43] N. Mailer, 'Letter to Castro', in *The Presidential Papers* (New York: Putnam, 1963), pp. 67–8.

[44] J.P. Sartre, *Sartre on Cuba* (New York: Ballantine Books, 1961), pp. 102–3.

I did not intend to overstate the similarities between political and religious pilgrimages. In the first place it is far more difficult to generalize about religious pilgrimages than about the political ones because they stretched over far longer periods of time, over many centuries, indeed millennia and took place in many divergent historical settings. In any event let me note important differences between religious and secular religious beliefs and the pilgrimages they respectively inspired: the sacralized political belief-systems (such as Marxism-Leninism) have nothing to say about life after death, they promise neither other-worldly rewards nor punishments, there is no deferred, compensatory gratification awaiting the political true believer after death.

Political and religious pilgrimages also differed insofar as the religious pilgrims usually retained their religiosity following their pilgrimage, whereas many political pilgrims after the pilgrimage gradually abandoned their fervent beliefs and hopes and the values which inspired their pilgrimage came to play a diminished role in their subsequent lives.

Religious pilgrimages, unlike the political ones, usually involved long, arduous journeys lasting for many weeks or months. Undertaking such a journey presumably also helped to confirm the sense of devotion and duty of the participants, providing reassurance of their rectitude, or in modern terminology, confirming or bestowing a positive self-conception. It is likely that there was a strongly felt connection between the hardships imposed by the pilgrimage and the rewards expected. Political pilgrimages did not require arduous, long or difficult journeys; modern means of transportation could be relied upon and the more important figures among the pilgrims were given luxurious treatment by the authorities.

The socio-demographic composition of the two types of pilgrimages also appears to be different. Most political pilgrims were intellectuals, whereas the social composition of religious pilgrims was and is far more heterogeneous, and a large portion of them were and are not intellectuals but ordinary people, with modest education.

Religious pilgrimages were more often a group phenomenon, while political pilgrims, especially those better known among them, often went by themselves. Political tourism was, of course, a group phenomenon. Religious pilgrimages were more narrowly focused on particular individuals (such as saints), objects or specific settings to be venerated whereas the political ones potentially involved large areas, different locations, a wide variety of sights and people to be met. Lastly religious pilgrims were not subject to what I called the techniques of hospitality, the deliberate, highly organized manipulative efforts designed to make sure that the visitors will only have positive experiences and impressions.[45]

To conclude, the most direct stimuli of the political pilgrimages were the economic crises of the late 1920s and early 1930s and the politico-cultural crises of the 1960s and 1970s. Both crises intensified the rejection of Western societies and especially the United States. But there were also deeper, less tangible but more important reasons for the pervasive political disillusionment which led to the search for alternatives and thus to the pilgrimages. The political pilgrimages were, for the most part, by-products of secularization and modernization that shifted the pursuit of meaning, sense of identity and spiritual needs from the religious to the political sphere. In other words modernization transformed religious needs into secular-religious, or quasi-religious ones, into the belief that there were political solutions or remedies for spiritual problems and deprivations. The fundamental source of these pilgrimages was the profound, strongly-felt disenchantment with, or alienation from, modern, commercial, secular and highly individualistic Western societies. The political pilgrimages reflect the unmet needs for self-transcendence, for belonging to a sustaining community, and the longing for sense of purpose, especially strongly felt by people we call intellectuals.

---

[45]   For a detailed examination of these manipulations see Hollander, *Political Pilgrims*, ch. 8, pp. 347–99 and A. Daniels, *Utopias Elsewhere: Journeys in a Vanishing World* (New York: Crown, 1991), especially the chapter on North Korea.

Chapter 5

Israeli Youth Voyages to Holocaust Poland: Through the Prism of Pilgrimage

Jackie Feldman

Walking through the Warsaw Ghetto

Guide book in hand,
Slim like a breviary
Our struggling column
Threads its way through the *bidon ville*
Where the ghetto once was.
Intoning texts of witnesses,
Maneuvering the map like a dousing rod
That might unearth the bodies
From under the pavement,
Locate the underground spring.
A passerby stops to show us –
There, over there, Pani
See, Pani, the fist painted in tar
On the crumbling plaster?
Didn't you read all about it?
Trace the tram tracks,
Count the cobblestones,
This side is inside, that one out.
The church there-
The Nazis built a wall around it
To keep it out of the ghetto, the church.
And, important,
It has a clean bathroom.
Just ask the nun
And she'll open it for you.

Youth voyages to Holocaust Poland have become one of the most important practices of Israeli collective memory, especially among high school youth. Since their inception in 1984, somewhere around half a million students have participated in these 8- to 10-day visits. In the course of their journey, they visit sites of concentration and death camps, former ghettos and Jewish towns. They follow Israeli guides through a strictly-defined itinerary, conduct a series of ceremonies at memorial sites, hear testimony of Israeli survivors, take photographs, cry together and hug each other in consolation.

Although the organizers speak of the voyage as an educational trip, I have chosen to analyse it as a civil religious pilgrimage. The perspective of pilgrimage, I find, enables me to focus on processes often marginalized by educational perspectives; the religious context of pilgrimage casts new light on the rhetoric and practices of the journey, and takes seriously the claim of the voyage to create worlds of meaning and shape identity.

I suggest that the pilgrimage perspective offers the following vistas:

1. *Pilgrimage is part of a personal quest.* Not only for the participants, but for myself as researcher as well. Reflexivity on pilgrimage can contribute to a deeper understanding of both the voyages to Poland and the significance of contemporary pilgrimage.

2. *Pilgrimage encourages us to take secularized cosmology seriously.* The ability of nationalism to craft coherent worlds of commitment and inculcate these into its citizens through performative practice can only be underestimated at our own risk.

3. *Pilgrimage perspectives place the spotlight on the way symbols are used, space is regulated, authoritative offices assigned, sanctity produced and retained.* The pilgrimage perspective fosters a deeper look at the inner aspects of ritual before seeking an interpretation through integration of the ritual with the social surround.[1]

4. *Analyses of the state ritual in terms of pilgrimage open the voyage to ideological critique.* This perspective makes the canonical voyage form no longer 'the way it is done', but one religious practice among many other possible ones.

5. By naming the voyage as a pilgrimage, we facilitate comparisons that may pose new questions for the research of other pilgrimages and nationalist practices throughout the world.

---

[1]   D. Handelman, 'Introduction: Why Ritual in Its Own Right? How So?', *Social Analysis*, 48/2 (2004), pp. 1–32.

Pilgrimage is Part of a Personal Quest

Pilgrimage is a metaphor and practice which has both influenced my own development and helped me to make sense of it. I grew up in a traditional Jewish home in New York, as a child of Holocaust survivors and refugees. My first pilgrimage to Israel at the age of 16 profoundly influenced me: there, I found that the Biblical texts I memorized as a child referred to a world rooted in nature – ruins and rocks, streams, and terraced mountains. I also sensed a feeling of expanse, camaraderie and freedom as a Jew in a majority culture. Shortly after my arrival, I enrolled in the Israel tour guide course. The landscape provided pegs to hang memories on, while the Bible stories I had learned as a child anchored my attachment to the new-old place I sought to claim as my own. I then began working as a licensed tour guide for Christian pilgrims to the Holy Land, mostly for Palestinian tour agencies. I became aware of the role of the imagination in moulding perceptions of the Holy Land, and how the practice of travel to a sacred site could create emotional and spiritual bonds among people of different faith communities. It also made me realize how, through presenting Judaism and Israel to Christians, I was defining myself to myself – working through my identities as American emigrant, no-longer-Orthodox Jew, new Israeli and – especially when guiding in places like Yad Vashem – as second-generation child of escapees from the Holocaust.

In 1991, after my father passed away, I went on pilgrimage by train to his birthplace, Ungvár in the Ukraine on the border with Slovakia. Guided by a map drawn up after a long talk with my father's last surviving sister, I followed Moskowicz, the *shlisl yid* – one of the last surviving members of the pre-war community, who held the key to the cemetery. Moskowicz waved his cane in the windswept *Soviet* streets, hailed a passing car to drive us to the cemetery, and navigated me, with the help of an old battered registry, through drifting heaps of fallen leaves to the tombstone of my grandmother. The next day, I visited my father's childhood home, trying in vain to match the decaying building of my grandfather's childhood home with the map I had drawn, based on the memories of my last living aunt.

When, after returning to Israel, I encountered Israeli youngsters travelling on organized tours to Holocaust sites in Poland, I surmised that they too were travelling on pilgrimages like mine, attempting to fill obscure voids and half-articulated stories with places one could touch, places of meaning. Here, I thought, at the very moment when the last survivors were dying out, at the peak period of *lieux de mémoire*,[2] the juncture between lived memory and transmission through representations, I was witnessing the birth of a religious, though non-traditional, pilgrimage ritual. Perhaps, I surmised, the voyages in search of half- or totally-effaced traces of the Jewish past and Holocaust destruction might become the canonical way for future generations to mourn the third *hurban*, the destruction of the Temple that was European Jewry.

The Pilgrimage Perspective Makes us Take Secularized Cosmology Seriously – as a Central Rite of Civil Religion in Israeli Society

The voyages began in the mid-1980s, after the gates of Poland were reopened to Israeli visitors and in a social situation in which common bases for national identity were weakened by the rise of ethnic identity and the emphasis on individual self-realization. The old mythical figures – the pioneer and the soldier – had lost much of their moral authority, and identity began to coalesce around smaller units – my ethnic group, my religious group, my social circle, myself.[3] The Poland visits were promoted as a reaction to the atomizing force of the media and global youth culture – as a means of shoring up loyalty to the national collective. As Oded Cohen, former head of the Education Ministry's Youth Division and the single most important organizer of youth visits to Poland said, '[as a result of the voyages] the State of Israel becomes better understood as an expression of revival, of independence, of the capacity for self-defense. This is the new message of responsibility in an age of eclipse of moral values'.

The trips are a means of recharging commitment to a particular cosmology, in which the State of Israel plays the central redemptive role in Jewish history. The role of the Holocaust within this cosmology reflects and promotes changing Israeli understandings and self-legitimations.[4] In the early stages of Israel's history, Holocaust victims were disparaged as those who went as lambs to the slaughter; only the Warsaw Ghetto fighters and the partisans were deemed worthy progenitors of the State of Israel. In recent decades, however, Israelis have increasingly identified with Holocaust victims, and all victims and survivors have

[2] P. Nora, 'Between Memory and History: Les Lieux de Mémoire', *Representations*, 29 (1989), pp. 7–25.

[3] See Y. Bilu and E. Ben-Ari (eds), *Grasping Land: Space and Place in Contemporary Israeli Discourse and Experience* (Albany: SUNY Press, 1997).

[4] For a survey of changing Israeli memories of the Holocaust, see D. Ofer, 'Israel', in D.S. Wyman (ed.), *The World Reacts to the Holocaust* (Baltimore and London: The Johns Hopkins Press, 1996), pp. 836–922.

been heralded as heroes.[5] The voyages' construction of contemporary Poland proclaims the doomed nature of the diaspora, the inherent and eternal nature of anti-Semitism and the need for a strong State of Israel as protector of Jews and antithesis to diaspora vulnerability.

As chief organizer of these visits Oded Cohen said:

> As we stand by the crematoria ... our heart sorrows and our eyes shed tears for the terrible destruction of European Jewry, and Polish Jewry among them ... But opposite the flag of Israel raised on high and over the death pits and ovens of destruction, our eyes fill with tears, but we stand erect and our lips whisper – the people of Israel lives! ... And we swear to the millions of our murdered brethren – if I forget thee, O Jerusalem, let my right hand forget its strength! In the ears of our spirit we hear their souls calling to us – through our death we have commanded you to live! Guard and protect the State of Israel like the apple of your eye! And we answer wholeheartedly – long live the State of Israel forever![6]

Pilgrimage Perspectives Place the Spotlight on the Way Symbols are Used, Space is Regulated, Authoritative Offices Assigned, and Sanctity is Produced and Retained

The conceptual framing of the voyage as a civil religious pilgrimage ritual shines a spotlight on the structuring tools, bodily experiences and potentials for transformation often overlooked by the Ministry of Education's classification of the voyages as 'study trips'. The latter perspective often emphasizes the pre-planned educational objectives, preparatory programmes and texts. The pilgrimage frame, by contrast, seeks the significant meanings of the voyage by observing the dynamic performance of the trip: the structure of the voyages' space-time, the emplaced testimony of the witnesses and the songs and ritual gestures of the ceremonies.

Through selected texts and the multi-sensory experiences of students at key sites, national conceptions become part of the natural order of things. As Victor

---

5   In a previous article, I suggest that the tendency to glorify the victim (rather than the fighter) was fortified by the events of the Second Intifada, in which the majority of Israelis were killed not as combatants on the front, but as civilians on buses and in cafes. J. Feldman, 'Between Yad Vashem and Mount Herzl: Changing Inscriptions of Sacrifice on Jerusalem's "Mountain of Memory"', *Anthropological Quarterly*, 80 (2007), pp. 1145–72.

6   Israel Ministry of Education, *It Is My Brothers I Am Seeking: A Youth Voyage to Poland* (Jerusalem: Youth Division, Ministry of Education, 1989), p. 3.

Turner emphasized in his studies of ritual, including pilgrimage, 'the action situation of ritual, with its social excitement and direct physiological stimuli ... effects an interchange of qualities between its poles of meaning. Norms and values on the one hand, become saturated with emotion, while the gross and basic emotions become ennobled through contact with social values'.[7]

The following patterns discerned by the pilgrimage perspective form the core of my analysis.

Organization and Security

In the course of the voyage, the Ministry of Education treats bureaucratic and logistic factors as neutral arrangements needed to ensure smooth operation of the voyage. Through my focus on the shaping of space and time, scheduling and bureaucracy become opaque and contingent. They may then be recognized as tools that implicitly convey ideologies by making certain experiences accessible and others not. The effort of organizers to render bureaucracy and security necessary and transparent is thus challenged by a critique that recognizes the ideological contents of bureaucratic systems and arrangements, making them visible and, hence, contingent.

The Poland trips are characterized by extremely tight security arrangements. Students on Ministry of Education visits travel together in guarded convoys of four or five buses each. They are almost never out of sight of the Israeli security personnel, who accompany each bus. Buses are checked for bombs each time the group enters, and students are prohibited from speaking to Poles they may encounter along the route for security reasons. The Israeli security personnel become perceived as essential for the safety of the group in what is painted as a dangerously hostile surrounding. Security is cited as the ultimate authority in determining itinerary choices and changes (even when, in fact, it is not), and becomes an effective disciplining agent, keeping the group together at sites and in their hotels at night. The additional – and to my mind, not unintended – effect of this security bubble is to paint Poland as a murderously anti-Semitic place in which the Holocaust could recur today, were it not for the protective power of the State of Israel. Some delegation leaders say this explicitly. In one case, a delegation was walking through Cracow on a Friday night, loudly singing Israeli songs as they returned from the Friday evening synagogue services to their hotel for dinner. The Polish police had stopped traffic along the route. One student turned to another, saying: 'Look! Who could imagine the "blues"

---

7   V. Turner, *The Ritual Process* (Chicago: Aldine, 1969), p. 30.

Table 5.1   The environmental bubble of the group

Inside the bus or hotel	Outside the bus or hotel
• Encompassing environmental bubble of the home world	• Alienation of the foreign terrain
• Warm temperatures	• Cold temperatures
• Hebrew spoken	• Foreign language spoken – Polish
• Israeli snack food and music	• Unfamiliar or poor quality Polish food; no music
• Security	• Danger
• Night	• Day
• Fun and socializing	• Mourning/serious demeanour
• Emotional 'decompression' sites	• Tension and sorrow
• Israel	• Holocaust Poland/diaspora Jewry
• Behave like teenagers	• Behave like representatives of Israel
• Hope	• Despair
• Present/future	• Past
• Life	• Death
• 'Us'	• 'Them'

[ghetto name for policemen] are protecting us from the Poles! If the State of Israel weren't around, this would never have happened!'

Students follow an extremely tight schedule which allows them practically no time to mingle with people outside the group or explore new territory on their own. Poland is essentially painted as a Holocaust-death world in contrast to the bus and hotel, which serve as the insulated life-world (= Israel) of the students. I schematically depict the separation and isolation of the group in Table 5.1.

While the 'environmental bubble' isolating the group from their surroundings is typical of many guided excursion groups – both of pilgrims and of tourists – on the Poland voyages this isolation is given moral value. The borders of the group represent the borders of righteousness and innocence, as opposed to the 'murderous' Polish environment outside.

The Power of Place

Place has tremendous power in bestowing guides' accounts and survivors' testimony with authority and power to convince. I found, as I knew from my experience guiding Christian pilgrims in the Holy Land, that the impact of the narrative often depended on the sensory setting of the site. The more the site could work on many senses at once (sight, sound, touch, smell), the more the significant past could be isolated from the 'noise' of present alternative uses of the space and seen as frozen in time – the more likely it was to leave an impression.[8] One veteran guide complained to me upon her return from Poland:

> Jackie, I spoke to them of the Bund, of Hasidim and Mitnagdim,[9] of the Jewish press between the wars. Two weeks after the trip, I asked them, "so how was it?" "Cool", they replied. "What made an impression on you?" I asked them. "The [piles of moldering victims'] shoes in Majdanek", they answered. Jackie, for this I had to work so hard and spill my soul? For the shoes in Majdanek?? They don't need me for that.

I answered: 'how do you expect to compete with the shoes in Majdanek?' In follow-up interviews, I found that students remembered the cold and the smell of a place, even if they had totally forgotten the explanation given there.

The Importance of Sequencing and Ceremonies

One of the prominent elements in the Turners' analysis of pilgrimage is the importance of the road.[10] Many pilgrimages construct the path to the sacred site as a series of way stations leading up to the central shrine; the road becomes sanctified as way stations are marked by traditions, buildings and devotional practice. These markings also intensify the sense of the pilgrim's teleological movement towards the sacred centre.

---

[8]   For an analysis of this in the context of Protestant pilgrimage to the Holy Land, see A. Ron and J. Feldman, 'From Spots to Themed Sites: The Evolution of the Protestant Holy Land', *Journal of Heritage Tourism*, 4 (2009), pp. 101–16.

[9]   Bund-A movement founded in October 1897 in Vilnius which sought to preserve Jewish culture and Jewish nationality in the context of socialism through speaking of Yiddish and perpetuation of Yiddish culture. Hasidism – a branch of Orthodox Judaism founded in eighteenth-century Eastern Europe by Rabbi Israel Baal Shem Tov, widespread in pre-Second World War Eastern Europe, that promotes spirituality and joy through the popularization and internalization of Jewish mysticism as the fundamental aspects of the Jewish faith. Mitnagdim – Ashkenazi Jews who opposed the rise and spread of Hasidic Judaism, emphasizing Torah study and exegesis over ecstatic practices, popular kabbalah or the mystical power of Hasidic rabbis.

[10]   V. Turner, 'The Center Out There: The Pilgrim's Goal', *History of Religion*, 12 (1973), pp. 191–230; V. Turner and E. Turner, *Image and Pilgrimage in Christian Culture* (Oxford: Oxford University Press, 1978).

In listening to group meetings held in the course of the trip and afterwards, and in analysing the transcripts of those meetings and the diaries of students, I saw how certain phrases repeated by guides and teachers found their way into students' discourse in the course of the eight-day voyage and after their return home. The gap between students' expectations of the voyage and the voyage experience is often great at the outset. In the course of the eight-day trip, students come to tune their expectations to the voyage experience and bridge the dissonance, learning how to look at sites and imagine (with the help of pictures and texts offered by the guide) what is not visible.

The redemptive structure of the voyage manifest in the sequencing of sites – from Warsaw to death camps to the preferred ending at the monument of the Warsaw Ghetto Uprising – is also manifest in the structure of each ceremony. The ceremonies move from the Kaddish – the mourning prayer – to texts of witnesses' testimony, to the Israeli national anthem and the raising of flags. As in many pilgrimages, the sequence of ceremonies at the death sites also draws the students in to become participants in a transformative rite of passage: from child to victim to survivor and to immigrant (*oleh*-ascender) to Israel and to empowered witness of the witness, who realizes his mission through service to the State of Israel.[11] As one student wrote:

> And when they performed the ceremony, all kinds of tourists saw us. They all have to see. And it was some consolation when they took pictures of us, and at the end, at the Hatikvah, many people stood and watched us … And, finally, with respect to walking with the flag, it reminded me a lot of what we saw in the film on Janusz Korczak, when they walk in slow motion with the flag with the Star of David, and when we walked through all the camps, I felt this, the pride with which we walk with the flag. *We're the same children who were there at the end* [of the film]. (Emphasis mine)[12]

The cumulative effects of death sites and the repeated ceremonies there also tune students' emotional expressions. The shedding of tears is often taken by both students and teachers as proof of the efficacious power of the sites and ceremonies to overpower the barriers of individual bodily resistance. Thus, when some students complained of their disappointment and frustration in not

---

[11]   For a detailed description of the ceremonies, see J. Feldman, *Above the Death Pits, beneath the Flag: Youth Voyages to Poland and the Performance of Israeli National Identity* (New York and Oxford: Berghahn, 2008), ch. 5.

[12]   Feldman, *Above the Death Pits*, p. 173.

shedding tears at the visit to Treblinka, the group leader consoled them, 'the coin always drops after the second death camp'.

The performance of commemorative ceremonies is central to the voyage programme and its redemptive structure. Some sites may be skipped because of time pressures; ceremonies – almost never. The ceremonies build on meanings that have already become part of students' life-world through participation in Israeli society and performance of school ceremonies from kindergarten on.[13] In this ceremonial sequence, the Holocaust is linked with the commemoration of fallen Israeli soldiers and national independence. In Israel, commemorative ceremonies, especially those marking the Holocaust and fallen Israeli soldiers, are 'mirrors', events which reflect, in a fragmented but concentrated form, the State's vision of itself; 'vivid and vibrant expositions, in which what was done was seen fully to happen'.[14] But when those ceremonies are positioned at particular 'authentic' sites of death and in a particular sequence, they are charged with sensory materiality and with new meaning. In Poland, they function not only as mirrors, reflections and reiterations of social values, but as models, rites of passage. As one teacher commented after the ceremony at Birkenau:

> In school, we perform many ceremonies. I hear murmurings during Hatikvah, students moving around. And here, I feel at Hatikvah ("The Hope" – the Israeli national anthem) how it uplifts everyone and connects us from a collection of individuals to a single conglomerate, to one nation. And here I felt this power. And we have power. And this force should accompany us everywhere.

The repeated performance of ceremonies at the death sites in Poland inscribes a trajectory of identification and corporealization of suffering, death and redemption. In a poem read at the close of the final ceremony in Warsaw a delegation leader proclaimed:

> And my heart expires, and my hands are too weak to save,
> And sometimes it is I that suffocated in the gas chambers,

[13]   L. Shamgar-Handelman and D. Handelman, 'Celebrations of Bureaucracy: Birthday Parties in Israeli Kindergartens', *Ethnology*, 30/4 (1991), pp. 293–312; A. Ben-Amos and I. Bet-El, 'Commemoration and National Identity: Memorial Ceremonies in Israeli Schools', in A. Levy and A. Weingrod (eds), *Homecomings: Unsettling Paths of Return* (Lanham: Lexington Books, 2004), pp. 169–99; O. Almog, *The Sabra: The Creation of the New Jew* (Berkeley: University of California Press, 2000).

[14]   For the distinction between models and mirrors, see D. Handelman, *Models and Mirrors* (Cambridge: Cambridge University Press, 1990), pp. 23–48. The quote is from p. 42.

And a minute later, I am the partisan in the forests
And again, I am a member of the Sonderkommando burning
bodies in the forest
And I am the Mussulman,
And I am the IDF paratrooper taking revenge against his enemies ...
And I know that this is my people. And I know
That the strength of this memory
Is what makes me what I am,
What gives me the strength
And the power and the courage, and the right,
The right and the obligation,
To remember, to do and to march onwards.[15]

The Role of the Israeli Survivor-Witness in 'Bringing Sites to Life'

The survivor-witness's personal story and physical presence authorizes the sites and interpretations, while the physical remains make his testimony effective. Although students and teachers often slept through testimony given by witnesses when travelling on the bus, when the survivor testified in the places of his suffering, especially in the camps, he commanded their undivided attention. While the witnesses tell their stories in a variety of settings, the story with the most impact is the one presented in the quarantine barracks at Auschwitz. There, students are squeezed into the long, narrow unheated wooden shack, between the mouldering bunk beds. The cold, the smell, the detachment from the outside world, the authentication of the remains by the witness's voice, body and his pointing to the well-preserved remains serve to efface the distance between Auschwitz and its relics. One student reported:

> We walked among all the barracks and they're all empty, just air. And they talk with you about the terrible smell and you smell the smell of nothing ... [but] when the witnesses were talking, I saw a flash of a picture in black and white and then it was gone. It was really scary. The actuality of the situation.

Thus, the survivor-witness serves as a kind of shaman, connecting the living and the dead, evoking the spirits of specific dead persons hovering around the extermination camps, and enabling authoritative contact with them. Sometimes

---

15 Omri, Nozhik Synagogue ceremony, 20 September 1995, in Feldman, *Above the Death Pits*, pp. 203–20.

the witness briefly loses touch with the current reality of the student voyage and speaks as if he were talking with his fellow-prisoners/survivors.

The witness frequently assumes a priestly role in the death-camp ceremonies. Thus, at one visit I observed at Birkenau, at the close of the visit, the 150 members of the delegation gathered opposite the remains of the gas chambers, clad in blue and white sweatshirts. The students formed a line atop the ruins of the crematoria, Israeli flags raised aloft. The Israeli survivor-witness climbed up onto the 'stage', took a flag from one of the students, and planted its staff firmly in the soil and ash. He raised his eyes towards heaven and cried: 'How long, will we Jews, your chosen children, be a victim and prey of the gentiles? How long? How long?' He then turned to the students: 'You know, you give me the strength to continue … I'm transmitting things that were sealed for 50 years, and I see that you thirst to know. And that's why we're here, so that you can be witnesses to what they did to the nation.' He concluded with the words: 'You, in this place, know that you are the correct answer to Nazism and anti-Semitism. On one side are the crematoria, in which hundreds of thousands were burned. And now children, girls and lads, bring many sons to the nation, so that we may live forever!'[16]

The emplacement of the significant testimony of the witness over the crematoria helps dissolve the distance between the original event and its ritual commemoration. At the same time, the *mise en scène* of the testimony in front of a large delegation of flag-carrying, blue-and-white clad youngsters nearly assures that the survivor will mention Israel as the redemptive end of his ordeal. The students are told that it is they who empower him to give his testimony, and provide the redemptive close to his story, his victory over death in the places where his family members were murdered.[17] The students become proof of Hitler's failure, the people of Israel's victory. Many students say that the witness reminded them of one of their own grandparents or stories of survival told within their families. Through this ceremony, students are told, they become 'witnesses of the witnesses'; their future service to the nation becomes the ultimate act of homage to and redemption of the Holocaust dead.

---

[16]   (H., 17 September 1995), in Feldman, *Above the Death Pits*, p. 170.

[17]   I discuss this at length in J. Feldman, 'Nationalizing Personal Trauma, Personalizing National Redemption: Performing Testimony at Auschwitz-Birkenau', in N. Argenti and K. Schramm (eds), *Remembering Violence: Anthropological Perspectives on Intergenerational Transmission* (New York: Berghahn Books, 2010), pp. 103–32.

The Pilgrimage Perspective Provides an Opening for Ideological Critique

My analysis of the Israeli trips to Poland, both here and elsewhere, contains two major critiques: an objection to the politicization of Holocaust memory to support a security-centred worldview, and the critique of the inability of many Israelis to think creatively with ritual. The latter failure results in the mindless replication of ceremonial forms by educators within the voyage and the adoption of the standardized voyage even by schools and parents who do not agree with the security orientations and isolationism built into its structure. The Poland trips continue to proliferate, while their form has hardly changed over the past two and a half decades. Educators seem to be too busy 'doing', recruiting ever-larger groups for the Poland voyage and overseeing logistics and collecting parents' money – to stop to reconsider the effective messages and rituals of the voyages that run so smoothly. As one of the chief organizers of the voyage once said to me in response to a minor criticism: 'the dogs bark and the convoy rolls on through'.

It is my hope that the pilgrimage perspective I have promoted can open the voyages to ideological and ritual criticism,[18] both by naming it as a civil religious pilgrimage and by showing how ritual tools work to convey particular messages. In contemporary Israeli society, religious forms are individual, sectarian or private. In any case, unlike rites of nationalism, these are not seen as necessary for good citizenship. A plurality of forms and practices is acceptable. Part of the mystification of nationalism, especially insofar as it demands blood sacrifice of its citizens, requires that it frame its demands as other than and superior to those of sectarian religion.[19] By classifying the voyage as a civil religious pilgrimage, I hope to create an opening for critique, a splintering of hegemony into a multiplicity of 'religious' traditions. While maintaining the sanctity of the Holocaust event and encouraging pilgrimage as an efficacious and rewarding practice, I hope to encourage the crafting of new ritual forms, reflecting a wider variety of understandings of the Holocaust, the State and the link between them.

---

[18] R. Grimes, *Ritual Criticism: Case Studies in its Practice, Essays on its Theory* (Columbia: University of South Carolina Press, 1990).

[19] C. Marvin and D.W. Ingle, *Blood Sacrifice and the Nation: Totem Rituals and the American Flag* (Cambridge: Cambridge University Press, 1999).

By Naming the Voyage as a Pilgrimage, we Facilitate Comparisons that May Pose Questions Relative to the Research of Other Pilgrimages and Nationalist Practices Throughout the World

As a universal and seemingly timeless phenomenon, pilgrimage presents a tremendous diversity of human experiences. Over the last two decades, much anthropological scholarship on pilgrimage has dwelt on its affinities with other forms of mobility, particularly tourism.[20] I hope I have demonstrated that civil religious pilgrimages are indeed pilgrimages. The voyages to Holocaust Poland have an emotional intensity and a transformative potential equal to that of many traditional pilgrimages. The inclusion of civil religious pilgrimages, including nationalist rites, within the purview of pilgrimage studies help us interrogate how place may authenticate narratives and what role witnessing plays in sanctifying space. It leads us further to interrogate the dynamics of *communitas*, group inclusion and exclusion in pilgrimages throughout the world.[21]

As for nationalism, while the religious nature of nationalism is hardly new,[22] the youth pilgrimages to Poland illustrate how ritual analysis and critique may be productive for understanding national practices. The performance of pilgrimages to a negative sacred site cosmicizes the nation by depicting foreign territory as the ultimate locus of evil and destruction. Particularly, the case studied demonstrates how rites of nationalism can endure, proliferate and continue to arouse people's emotions and commitments, even in an era of individualism and (seemingly) porous borders. Thus, the Israeli youth voyages to Poland should alert us to the potential of political powers to shape pilgrimage

---

[20]   E. Badone and S.R. Roseman, 'Introduction', in E. Badone and S.R. Roseman (eds), *Intersecting Journeys: The Anthropology of Pilgrimage and Tourism* (Urbana and Chicago: University of Illinois Press, 2004), pp. 1–25; S. Coleman and J. Eade, 'Introduction: Reframing Pilgrimage', in S. Coleman and J. Eade (eds), *Reframing Pilgrimage: Cultures in Motion* (New York: Routledge, 2004), pp. 45–68; D. Eickelmann and J. Piscatori (eds), *Muslim Travellers: Pilgrimage, Migration and the Religious Imagination* (Berkeley: University of California Press, 1990); E. Cohen, 'Pilgrimage and Tourism: Convergence and Divergence', in A. Morinis (ed.), *Sacred Journeys: The Anthropology of Pilgrimage* (Westport and London: Greenwood Press, 1992), pp. 47–61.

[21]   This was a major theme in the critiques of the work of Victor Turner, especially those assembled in J. Eade and M. Sallnow (eds), *Contesting the Sacred: The Anthropology of Christian Pilgrimage* (Chicago: University of Illinois Press, 1991).

[22]   To cite three works that have influenced me on this matter: B. Kapferer, *Legends of People, Myths of State* (Washington, DC: Smithsonian Institute Press, 1988); D. Kertzer, *Ritual Politics and Power* (New Haven: Yale University Press, 1988); Marvin and Ingle, *Blood Sacrifice*.

by harnessing the transformative forces of place, testimony and performance to make their hegemonic views of the world natural and acceptable.

Chapter 6

The Pilgrimage to the Hill of Crosses: Devotional Practices and Identities

Darius Liutikas and Alfonsas Motuzas

Introduction

You will never meet such popular piety or indeed hear such expressions of spirituality, as those that exist today in the Lithuanian cult of the Hill of Crosses, a phenomenon unique in the whole world. More than 160 years ago, when the Hill was first declared to be a sacred place, pilgrims began to flock there from every part of Lithuania. During the period of Soviet occupation, pilgrims secretly erected crosses at night despite the threat of persecution, but in 1990, following the restoration of Lithuanian independence, visitors returned in huge numbers. Today the Hill of Crosses (in Lithuanian – *Kryžių kalnas*) comes under the jurisdiction of the diocese of Šiauliai and is often referred to as the Mound of Jurgaiciai or Domantai, in other words, the Castle Hill, the Holy Hill. Pilgrims come here to observe particular devotional practices but their widespread geographical origins offer a variety of narratives and explanations for the crosses that they leave behind. The tradition of erecting crosses on the Hill of Crosses is intertwined into several layers and related to the commemoration of the dead, folk beliefs and geo-political practices. Our research is based on the assumption that the identity of the Hill of Crosses derives from its unique historical origins, including diverse folk devotions, prayers, hymns and music from a wide variety of liturgical, Holy Land, Polish and local sources.

The cult of the Hill of Crosses is also well-established in north-eastern Poland, where the Holy Mount of Grabarka, located in the Podlasie Voivodship between the two historic towns of Mielnik and Drohiczyn, has become the main pilgrimage site for the Polish Orthodox Church. Some devotional practices by the faithful on this Mount, such as the erection of crosses, washing in the nearby stream, crawling on their knees and hymn-singing, are similar to traditional Lithuanian devotional practices which take place on the Hill of Crosses.

Research on pilgrimage sites was forbidden during the Soviet occupation and, in general, academic research on the topic is still in its infancy.[1] However, several valuable publications are now attempting to analyse and explain different aspects of this extraordinary phenomenon, including the motivation underlying such pilgrim journeys.[2]

The aim of this chapter is to discuss the origin of the Hill of Crosses and to illustrate its devotional practices and identities. Together with several other pilgrimage sites of international significance in Lithuania, namely the Gate of Dawn and the Cathedral, both in Vilnius, and Šiluva, which witnessed the apparition of the Virgin Mary, the Hill of Crosses, in particular, is firmly embedded into a network of Catholic pilgrimage sites.

The Network of Pilgrimage Places in Lithuania

In pagan Lithuania, the network of sacred places focused on natural objects, such as mounds, forests, trees, stones and springs. This country, the last in Europe to be converted to Christianity, was evangelized from 1387 by the Lithuanian Grand Duke, Jogaila (1377–1434), married to the Catholic Jadwiga of Poland, and by Vytautas, his cousin. The late Christianization of the country meant that pilgrimage did not begin to take root until the end of the sixteenth century. Indeed, the rapid building programme which followed the conversion resulted in more than a hundred churches being constructed throughout Lithuania by the early sixteenth century while, in the seventeenth century, a network of Catholic pilgrimage places was intensively developed, the number of pilgrimages increasing accordingly.[3]

The first recorded pilgrimage in 1604 was that organized by the Jesuits of Vilnius to the miraculous image of the Mother of God and Child at Trakai and led by Benediktas Vaina, bishop of Vilnius (1600–15). From this year, pilgrimages from Vilnius to Trakai were organized annually. After the apparition of the Blessed Virgin in 1608, pilgrims began to visit Šiluva where a

---

[1]   D. Liutikas, *Piligrimystė. Vertybių ir tapatumo išraiškos kelionėse* (Vilnius: Lietuvos piligrimų bendrija, 2009); D. Liutikas, 'Piligrimystės vietų tinklas Lietuvoje: geografinė retrospektyva', *Geografijos metraštis*, 38/1 (2005), pp. 147–63.

[2]   D. Mačiulis, 'Kryžių kalno ir jį supančio kraštovaizdžio istorinė raida', *Kultūros paminklai*, 6 (2000), p. 88; A. Motuzas, 'Kryžių kalno apeiginiai papročiai', *SOTER*, 13/41 (2004), pp. 189–208; A. Motuzas, 'Kryžių kalno sakralinė muzika', *Žiemgala*, 2 (2005), pp. 8–14.

[3]   Liutikas, 'Piligrimystės vietų tinklas Lietuvoje', pp. 149–52.

new Catholic church was built in 1627. As early as 1629, about 11,000 received the Holy Sacrament at Communion during the annual Indulgence feast.

The Samogitian Calvary (Žemaičių kalvarija), one of the most important centres of pilgrimage in Lithuania, was created between 1637 and 1642 on the initiative of Jurgis Tiškevičius, bishop of Samogitia. In 1649 a significant relic, a small piece of wood from Christ's Cross, was brought from the Dominicans' convent in Lublin and, in the following years, the Calvary also became famous for a miraculous image of Mary and the Child Jesus.

The Calvary in Vilnius at Verkiai was created between 1662 and 1669. The Way of the Cross is located in a hilly area between the river Neris and the pinewoods of the Baltupai and Jeruzalė regions. This Calvary became a popular destination for pilgrims and most of them walked the Way of the Cross at Pentecost. In general, almost all the Calvaries established in Lithuania became places of pilgrimages of regional or national importance. In the eighteenth century, the Bernardine monks of Telšiai built the Stations of the Cross on the hills of Beržoras. From 1771 to 1780, the Stations of the Way of Cross were also erected in the cloister (*kluatr*) of the Bernardine monastery of Tytuvėnai.

In 1636, St Casimir (1458–84) was declared the patron of Lithuania and many pilgrims came to visit his tomb in Vilnius Cathedral. As early as the beginning of the seventeenth century, the tomb of St Casimir was already covered with a large number of wax and silver votive offerings. In the second part of this century, the miraculous image of Mary, Mother of Mercy, at the Gate of Dawn in Vilnius became famous.

In general, the main pilgrimage centres of Lithuania were established in the seventeenth century. However, in the middle of the nineteenth century, the Hill of Crosses, a unique sacred place, was set up and in the twentieth century places where there had been apparitions of the Blessed Virgin Mary were added to the Lithuanian pilgrimage map. Places such as Gulbinėnai, Imbradas, Keturnaujiena and Skiemonys are not officially recognized by the Catholic Church but are very popular as pilgrimage destinations for simple devotees.

During the Soviet occupation, various obstructions were imposed to prevent people from visiting sacred places, and a campaign of their physical destruction was carried out. On 20 April 1959, the Central Committee of the Lithuanian Communist Party, having received a directive from Moscow, issued a resolution entitled 'Considering measures to stop the visiting of so-called sacred places'. The document set out methods for reducing the numbers of pilgrims at Šiluva, as well as the Samogitian, Vilnius and Vepriai Calvaries. The sanctity of these places was 'denounced' in the media and huge secular events were organized during the indulgence Feast days. For example, bus traffic was cancelled, roads leading to the town of Šiluva were blocked, some drivers' licences were taken away, and passengers were forced to get out and walk. The organizers of several pious processions to Šiluva were sentenced to three years in prison. The Stations the Cross of the Vilnius and Vepriai Calvaries, as well as the crosses on the Hill of Crosses were physically destroyed.

During the period of Lithuanian revival between 1988 and 1989, and after the restoration of Lithuanian independence in 1990, pilgrimages to the most important sacred places such as those of the apparition of the Virgin Mary in Šiluva, the miraculous image of Virgin Mary in Pivašiūnai, the Gate of Dawn, Vilnius Cathedral, the Hill of Crosses, the Samogitian Calvary, etc., were particularly popular.

In general, sacred places of Christianity vary according to their origin, whether natural or cultural, the object of veneration, such as the cult of Virgin Mary, Christ, the saints, spiritual authority, the events commemorated, such as historical events from the life of Jesus, the saints, events from one's personal life, apparitions. Tanaka suggested two factors that help to identify the importance of sacred places – the radius within which the place is known and from which pilgrims are drawn, and the total number of pilgrims during the year.[4]

Nowadays we can identify 20 major Catholic pilgrimage places in Lithuania (Figure 6.1). This identification is based on the places visited by contemporary pilgrims as well as taking into consideration the historical traditions, the geographical area of attraction, the number of pilgrims who visited the place, the hierarchical importance of sacred places and their significance. Most are related to the cult of Virgin Mary (Šiluva, the Gate of Dawn, Pivašiūnai, Trakai, Pažaislis, Imbradas, Keturnaujiena, Krekenava, Skiemonys, the Cathedral of Kaunas). A second group consists of Calvaries (Vilnius Calvary, Vepriai Calvary, Beržoras Calvary, Tytuvėnai Calvary, Samogitian Calvary), places related to saints and the cults of holy persons (St Casimir at the Cathedral of Vilnius and Blessed Jurgis Matulaitis in Marijampolė), a place where the Cross is venerated (the Hill of Crosses), a holy spring (Alksnėnai) and the Shrine of Divine Mercy at Vilnius which contains the first image of Merciful Jesus which was painted according to the visions of St Faustina.

From 4–8 September 1993, Pope John Paul II visited Lithuania. He prayed at the most important Lithuanian pilgrimage places: the Gate of Dawn in Vilnius,

---

    4   H. Tanaka, 'On the Geographic Study of Pilgrimage Places', *Geographia religionum*, 4 (1988), pp. 21–40.

Figure 6.1   Religious pilgrimage places in Lithuania

the cathedrals of Vilnius and Kaunas, the Hill of Crosses, and the place of the Apparition of the Virgin Mary in Šiluva. During his stay in Vilnius, the Pope also visited the Church of the Holy Spirit where a meeting with the members of the Lithuanian Polish community was held and the Vilnius University Church of St John the Baptist and St John the Evangelist and Apostle where there was a meeting with the representatives of the Lithuanian cultural and academic community.

With the coming of the fifteenth anniversary of the Pope's visit to Lithuania, the Conference of Lithuanian Bishops decided to link all the sanctuaries which were visited by the Pope to form the pilgrimage route of Pope John Paul II. In 2007, the Lithuanian government confirmed the programme of the pilgrimage, which included the Hill of Crosses, and this programme gained a status of national importance.

Table 6.1   The main Catholic pilgrimage places in Lithuania

No	Place	The goal of pilgrimage							District, town	Diocese
		Miraculous image of Virgin Mary	Apparition place of Virgin Mary	Calvaries – the Way of Cross	The cult of saints and spiritual authorities	The cult of the Cross	Miraculous image of Jesus	Holy spring		
1	Alksnėnai							+	Vilkaviškis	Vilkaviškis
2	The Gate of Dawn	+							Vilnius	Vilnius
3	Beržoras Calvary	+		+					Plungė	Telšiai
4	Vilnius Divine Mercy Shrine						+		Vilnius	Vilnius
5	Imbradas		+						Zarasai	Panevėžys
6	Kaunas Cathedral	+							Kaunas	Kaunas
7	Keturnaujiena		+		+				Šakiai	Vilkaviškis
8	Krekenava	+							Panevėžys	Panevėžys
9	The Hill of Crosses					+			Šiauliai	Šiauliai
10	Marijampolė				+				Marijampolė	Vilkaviškis
11	Pažaislis Monastery	+							Kaunas	Kaunas
12	Pivašiūnai	+							Alytus	Kaišiadorys
13	Skiemonys		+						Molėtai	Panevėžys
14	Šiluva	+	+						Raseiniai	Kaunas
15	Tytuvėnai			+					Kelmė	Šiauliai
16	Trakai	+							Trakai	Vilnius
17	Vepriai Calvary			+					Ukmergė	Kaunas
18	Vilnius Cathedral	+				+			Vilnius	Vilnius
19	Vilnius Calvary			+					Vilnius	Vilnius
20	Samogitian Calvary	+	+						Plungė	Telšiai

The 16 main Catholic pilgrimage places of Lithuania were linked:

1. Vilnius Cathedral Basilica. Chapel of St Casimir
2. Gate of Dawn Chapel and St Teresa's Church (Vilnius)

3. Vilnius Calvary
4. Trakai Church of the Visitation
5. Kaunas Cathedral Basilica
6. Christ's Resurrection Church in Kaunas
7. Pažaislis Church and Monastery
8. Shrine of Šiluva
9. Tytuvėnai Church and Monastery
10. Šiauliai Cathedral
11. Hill of Crosses
12. Samogitian Calvary Shrine
13. Marijampolė Basilica and Chapel in Lūginė
14. Pivašiūnai Church of the Assumption
15. Divine Mercy Shrine in Vilnius
16. Krekenava Shrine.

The John Paul II pilgrimage route includes not only the sanctuaries which the Pope visited in Lithuania, but also other sites of pious renown which received the Holy Father's attention and are somehow connected with this Pope. Today the network of Lithuanian pilgrimage places is clear and well established. The pilgrimage shrines falling into this network have spiritual significance and long-standing cultural and religious traditions of piety and visits.

The Hill of Crosses: Origin of the Pilgrimage

The Hill of Crosses is located 12 km north of the city of Šiauliai, not far from the main road to Riga. The Hill is on the left bank of the Kulpe brook, surrounded by its small nameless tributary. It is 70 m long, 60 m wide and the height of a two-storied house. Geologically, it is the highest point of the area. The first evidence concerning the Hill comes from archaeological excavations and the discovery of many human skeletons, Swedish swords and medals, supplemented by ethnological and historical materials. The Livonian Chronicles mention that, in pre-Christian Lithuania, there was a castle Kula or Kulen that was burned by Crusaders in 1348. The name of the castle could have derived from the nearby Kulpe brook. With the coming of Christianity, the pagan altar was destroyed, but Lithuanians continued to worship at the Hill.

People began to place crosses on the Hill in the middle of the nineteenth century. There is no exact record of why the first crosses were erected there, but one local story relates that a father had a sick daughter, and that nobody could help her. Once, when he grew tired after nursing her and fell asleep, in a dream a lady in a stream of light came to him and said:

> "If you wish your daughter to be healed, you have to make a cross yourself, bring it to the Hill of the Castle and plant it in the ground". The father did so. His cross was very heavy, and took him thirteen hours to carry up the Hill and erect. Then he kissed the cross and returned home. On his way back, he met his daughter who had recovered. She said that when he left home with the cross, she felt better and when he reached the Hill, she got out of bed.[5]

A similar story comes from M. Hriškevičius, the treasurer of the region of Šiauliai who, in 1850, wrote a description of the manors of the Šiauliai region. According to him the first cross was erected to ask God for health:

> Now people regarded the mound of Jurgaiciai as holy. This Hill has never been a Christian cemetery and never had any crosses until 1847. Now twenty crosses stand there. According to local records, this happened in 1847 when a local man from Jurgaiciai promised God that if he survived his unpleasant illness, he would erect a cross on the Hill. He built a cross on the Hill and recovered. This message spread among the people and in the course of the next three years, many crosses were erected there from people from local villages and those farther away. We can now see how numerous they are.[6]

Stories such as these encouraged people to make promises in difficult situations and later to build crosses as a sign of gratitude. Another legend recounts the existence of the chapel on the Hill. Rebels against the tsarist authorities came to pray there in 1863. When the Cossacks discovered this, they bolted the door and in three days buried the rebels underground together with the chapel. In the course of time, the joists of the chapel rotted and collapsed, the land subsided and a pit or a hole appeared where people started to build crosses in commemoration of the rebels, who had been buried alive.[7]

There is also a story about the pit on the summit of the mound. At one time there was a pastor from Meškuičiai who became interested in the Hill.

---

5   V. Puronas, *Kryžių kalnas* (Šiauliai: Interstatyba, 1993), p. 12.

6   Mačiulis, 'Kryžių kalno', p. 73.

7   B. Kviklys, *Lietuvos bažnyčios* (6 vols, Chicago: Amerikos lietuvių bibliotekos leidykla, 1983), vol. 3, p. 256.

Together with some other men, he started to dig on the summit and found the moulded roof of the church; and one digger went inside and brought out some candlesticks. At night the pastor was warned in a dream to return the findings. But he was not afraid and continued the excavations. Whilst excavating, one digger was struck down by disease. Then the pastor grew frightened and stopped the work, returned the objects, sprinkled them with holy water and then buried them. The unfortunate digger built a cross and recovered.

Another folk witness account exists, concerning the Appearance of the Blessed Virgin there to some local children in 1870. She promised to appear the next day at noon again and asked the children to bring some adults along as well. The Blessed Virgin appeared again and asked them to build a cross there as a sign of faith. She warned them about hard times to come, asked them to build crosses on the Hill and promised her intercession. After that, she disappeared. Later, rich farmers built a chapel in the place where she had appeared.

The most popular version of the story of the Hill's origin is related to the rebellions against tsarist Russia. In the nineteenth century, Lithuania-Poland was under the oppressive rule of tsarist Russia. In 1830 the Poles were the first to organize a revolt in order to liberate the occupied territories from Russian power. On 25 March 1831, they were joined by the Lithuanians. The heaviest loss of life of the rebels was near Šiauliai. It is related that in 1831 the chapel was built by the relatives of those killed because the tsarist powers did not permit them to pay proper tribute to their dead. From 1850, indulgence feasts started on the Hill of Crosses. The strict tsarist regime further provoked Lithuanian and Polish religious and national manifestations. In 1863, there was a major revolt which included the whole of Lithuania and Poland, but at the end of that year it was defeated. Many stories tell of executions during the suppression of the revolt on the Hill of Crosses. On the western slope, four rebels were rumoured to have been shot. Another story relates that after the suppression of the revolt, the tsarist general Muravjov, the Hangman, built something similar to a concentration camp where about 1,000 rebels died of famine and harsh weather conditions. Only 11 martyrs survived. They were put to death on the western slope and their bodies thrown into the pit on the Hill where the tsarist army trampled their grave in order not to leave any sign. Local people and pilgrims from the neighbouring parishes had crosses built, but they were destroyed by the authorities. In 1888, the American Lithuanian paper, *Lithuanian Voice*, wrote that the Stations of the Cross (14 of them) were placed at the foot of the Hill in commemoration of those killed and all the dead.

Two principle reasons account for the first crosses on the Hill of Crosses. The first is as a sign of popular devotion, leaving votive offerings out of gratitude to God. The alternative was a wish to commemorate the rebels of the uprising and to resist tsarist authority, which prohibited and prevented the erection of crosses. According to research on the Hill of Crosses by the Polish archaeologist, L. Krzywicki, 130 crosses were standing on 22 August 1900, but by 2 July 1902, there were 155 crosses and an old brick chapel on the summit of the Hill. The chapel was destroyed during the Second World War with only the foundation remaining. Between the two world wars, the Hill of Crosses flourished. From 1918 to 1940 Lithuania was an independent country and many pilgrims came to pray at the Hill of Crosses, Masses were celebrated, and during the Hill of Crosses indulgence feast in July large crowds were especially prominent.

During the Soviet occupation, building crosses on the Hill was strictly forbidden. Moreover, communists and atheists organized the destruction of the Hill of Crosses on no fewer than five occasions. The first occurred on 5 April 1961 when 14 Stations of the Cross and about 5,000 crosses were destroyed. The second was on 26 April 1973 when about 400 crosses were destroyed. The third was on 23 November 1974, and the fourth was at Christmas of the same year when again about 400 crosses were destroyed. People were threatened with arrest and punishment for building the crosses. The fifth destruction was in the summer of 1976 when the whole Hill was destroyed, even the part of it that was under cultivation. But believers continued to pray at the place, and erected crosses at night. During the period 1980 to 1990, numerous devotional processions were organized with a significant participation of young people, all of whom were under threat of persecution.

During John Paul II's visit in 1993, he was taken to the Hill of Crosses on 7 September where he offered a Holy Mass in a nearby chapel. This event made the Hill of Crosses popular throughout the world. The Pope celebrated the Lithuanian struggles for national and religious freedom by his words on the Hill of Crosses: 'Climb the Hill and remember all the sons and daughters of this country who were sentenced, put into prison, sent to concentration camps, exiled to Siberia or Kolyma, or put to death'.

On 9 September 1995, about 20,000 young people gathered at the Hill of Crosses to celebrate the second anniversary of John Paul II's visit. On 28 May 1997, the Pope established the diocese of Šiauliai, and on 20 July of the same year Eugenijus Bartulis, Šiauliai's first bishop, revived the indulgence feast of the Hill of Crosses which is celebrated on the last Sunday of July. During his visit to the Franciscan convent at La Verna (Italy) in 1997, the Pope spoke of the spiritual bond between these two places. When the Franciscans of Lithuania and those of the Italian province of Tuscany met in the Vatican, the Pope blessed the future project of the Lithuanian Franciscan brothers to build a new house for the Franciscans vice-province of St Casimir. They bought a site near the Hill of Crosses in 1998 and built a convent completed on 8 July 2000.

In 2003, on the tenth anniversary of Pope John Paul II's visit to Lithuania, there was a 68 km pilgrim march from the Hill of Crosses to another Lithuanian sanctuary in Šiluva, as if linking both shrines. On 25 July 2004, more than 4,000 young people who had assembled at the Lithuanian youth days in Šiauliai marched to the Hill of Crosses. Every year larger or smaller pilgrimages are organised to the Hill of Crosses while annual three-day pilgrimages on foot from the Hill of Crosses to Šiluva carried out at the beginning of September became a pleasant tradition.

Devotional Practices of the Hill of Crosses

Today the Hill of Crosses is visited in groups or individually with organized or private devotions. People build crosses or leave other signs such as paintings or rosaries, etc. Some come with promises; others pray or sing the Rosary in the Holy Name of Jesus or climb the Hill on their knees. Other pilgrims pray for their dead, singing and playing a variety of musical instruments.

Earlier during the traditional feast of Our Lady of Mount Carmel in July, thousands of pilgrims gather and some devotions are performed. Some of them washed in the nearby unnamed spring, while those who had sick relatives or friends took bottles of this water and brought it home.[8] And today the majority of pilgrims from nearby or distant villages and towns come with their pledges, build crosses, go around or climb the Hill on their knees[9] singing the Rosary of the Holy Name of Jesus. Other pilgrims, praying for their dead, follow the 14 Stations of the Cross or sing, some of them accompanying hymns with musical instruments. It is the custom before following the Stations of the Cross that pilgrims stop at the statues of Jesus Christ and Our Lady, bow their heads or kneel down in prayer and light candles around the crosses.[10]

---

[8] Kviklys, *Lietuvos bažnyčios*, p. 256.

[9] A. Motuzas, *Katalikų liaudies pamaldumo praktikos Lietuvoje* (Kaunas: Vytauto Didžiojo universiteto leidykla, 2004), pp. 100–102.

[10] D. Striogaitė, 'Po aukštu dangum', in A. Ostašenkovas (ed.), *Kryžių kalnas* (Šiauliai, Interstatyba, 1993), p. 1.

In general we can identify major cult or devotional practices performed at the Hill of Crosses:

1. Erecting or leaving crosses
2. Celebration of the indulgence feast
3. Processions of walking pilgrims
4. Commemoration of the dead
5. Crawling on the knees (climbing the Hill or walking around it)
6. Praying
7. Singing hymns (sometimes accompanied by musical instruments)
8. Walking the 14 Stations of the Way of the Cross.

It is important not only to identify ritual customs related to the Hill of Crosses, but also to discover their origin, which in turn could help researchers to trace transitions of Catholic ritual as they evolved into the pilgrims' devotion of the Hill of Crosses.

Erecting Crosses

The tradition of erecting crosses in prominent places or near houses is venerable and widespread in many Catholic countries. In the medieval period soldiers who died on the march were buried and simple crosses were built to mark the site of their graves. In Lithuania pillar-type crosses or miniature chapels used to be built on farmsteads, by the roadside, at crossroads, on riverbanks, in cemeteries, churchyards, streets and squares of towns, villages and hamlets.

Some authors argue that the origin of the tradition of placing crosses lies far back in primitive pre-Christian beliefs. Trunks of trees, often rudimentary stems, were placed in prehistoric cemeteries.[11] Lithuanian crosses are very ornamental and most decoration is related to pre-Christian times. With pillar structures each cross is typically carved with floral and geometric motifs. In 2001, the traditional Lithuanian crafting of wooden crosses was included in the UNESCO list of the Intangible Cultural Heritage of Humanity. Eventually, in the eighteenth and nineteenth centuries crosses and miniature wooden chapels became so widespread that the country, and particularly Samogitia, used to be called the homeland of crosses and chapels, the sacred land of crosses or

[11]   J. Baltrušaitis, 'Crosses and Chapels', in T.J. Vizgirda (ed.), *Lithuanian Folk Art* (Munich: Aufbau, 1948), pp. 36–54.

simply the cross-marked Lithuania.[12] Today it is still a common practice to erect crosses at different places to commemorate significant events and dates in the lives of families, village communities and the political, social and cultural life of the nation. Roadside crosses are mostly placed to remember a loved one who has died in a traffic accident, or to commemorate tragic historical events which have happened there.

Celebration of the Indulgence Feast

One of the most traditional customs of the Hill of Crosses is the celebration of indulgence feasts. Religious feasts are visual expressions of spiritual life in different rituals. After the introduction of Christianity to Lithuania, the feasts of the Church were also established. There were numerous feasts in neighbouring Poland: apart from the universal feasts, some celebrations of patron saints of the country were added. At first the patron saints of Poland and Lithuania were the same but during the episcopate of Benediktas Vaina, bishop of Vilnius, the synod chose different patrons: St George, St Casimir and St Nicolas.[13] In 1634, during the pontificate of Pope Urban VIII, the Congregation of Divine Worship in Poland and Lithuania permitted the faithful to move the feasts from working days to Sundays during the spring and summer months of June, July, August and September but the feasts of Holy Mary and apostles were not allowed to change.[14] Pope Pius VI in 1775 published the bull '*Paternae Caritati*', granting permission to celebrate some feasts of the country and dioceses – St Casimir, Our Lady of Mount Carmel and others in Poland and Lithuania.[15] So the indulgence feasts in Lithuania came from Poland as a heritage of religious culture as expressed in different feasts of the Church calendar.

The feast of Our Lady of Mount Carmel on the Hill of Crosses was traditionally celebrated on 16 July. The first Carmelites arrived in Lithuania from Poland in the seventeenth century, and this feast was spread by the sodality or confraternity of Our Lady of Mount Carmel. In Lithuania, this feast was

---

[12]   A. Stravinskas, 'Introduction: Lithuanian Folk Art. Small-Scale Architecture', *Old Lithuanian Sculpture, Crosses and Shrines*, at http://www.tradicija.lt/Kryziai/A_Stravinskas_Small_scale.en.htm (accessed 15 February 2011).

[13]   J. Kurczewski, *Kosciol Zamkowy* (Wilno: nakł. i druk Józefa Zawadzkiego, 1908), vol. 1, p. 102.

[14]   M. Wolonczewskis, *Žemajtiu Wiskupiste* (Wilniuj: spaustuwieje Juozapa Zawadzki, 1848), vol. 2, p. 223.

[15]   J. Vaišnora, *Marijos garbinimas Lietuvoje* (Roma: Lietuvių katalikų mokslo akademijos leidinys, 1958), p. 40.

also celebrated at the Calvary of Beržoras, which was established in 1775 and fostered by the Bernardines of Telšiai.

In general, indulgence feasts were an important reason for pilgrimages in Lithuania. Pilgrims even came from remote parishes to various indulgence feasts in different churches where they participated in the Holy Mass, received the Holy Sacrament, and completed other conditions in order to receive indulgences. The indulgence feast on the Hill of Crosses was revived in 1997 when the Šiauliai diocese was established and Bishop Eugenijus Bartulis became its leader. The date of the indulgence feast of the Hill of Crosses was moved from 16 July to the last Sunday of July.

Processions of Pilgrims on Foot

According to different sources, midsummer processions of pilgrims from Šiauliai to the Hill of Crosses were organized during which a cross was carried and the Rosary in the Holy Name of Jesus and the Stations of the Cross were sung. Also nowadays during the indulgence feast or at other times pilgrims march in processions on foot from the Cathedral of Šiauliai to the Hill of Crosses (12 km).

In pre-war periodicals, we discover that organized processions carried a cross to the Hill of Crosses in the middle of summer in addition to individual pilgrimages.[16] Such processions also survived during the Soviet period.

> On 19 May 1973, young people from the city of Šiauliai carried a cross as a sign of victory to the Hill of Crosses, reciting the Rosary. On 28 May 1977, on the vigil of Pentecost a group of Lithuanians again solemnly carried a new cross to the Hill of Crosses. Another historical fact is about bringing crosses from different places as, e.g. on 22 July 1979 from the church of Meškuičiai. Father Algirdas Mocius carried a cross for 8 km and then pronounced a homily on the Hill and offered Holy Mass. During the procession and the Mass, hymns were sung.[17]

The origin of the ritual custom of processions or pilgrimages is related to the Old Testament, when the Ark of the Covenant was carried in solemn processions. In the New Testament, Jesus Christ was followed by a solemn procession to the Temple of Jerusalem before Easter. Ecclesiastical sources state that the rituals of the first processions following the Way of the Cross in Jerusalem were introduced

---

[16]   'Žinutė', *Momentas*, 4 (1928), p. 3.
[17]   Kviklys, *Lietuvos bažnyčios*, pp. 260–63.

in the fourth century.[18] In the sixteenth century, these solemn processions were led by Franciscan friars, guardians of the Holy Places: 'In the Church of the Holy Sepulchre Franciscan friars organised a procession with banners.'[19]

Traditional rituals involve carrying a cross on the shoulders and playing musical instruments during processions. As historical sources show, three social groups, namely hired musicians, pilgrim-musicians and beggar-musicians, followed the custom of singing hymns accompanying themselves on musical instruments. Playing musical instruments in pilgrim processions has its prehistory in Lithuania. Historical sources state that in 1525, in Vilnius, music was performed by pilgrims during one of the most popular processions of Corpus Christi, which usually started in the Cathedral and moved to the Bernardine Church. In 1586, Jesuits followed this Franciscan example by inviting the academic youth of the city to join in the processions.[20] From 1628, the tradition of instrumental music in the Cathedral was transformed into mass singing during different processions. Historical sources show that only what were known as sacred instruments were used in processions – brass instruments and drums, while string instruments were unacceptable in the rituals. In the seventeenth century, ensembles of St John, St Casimir and the Trinity were created. Sometimes the choirs of these chapels played together during the ceremonies. Musicians called such practice 'hunting for Mass' – it is known that they were supported by parishes, and sometimes by the Jesuit Academy of Vilnius. From the seventeenth century, alongside the pilgrim-musicians, a new social group appeared – hired musicians, who performed traditional rituals for wages. The use of loud, effectively sounding brass instruments was typical of those times. Brass and percussion instruments were probably also used in processions because the Lithuanian nobility, grandees and clergy, following the Polish example, started to form professional chapels.

Commemoration of the Dead

Ritual customs of commemorating and praying for the dead go back to ancient times. Franciscan friars introduced the practice of praying for the dead in Jerusalem, on the way of Christ's Passion. One of the first to describe this was M.K. Radvila (the Orphan), a Lithuanian pilgrim, in 1582–4: 'In those sacred

---

[18]   J.J. Kopec, *Droga Krzyzowa. Dzieje nabo-zenstwa i antologia wspolczesnych tekstow* (Poznan: Księgarnia Św. Wojciecha, 1987), p. 17.

[19]   M.K. Radvila, *Kelionė į Jeruzalę* (Vilnius: Mintis, 1990), pp. 73–7.

[20]   V. Gidžiūnas, 'Pranciškonų observantų-bernardinų gyvenimas ir veikla Lietuvoje XV ir XVI amž', *Lietuvių katalikų mokslo akademijos Suvažiavimo darbai*, 9 (1982), p. 84.

places Franciscan friars perform devotions for dead parents and family members. Others ask a priest to perform devotions for their dead on the Mount of Calvary or some other place according to their inspiration.'[21] In the course of time, this practice also moved to Europe where it was spread by different sodalities or confraternities within Bernardine or Franciscan orders or churches. This custom of praying for the dead came to Poland from Italy[22] and from Poland to Lithuania it came through various confraternities run by the orders or churches. The devotions of prayer and singing hymns for the dead were spread by those of St Anne in Vilnius, the Holy Rosary, and the Franciscans of the Third Order in the Samogitian Calvary; also by travelling beggar-musicians, parish servants and the residents of 'prayer-homes' in Samogitia.[23] In 1726, Pope Benedict XIII granted indulgences for the 14 Stations of the Cross to all believers, especially those who prayed for the souls of the dead.[24] After the Uprising of 1831, this folk devotion of praying for the dead became very popular in Poland, and later in all Catholic countries.[25] So we may argue that this devotion at the Hill of Crosses came from Poland.

Walking on the Knees (Climbing the Hill or Walking around the Hill)

The liturgical position – kneeling before the high altar or at the chapels – is an old Christian tradition. The ritual custom of praying at the Stations of the Cross while crawling on the knees has its roots in the Holy Land and pilgrimages there. The ritual custom of climbing the Hill of Crosses on one's knees was identified with people's respect for a sacred place. Climbing on one's knees was known since the dawn of Christian culture. This devotional practice is also connected with the custom of climbing the stairs of the chapel of the Holy Staircase (*Scala Sancta*) in Rome. In Lithuania, this devotional practice was also performed in special chapels in the church of St Francis in Vilnius and in the Bernardine convents of Telšiai and Tytuvenai. This devotion came to Lithuania from the Polish Calvary of Zebrzydowska.[26]

21 Radvila, *Kelionė į Jeruzalę*, p. 76.
22 Kopec, *Droga Krzyzowa*, p. 69.
23 A. Motuzas, 'Katalikiškos pridedamosios pamaldos Lietuvoje. Švč. M. Marijos kalbamasis bei giedamasis rožinis. Vėlinės. Šermenys ir mirusiųjų minėjimai', *Liaudies kultūra*, 5 (2000), p. 10.
24 B. Ramanauskas, *Aš savo dalį atlikau* (Brooklyn: Franciscan Press, 1983), p. 110.
25 A. Chadam, *Spiewnik Kalwaryjski* (Kalwaria Zebrzydowska: Wyd. 'Calvarianum', 1984), p. 18.
26 A. Motuzas, *Lietuvos kalvarijų Kryžiaus kelių istorija, apeiginiai papročiai ir muzika* (Kaunas: Vytauto Didžiojo universitetas, 2003), pp. 26–33, 115–20, 166.

Praying

There are today many forms of prayers and praying. One particular Catholic devotion in which Christ's life, death and resurrection are meditated upon, is reciting the Rosary in honour of the Holy Name of Jesus. This Rosary was very popular at the Hill of Crosses, although it is a personal prayer and not part of liturgical prayers. It is not an official prayer of the Church as are Holy Mass or the Liturgy of the Hours, but is connected with the Mass on account of its meditation on the life, death and resurrection of Christ – the sacrifice of the Mass which leads to work of Salvation.

Praying in the prone position is an act of total humility, and rather unusual except for priests and religious who, in the presence of God's people, express their humble love before Him in this way on special occasions such as taking Holy Orders or religious vows. Praying with raised hands is not only a priestly rite. It expresses prayer as a symbol of change where there is giving and taking, pleading and thanksgiving.[27] It is a biblical way of praying, older and more expressive than conventional forms of prayer.

Singing Hymns (Sometimes Accompanied by Musical Instruments)

Another ritual custom, or rather two complementary customs, are praying and singing. The ritual of singing hymns while walking came from the late Middle Ages when ritual folk music used in the cult of the Passion of Christ and the burial of the Christian dead developed from Gregorian chant. Walking from one station to another and singing hymns was not only a physical action but also an act of prayer, reminding the faithful of the Way of the Cross, and that people are always journeying towards God's nation.[28]

The custom of accompanying hymns with folk musical instruments is connected with pre-Christian rituals. In the Samogitian diocese, they were integrated into Catholic ritual culture. Bishop Motiejus Valančius, in his 'Samogitian diocese', states that from the times of Bishop Merkelis Giedraitis (1576–1609), singers gathered in the Cathedral of Varniai as well as those who played the 'kanklės', the national instrument, and who, at the request of the bishop, were paid by the king, Stephen Batory.[29] In 1618, the Jesuit Chronicles, *Annuae Litterae S. Iesu*, record that the Samogitians, who were baptized and had

---

27 J. Lebon, *Kaip suprasti liturgiją* (Kaunas: Lietuvos Katechetikos centras 1998), p. 86.

28 Lebon, *Kaip suprasti liturgiją,*, p. 86.

29 M. Valančius, *Raštai* (Vilnius: Vaga, 1972), vol. 2, p. 161.

become Catholics, took the instruments such as 'kanklės', reed-pipes, whistles and wooden trumpets from pagan priests. Those playing the 'kanklės' and trumpets took part in the earliest processions.[30] Witnesses also attest to the use of drums in processions: 'Some of them have an orchestra accompanying their hymns or just a drum so liked by Samogitians.'[31] Evidence from the turn of the twentieth century suggests that in Samogitia, hymns were accompanied by 'kanklės' used by priests, monks and beggar-musicians. So perhaps we may suggest that the ritual custom of accompanying hymns with musical instruments on the Hill of Crosses is much older than Christianity itself. According to the facts mentioned here, we can state that the practice of playing traditional musical instruments on the Hill of Crosses came from Western Europe, while playing folk instruments is of local origin.

Walking the 14 Stations of the Way of the Cross

The 14 Stations of the Cross were installed at the Hill of Crosses at the end of the nineteenth century but the practice of following the stations of the Via Dolorosa comes from Jerusalem and the Way that Jesus Christ took to the place of His death. Building the stations in Europe became popular when, in the sixteenth to seventeenth centuries, pilgrimages to the Holy Land decreased. Dominicans started to build multi-stage calvaries in Europe at that time. Later, the 14 Stations of the Cross appeared as another form of commemorating Christ's Passion. Spanish Franciscans approved this cycle of 14 stations and, in 1628, Franciscan Capuchins built the Stations of the Cross on Monte Varverdo in Sardinia. In 1686, Pope Innocent XI issued a special decree authorizing the Franciscan Order to set Stations of the Cross in all their churches. This privilege was confirmed by Pope Innocent XII in 1695, with the explanation that Franciscans all over the world had the right to set stations in all their churches and to encourage people to pray to them. Pope Benedict XIII in 1726 granted indulgences of the Stations of the Cross to all believers, especially those who pray for the souls of the dead. In 1741, Pope Benedict XIV encouraged all the priests to set the stations in their churches because many did not possess them. Not all the monasteries had them either. St Leonard, who instituted the stations in the church of the monastery of St Bonaventure, was the first to do this in Rome. Under the guidance of Pope Benedict XIV, and the efforts of St Leonard,

---

[30]   B. Bagužas, *Alsėdžių parapijos 500 metų istoriniai bruožai* (Telšiai: Telšių kunigų seminarija, 1976), p. 23.

[31]   J. Totoraitis, *Žemaičių Kalvarija* (Marijampolė: Marijonų leidinys, 1927), pp. 5–6.

on 27 December 1750, a huge wooden cross with 14 stations around it was erected in the middle of the arena known as the Coliseum and was blessed by Cortonian, the papal legate.[32] From 1775, the 14 Stations of the Cross began to be built in all the churches and churchyard chapels of the world. They are followed with prayers and hymns on Fridays or in commemoration of Christ's passion and death. The sources of the expeditions show that pilgrims usually begin the Stations of the Cross on the Hill on their knees after making the sign of the Cross. The stations are also followed with the intention of praying for the dead.[33]

Other Rituals

The custom of almsgiving to beggars at the Hill of Crosses is related to the piety of the beggars whose prayers were regarded as being particularly effective. The intentions of almsgiving were as follows: compassion for the poor, following traditions, belief in the powerful prayer of a beggar which could intercede for a sick person or animal. Beggars were asked to pray for successful farming, good weather or for the dead and it was believed that their prayers helped souls in the purgatory as they were regarded as intercessors between the living and the dead.[34]

Some other rituals and customs at the Hill of Crosses:

– *Standing during a pilgrimage* was a sign of respect. This prayer position is seen in paintings in catacombs and works of early Christian writers.[35] A special painting where the believers stopped and prayed marked each place of Christ's stopping.[36]

– *Offering and lighting candles* on the Hill of Crosses together with Christianity came from the Roman Catholic liturgy.

– *Beating one's breast* is a sign of repentance and humility found in the books of the Prophets of the Old Testament (*Jeremiah* 31:19; *Ezra* 21:17). The first Christians in Jerusalem adopted this custom with enthusiasm.

---

[32]   Ramanauskas, *Aš savo dalį atlikau*, p. 261.

[33]   Motuzas, *Katalikų liaudies*, pp. 100–102.

[34]   A. Simoniukštytė, 'Elgetos ir elgetavimas', *Liaudies kultūra*, 5 (1994), p. 17.

[35]   A. Kajackas, *Bažnyčia liturgijoje. Liturgijos raida istorijoje* (Kaunas: Lietuvos katechetikos centras, 1997), pp. 29–30.

[36]   D. Ramonienė (ed.), *Krikščioniškosios ikonografijos žodynas* (Vilnius: Vilniaus dailės akademijos leidykla, 1997), p. 166.

– *The ritual custom of bowing one's head* comes from the Church's liturgical position and expresses respect, repentance, invitation and agreement. At the Hill of Crosses, pilgrims bow their heads facing the statues of Jesus Christ and Our Lady.

– *The ritual custom of preaching on the Hill of Crosses* comes from the Church tradition of the fourth century. According to this, excerpts were read aloud from the books of the New and Old Testaments.[37] So this custom is related to the liturgy of the Church.

The ritual customs related to the water had been implemented before the Soviet occupation. During this occupation the Kulpe brook was polluted by sewage water and the first sewage treatment plants were built only in 2004. The custom of washing with water from the nameless tributary around the Hill of Crosses can be related to the sacredness of water, considered to be so because of the sacrament of Baptism. In the Christian Church, only blessed water gains such power. Such water is called holy and people are aspersed as a reminder of their Baptismal water with its power to forgive sins.

Non-traditional rituals were also performed at the Hill of the Crosses. The Lithuanian media were the first to describe such non-traditional feasts on the Hill of Crosses which began on 17/18 July 1998 when there was a nocturnal vigil with a concert singing non-traditional hymns praising the Lord on the Hill. The Franciscan friars of Kretinga in western Lithuania hosted the ceremonies and the music. Some were happy, others expressed their disapproval. Most of the beggars, tourists and devout elderly people agreed with the Franciscan friars that

the Hill of Crosses is not a place of sorrow but of joy. Joyful hymns were performed accompanied by the guitar. In the morning traditional pilgrims took part in the liturgy of the Mass, and those non-traditional were walking around.[38]

Identity

The Hill of Crosses constitutes and represents multiple positions of different identities, reflects various aspects of attraction, and creates forms of legibility, or ways in which its place identity can be imagined, understood and experienced

37   Kajackas, *Bažnyčia liturgijoje*, p. 91.
38   N. Salmininkienė, 'Atlaidai', *Lietuvos žinios*, 166 (1998), p. 14.

from diverse points of view. Places do not exist as such, but are actively constructed by social processes,[39] including religious devotion and pilgrimage. According to Lefebvre 'every society produces a space ... its own space'.[40] Zukin draws attention to the 'production of space', alongside the parallel 'production of symbols'.[41] Indeed, the identity and understanding of the Hill of Crosses cannot be the same for different individuals because each has had a particular interaction with the Hill; their knowledge, their symbolism of the Hill, and their personal relationship to the Hill differs.

Understanding the identities and meanings of the Hill of Crosses depends in part

> on understanding subject positions and subject formations of the touring, the toured, and those who would work at being both or neither, and from one moment or place to the next. In such contexts, ideas people hold about places substantially inform identity formation, human agency, and questions of subjectivity.[42]

Therefore, landscapes mean different things to different people. This particular place could symbolize various power relations and could be an instrument of national, cultural or religious power. The crosses erected at the Hill of Crosses are symbols of personal (spiritual, mental or physical) or communal (national historical, social, cultural or religious problems and memorials) circumstances which are closely intertwined with the motives of pilgrimage.

The two main groups of crosses can be identified according to the inscriptions on them:

1. gratitude or supplication crosses (for health, success, happy marriage, religious freedom, independence of Lithuania, other graces);
2. memorial crosses (in remembrance of the dead, exiles, convicted or in remembrance of historical events, jubilees, etc.).

After the evaluation of the meanings of the identity of the Hill of Crosses, four essential symbolic identities of the Hill of Crosses can be identified:

---

[39]   G. Shaw and A.M. Williams, *Tourism and Tourism Spaces* (London: SAGE, 2004), p. 186.

[40]   H. Lefebvre, *The Production of Space* (Oxford: Blackwell, 1991), p. 31.

[41]   S. Zukin, *The Cultures of Cities* (Oxford: Blackwell, 1995), p. 24.

[42]   C. Cartier, 'Introduction: Touristed Landscapes/Seductions of Place', in C. Cartier and A.A. Lew (eds), *Seductions of Place: Geographical Perspectives on Globalization and Touristed Landscapes* (London and New York: Routledge, 2005), p. 18.

1. The Hill of Crosses as a symbol of national and religious freedom and resistance to the occupiers.

The Hill of Crosses is not only a religious object but also a symbol of national and religious freedom. This symbolism began as a result of historical, religious and political events (the 1831 and 1864 rebellions against tsarist Russia, resistance to the Soviet occupation) which strengthened this type of symbolic identity of the Hill of Crosses.

According to Mačiulis, during the Soviet era, the Hill of Crosses was a place for self-expression of unrestricted individual religious beliefs. Often crosses were placed as a sign of resistance against the Soviet regime and its anti-religious policy.[43] In Soviet times, pilgrimages, and especially the crosses raised, were challenges to the atheist authorities. Large numbers of young people and students generally took part in pilgrimages and several people were detained and convicted for organizing these.[44] The more intense the efforts to destroy the Hill of Crosses became, the more energetically was it regenerated. People would place crosses at night, disregarding dangers, bans and persecution.

2. The Hill of Crosses as a symbol of personal or national rebirth.

The Hill of Crosses is a sacred place where pilgrims negotiate their identity, seeking renewal or exploration, the possibilities of change and shift of liminal identity (such as on wedding day visits).

According to several sources, the origin of the Hill of Crosses is related to miraculous healing. Now people ask for God's grace, health, as well as spiritual renewal there. They believe that erecting a cross will be a sign for a new stage in their spiritual, physical or communal life. For young married couples it is not only a place for taking wedding day photos, but a symbol of passage to a new stage of their life. After success or recovery from illness, it is a place for expressing gratitude to Jesus or the Virgin Mary. During the Lithuanian revival in 1988–9, the people of Lithuania demonstrated their will to be independent by leaving crosses there. After Lithuania had gained independence, it was a place where everyone could leave the mark of their personal gratitude for independence.

---

[43] Mačiulis, 'Kryžių kalno', p. 88.

[44] *Pilgrim Route of John Paul II in Lithuania: Guidebook* (Kaunas: Lithuanian Bishops Conference, Catholic Internet Service, 2009), p. 245.

3. The Hill of Crosses as a place of religious devotion.

The Hill of Crosses is an excellent illustration of how people persevered in their faith during the Soviet years. With its unique historical origin and continuity of pilgrimages with the indulgence feast and different folk devotional practices, prayers, hymns and music, the Hill of Crosses is a place for religious devotion. The Cross is a symbol of Christianity, and the Hill of Crosses is a unique place of the exaltation of the Cross.

4. The Hill of Crosses as a cultural space.

The leaving of crosses is no longer just a religious act, but also a cultural phenomenon and a sign of respect.[45] The Hill of Crosses is included in many tourist itineraries in Lithuania or the Baltic States. Tourists usually buy a small cross and leave or hang it on the bigger crosses on the Hill. The Hill of Crosses itself has unique picturesque and aesthetic value, and some of the crosses have been declared as cultural monuments. Tourist authorities often regard the Hill of Crosses as a complex cultural monument valuing its cultural and public aspects.

Therefore, the Hill of Crosses is open for different identities and various social interactions. Many places are open for different place identities, but the degree of openness has changed with history:

> Places are constantly changing over time, through both their internal dynamics and the manner in which these interact with external and increasingly globalized processes of change ... They negotiate their engagement with tourism, albeit in the context of unequal power relationships and they contest their roles in the world.[46]

Nowadays the Hill of Crosses could accumulate different narratives. We have to enter into discourse with the institutionalised understanding of the Catholic Church, meanings of Lithuanians socialized by family, culture and historical traditions, and religiously, culturally or tourist motivated senses of foreign visitors (as tourists and pilgrims).

Narratives are usually shaped, refined and distilled by social interaction and official promotion of power institutions. Knowledge and institutional power has a role in the management of narratives and leads in the attempts to homogenize meanings.

---

[45] *Pilgrim Route of John Paul II in Lithuania*, p. 247.
[46] Shaw and Williams, *Tourism and Tourism Spaces*, p. 187.

Conclusions

Having analysed the data, we can draw the following conclusions:

1. The network of Lithuanian pilgrimage places consists of the 20 most important pilgrimage places related to the cult of the Virgin Mary, saints and cults of holy persons. Lithuanian Calvaries are also included in this network. Besides the Hill of Crosses, one holy spring and the Divine Mercy Shrine at Vilnius, which contains the first image of the Merciful Jesus, are also included in this network.

2. Two main reasons for the first crosses on the Hill of Crosses could be identified. The first was signs of folk faith, votive signs of gratitude to God. Or alternately, it could be a wish to commemorate rebels of the uprising and to resist tsarist authority, which prohibited and prevented crosses from being built. The first group of explanations contain a miraculous element (miraculous healing of a local man, the apparition of the Blessed Virgin), while others are related to tragic historical events (commemoration of people who died in the 1831 and 1863 uprisings against tsarist Russia).

3. The most important devotional practices of the Hill of Crosses are erecting and leaving crosses, the celebration of indulgence feasts, processions, commemoration of the dead, walking on one's knees, praying, singing hymns (sometimes accompanied by musical instruments), and walking the 14 Stations of the Way of the Cross.

4. According to the inscriptions on the crosses, the two main groups of them are identified as follows – gratitude or supplication crosses and memorial crosses. The four essential notions of the symbolic identity of the Hill of Crosses are: 1) the Hill of Crosses as a symbol of national and religious freedom and resistance to the occupiers; 2) the Hill of Crosses as a symbol of personal or national rebirth; 3) the Hill of Crosses as a place of religious devotion; 4) the Hill of Crosses as a cultural space.

5. The Hill of Crosses is a sacred location for the veneration of the Cross and religious unity and devotion, as well as a burial place for heroes. Inscriptions in foreign languages and the increased number of foreign visitors demonstrate its international importance.

Chapter 7

The Saint and His Cat: Localization of Religious Charisma in Contemporary Russian Orthodox Pilgrimages[1]

Jeanne Kormina

I came to the island of Zalita in Pskov oblast' with a group of pilgrims from St Petersburg for the first time in 2004. After six hours overnight in an old rented bus and almost an hour on a shabby boat which was obviously and dangerously overloaded we found ourselves in a small village which had three streets of tiny houses, one semi-empty food store, a deserted community centre with statues of Lenin and local communist hero Zalit, after whom the island was renamed in the Soviet period, a church and a cemetery. The leader of the group, a kind of individual entrepreneur who was active in a recently developed pilgrimage market, regularly organized trips to this place. The main destination of these pilgrimages was the grave and a house of recently deceased *starets* (the elder) Nikolay Gurianov.

As I soon realized, some of pilgrims from the group used to visit Father Nikolay when he was alive. One could easily distinguish them among the visitors because of the bunches of white lilies in their hands. They explained that these were his favourite flowers. They spoke about him in a special, very sweet manner and the first thing which two of them asked the local priest in the church was about the *starets'* cat. Their question 'How is his cat Lipa doing now?' was not properly answered, as the priest started passionately explaining to the pilgrims the stupidity of venerating the cat and, by extension, the person who was not canonized by the Church.

Two things amazed me in this conversation: the question about a cat and the answer of a priest who pretended that he did not understand the question. In fact, the stories about that cat were quite widespread among those who venerated

---

[1] This research was supported by the National Research University Higher School of Economics' Academic Fund Program in 2012/2013, research grant #11-01-0126.

Father Nikolay as *starets*, including the tale of how he miraculously resurrected Lipa, but I could not imagine that his pet was so important that it could become the subject of a rather dramatic discussion.

Religious pilgrimages to the Orthodox sacred places have become increasingly popular in Russia since the mid-1990s. For many people, especially for non-churchgoers, these organized religious trips have become one of the most acceptable ways of practising their religion. These believers want to be religious outside the walls of the church, escaping the need to follow the commands of a parish priest in his role as confessor and the social control exercised by a church congregation.

The sacred sites visited by pilgrims in contemporary Russia can be roughly divided into two categories: traditional and new. Traditional pilgrimage destinations are large monasteries, which used to be pilgrimage centres before the 1920s, until religion was virtually prohibited in the Soviet Union. In the post-Soviet period many of these places have become pilgrimage destinations once more. However, a significant number of the sacred places visited by contemporary pilgrims in Russia have appeared quite recently – within the last two decades. Some of them are village shrines which, thanks to the joint efforts of a local priest, village 'keepers of a shrine' and a leader of a pilgrimage agency from the city, became a part of a pilgrimage route. A typical village holy site, or rather a holy landscape of this sort, is usually made up of a set of physical objects, for example, a stone with a footprint of a saint on it, a stream or a cave, and by a set of belief narratives explaining why this particular place is a sacred one.[2]

Alongside traditional village sacred places and officially recognized holy places like monasteries, one more type of holy site started to appear on the map of the pilgrims' routes in the 1990s: person-centred holy sites. Eade and Sallnow have discovered a similar trend in Catholic Christianity, namely a 'shift from place-centred to person-centred sacredness'.[3] The material 'container' of sanctity at these places is not a landscape as in the village sacred sites nor an ensemble of monastery buildings where holy icons are kept, but a person, a sort of living saint called '*starets*', meaning 'the elder'.

[2] For more detail about these sacred places see: J. Kormina, 'Pilgrims, Priest and Local Religion in Contemporary Russia: Contested Religious Discourses', *Folklore*, 28 (2004), pp. 25–40.

[3] J. Eade and M.J. Sallnow, 'Introduction', in J. Eade and M.J. Sallnow (eds), *Contesting the Sacred: The Anthropology of Christian Pilgrimage* (Urbana and Chicago: University of Illinois Press, 2000), p. 7.

The tradition of *starchestvo* and the practice of veneration of 'living saints' are not absolutely new aspects of the Russian Orthodox tradition.[4] There is much evidence about hermits – people, not necessarily monks or nuns, who were venerated as living saints by the local population – in late Imperial and even Soviet Russia.[5] *Starchestvo*, as it is understood by many now, is in fact an umbrella term covering quite heterogeneous religious phenomena. 'Starets', theoretically, is a monk and spiritual father of a large monastery.[6] However, in the ethnographical reality *starets* and especially *staritsa* (female elder) is usually a layperson who has neither taken a monastic vow nor been ordained as a priest. They share not only the regular spiritual guidance of a group of believers who are their spiritual children but also their perception and function as prophets and forecasters who can give sage spiritual advice in difficult personal circumstances. As an anonymous compiler of the recently published collection of biographies of female elders wrote:

> Since the old days an elder always played the role of mediator between a novice and God. For that, together with other necessary virtues, the elder has to be possessed of the gift of spiritual reasoning, that is, the talent to recognize God's will through prayer. This makes his answers spiritual and "prophetic". As a

---

[4]   Pilgrimage to the living saints was already quite widespread in Christian Late Antiquity. See G. Frank, *The Memory of the Eyes: Pilgrims to Living Saints in Christian Late Antiquity* (Berkeley, Los Angeles and London: University of California Press, 2000).

[5]   Biographies of the unglorified Russian Orthodox devotees of the eighteenth and nineteenth centuries, some of whom were venerated as living saints, were published in the 12-volume collection in the Russian Monastery of St Panteleimon in Athos, see Nikodim, *Zizneopisaniya otechestvennykh podvizhnikov blagochestiya XVIII i XIX vekov [Biographies of the Russian Zealots of Faith of the 18th and 19th Centuries]* (Moscow: The Russian Monastery of St Panteleimon in Athos, 1906–12). Amongst many publications of biographies of the zealots of faith (also unglorified) who lived in the twentieth century, are two of the largest collections according to gender. The 'male' collection includes 115 biographies of prospective saints, see S. Deviatova (ed.), *Velikie startsy dvadtsatogo stoletiya [Great Elders of the 20th Century]* (Moscow: Artos-Media, 2007 [2006]). The 'female' collection has 70 biographies: S. Deviatova (ed.), *Pravoslavnye podvizhnitsy dvadtsatogo stoletiya [Orthodox Zealots of Faith of the 20th Century]* (Moscow: Artos-Media, 2007).

[6]   For a detailed history of Russian *starchestvo* see the recently published book: I. Paert, *Spiritual Elders: Charisma and Tradition in Russian Orthodoxy* (DeKalb: Northern Illinois University Press, 2010).

mediator in transmitting God's will the elder is considered a successor to Christ Himself and a prophet equal to Moses.[7]

Many people believe that it is absolutely obligatory to follow advice given by the elder, even if it seems barely acceptable, because he or she foresees the consequence of every action or decision of those who come to him or her.[8]

The aim of this chapter is to analyse the meanings ascribed to the concept of *starchestvo* by various groups of pilgrims to one particular person venerated as *starets*, Father Nikolay Gurianov (1909–2002). It focuses on the narrative strategies used by different groups of believers in representing the holiness of the place which they visit as a pilgrimage destination. In their stories about pilgrimages to a particular *starets* or his or her grave, people discuss (either consciously or implicitly) many 'big issues' such as qualities of sanctity, the boundary between the religious and the secular, ethnic and national identities, and many others. In this chapter, I will briefly outline the main types of stories about the sanctity of the *starets* Nikolay Gurianov and describe groups of believers generating and promoting a particular version of these stories. These include a Christian legend from a secular newspaper, stories of pilgrims about 'small miracles' which they experienced as a result of their visits to the elder, pseudo-historical narratives by representatives of Orthodox fundamentalists, and stories of locals who do not believe that their parish priest is a living saint.

The chapter is based on field research conducted on an island during the course of my trips with groups of pilgrims from St Petersburg in 2004, 2006 and 2010, and participant observations made in July and August 2008 in collaboration with my colleague, Yulia Andreeva. Printed materials and Internet resources are also an important part of the data.

A Christian Legend in a Secular Newspaper

On 24 October 2002, Nikolay Gurianov, a celibate village priest from Pskov oblast, died. Information about his death appeared in both secular and Orthodox media of different political orientations, both national and provincial. Many

---

[7]   *Sviatye matushki i podvizhnitsy zemli Russkoy v XX veke prosiyavshie. Zhitiya, chudesa, vospominaniya* [*Venerable Female Ascetics of the Russian Land of the 20th Century: Biographies, Miracles and Memories*] (Nikolaev: Litopis, 2010).

[8]   These effects only apply to earthly life. I never heard from my informants or read about an elder helping in the afterlife. The earthly-life orientation of those who venerate *startsy* provides quite a good characterization of an average contemporary Orthodox believer.

important public figures, representatives of religious and secular elites from the city of Pskov and the capital Moscow, as well as from other places came to his funeral on the tiny island of Zalita (Talabsk) in Pskov oblast,[9] where Father Nikolay had served as a priest in the village church of St Nikolas since 1958. The list of VIP visitors included the archbishop and the governor of Pskov, the influential archimandrite Tikhon Shevkunov, superior of the Sretensky Monastery in Moscow, and 'Orthodox banker', billionaire and politician Sergey Pugachev. Local people say that the wife of President Putin was to attend the burial ceremony but for some reason she did not come.

It is not surprising that an article about Father Nikolay has appeared in the Russian version of Wikipedia; he was a famous figure since the mid-1990s, when people of different social backgrounds started visiting him en masse. The Wikipedia article includes a story about the miraculous help provided by Father Nikolay, a story that was published in one of Russia's national newspapers, *Izvestija* (*The News*), in 2001 and reproduced many times in secular media:

> He acquired a reputation as a miracle-worker after he had been found by Igor Stoliarov, the survivor of the nuclear-powered submarine Komsomolets.[10] Some years after the disaster, the seaman from Siberia, who heaven knows how happened to survive, came to the island of Zalita and immediately recognized father Nikolay. He was a *starets* who had appeared to him when he had been fainting in the icy waters of the Atlantic. The grey-bearded old man had identified himself as archpriest Nikolas and said to him, "You swim, I am praying for you and you will escape". Then he vanished. Suddenly, a log had appeared from somewhere; shortly after that a rescue boat arrived.[11]

This text is an easily identifiable Christian legend about Saint Nikolas the Miracle-Maker, who 'specializes' in helping seamen. Obviously, the story about miraculously helping the sailor from the last Soviet submarine makes Nikolay Gurianov a holy person on a significant national scale. It also puts the saint back in the Soviet period, thus building a bridge between Soviet and post-Soviet

---

[9]   The island is inhabited by fishermen, pensioners and, since the 1990s, Orthodox migrants from cities. The latter moved from Moscow (mostly) and St Petersburg, alone or with their families and spend every summer or the whole year on the island. These people are known as 'Orthodox *dachniki*'.

[10]   The nuclear-powered submarine *Komsomolets*, which means 'Komsomol member', sank in the Norwegian Sea in April 1989. This tragedy symbolizes the end of the Soviet epoch.

[11]   *Gurianov, Nikolay Alexeevitch*, at http://en.wikipedia.org/wiki/Nikolay_Guryanov (accessed 17 June 2011). Incidentally, there was nobody on the submarine with this name.

Russia. In other words, the narrative gives the reader an idea that this holy person used to live before the de-secularization of Russia had started. Hence, the central message of this narrative can be formulated as follows; he and other *startsy* served as vessels preserving religious tradition, meaning that the authenticity of religious tradition in Russia had not been interrupted during the Soviet period.

However, I have never heard this story from pilgrims or local people living on the island. Instead, some pilgrims and newcomers who came to the island from the cities and have settled there in the last 10 to 15 years recite a different narrative about a seaman from a submarine. This story tells of a man who had become infertile as a result of serving on the atomic submarine. He visited the *starets*, who prayed for him and subsequently his wife gave birth to a son, while other men from the same submarine remained childless. This type of narrative about miraculous help in solving health problems as a result of pilgrimage to a shrine or a holy person is a very typical one. It reproduces a widespread scheme of reciprocal exchange with the sacred, one that is well known in many religious traditions. It should be added in this context that, traditionally, infertility used to be one of the most typical health problems to be solved with the help of the divine. However, this problem used to be seen as linked only to female health. The narrators of these stories reveal not only their modern attitudes towards the source of fertility problems but also their quite modern social phobias and fantasies about atomic energy.

However, this tale is almost unusual because the stories about healing as a result of pilgrimage to a shrine are quite rare in the contemporary Orthodox narrative repertoire. They have probably disappeared together with the idea of a personal vow, which was very common in pre-revolutionary Russia, and even later, in small pilgrimages to local village shrines practised secretly in the Soviet countryside, at least in north-western Russia.[12] Instead of asking God or a saint for miraculous recovery from some illness, contemporary believers usually ask for divine intervention in their social relationships, such as problems with family members, colleagues or representatives of the state and in situations of uncertainty, such as trials, exams, etc. Visitors with health problems come to *starets* in search of help to make serious decisions about whether or not they

---

[12]   The tradition of making *obet* or *zavet* in Russia is discussed in T.B. Shchepanskaya, 'Krizisnaya set' (traditsii dukhovnogo osvoeniya prostranstva') ['A Crisis Network (Traditions of Creating Religious Landscape)'], in *Russaky Sever. K probleme lokal'nykh grupp* [*Russian North: The Study of Local Groups*] (St Petersburg: Musei Antropologii i Etnografii, 1995), pp. 110–76 and A.A. Panchenko, *Issledovanie v oblasti narodnogo pravpslavija: derevenskie sviatyni Severo-zapada Rossii* [*Study of Russian Orthodoxy: Village Sacred Sites of North-western Russia*] (St Petersburg: Aleteya, 1998), p. 82.

should trust their doctors. They would ask *starets* whether they should follow the doctor's prescriptions for a particular medicine or have an operation rather than ask for immediate miraculous recovery. Correspondingly, in the narrative repertoire of pilgrims, 'real miracles' about healing are replaced by the 'small miracles' which focus on consolation and harmonization of the self.

'I Became an Absolutely Different Person': Pilgrims' Narratives

Since at least the early 1980s Nikolay Gurianov has attracted the attention of members of the young Orthodox intelligentsia and neophytes from metropolitan bohemian circles.[13] It must be mentioned here that the Pskov region was one of those which were unintentionally promoted by the Soviet state as a representation of Russianness and of Russian spirituality. One of the reasons for this is that Pskov is an ancient city founded before the tenth century, preserving much of its medieval fortifications and churches, which date mainly from the fifteenth and sixteenth centuries. Since the 1960s the Soviet state organized excursions in the Pskov region for foreign delegations, which were allowed to visit very few places in Russia. These trips included visits to the local Orthodox churches and to the Pskovo-Pechersky monastery, the only one in Russia which was never closed, to demonstrate 'religious freedom' in the USSR. At the same time, specialists in Russian architecture and icon-painting from Moscow and St Petersburg started going to Pskov as part of expeditions from art museums and academies of sciences, hunting for ancient Russian pieces of art and manuscripts or as restorers of old churches.[14] Unsurprisingly, almost half of the material for the first documentary about the Russian Orthodox Church called 'Khram' (Temple), produced in 1988 to mark the millennium celebration of the Christianization of Russia, was filmed in Pskov oblast. In particular, this film contained a short scene with village priest Father Nikolay sipping tea at a table in his small house. The documentary was shown several times on TV, and was also screened at various film festivals. In addition, an article with a portrait of Father Nikolay was published in the popular illustrated magazine *Sovetski ekran* (*Soviet Screen*). It is entirely possible that this film and article played a role in

---

[13]   In Pskov oblast, Orthodox believers from Moscow and other cities also visited the monk-priest Ioann Krestiankin (Pskovo-Pecherski monastery) and Father Vassili Shvets, who served in the village of Kamenny Konets.

[14]   For information on the influence that this kind of expedition had on the reshaping of local and religious identities, see the recently published book: D. Rogers, *The Old Faith and the Russian Land: A Historical Ethnography of Ethics in the Urals* (Ithaca: Cornell University Press, 2010).

the popularization of the figure of Father Nikolay. Interestingly, he was not yet called a *starets* in the article, just a *sel'ski pravednik* (righteous village man).[15]

Mass pilgrimage to the island began in the mid-1990s, when Father Nikolay was already an elderly man in his late eighties. People, who came either in groups organized by parish priests or lay religious activists or separately, had to queue for hours to have a very brief talk with Father Nikolay. At the end of the 1990s, access to Father Nikolay was restricted in his everyday routine by his *keleinitsy* (the term derives from the word '*kellia*' – monastic cell).[16] The personal narratives of visitors to Father Nikolay about his sanctity usually have two central points. First, stories about visits to the *starets* contain evidence of his gift of foresight; he can see who his visitors are, in terms of profession and personal qualities, without asking them and he can foretell their future. Second, the visitors believed that as a holy person he could give wise advice in difficult personal circumstances or at a crucial moment when an important choice had to be made. For Orthodox seminary graduates it is often about marriage and thus whether to become a secular priest or to take monastic vows, for example. As it is believed to be appropriate for a real *starets*, Father Nikolay usually spoke in riddles. For example, he told a nun that she would receive a marriage proposal and should not reject it; later she was invited to become a Mother Superior of a nunnery, 'and realized then what kind of marriage proposal he was talking about'.[17] Sometimes he did not give any answer to a visitor, and this was also perceived as a riddle. The interpretation of his answers is a specific topic in the personal narratives of the pilgrims who visited him.

As mentioned above, the personal narratives about communicating with the *starets* very rarely contain evidence of miraculous healings or miracles of a different sort. However, the holiness of a living saint can be pronounced in another way. In the documentary *Why Are We Orthodox?*, shot on the island in 1997 by 'Orthodox director' Alexandr Alexandrov, one of the pilgrims queuing at the door of Nikolay's small house is demon-possessed. It is well known that a demon

---

[15] Y. Tiurin, 'Put' dlinoju v tysiacheletie' ['The Way that Lasted for a Thousand Years'], *Sovetskii ekran*, 11 (1988), pp. 6–8.

[16] A *keleinik* lives with an elderly monk or high-ranking church official as his servant, pupil and personal secretary. *Startsy* also have their *keleiniki* (male) or, as in case of Father Nikolay, *keleinitsy* (female), who act as gatekeepers controlling the sacred embodied in the living saint. It so happened that the *keleinitsy* of Nikolay Gurianov were representatives of the fundamentalist movement in the Russian Orthodox church, who continued their fight for the *starets'* legacy after his death.

[17] N. Hieromonk, *Starets Nikolay Zalitsky* [*Nikolay of Zalit, the Elder*] (St Petersburg: Satis, 2002), pp. 13–14.

reveals its presence in the body of the possessed when that person approaches holy things and places. In particular, they start blaspheming the Church and faith, and can only be exorcised by a religious specialist.[18] Although there are some places (monasteries) in Russia where people go to participate in the rituals of exorcism, Father Nikolay never practised it.[19] So the story, which probably began as a narrative about a miraculous recovery from demon possession, turned out simply to be evidence of the holiness of Father Nikolay. This evidence is articulated by the possessed women or, rather, by the demon who was speaking from her lips, in the last part of the documentary, 'Revelation of *the* Demon':

> I hate the Orthodox people! I hate them! The nastiest faith is the Orthodox faith! All the other religions will go to hell. You are idiots, why do you listen to him? Kol'ka (variant of the name Nikolay, pejorative in this context). He is a fool! Kol'ka, I hate you! You teach them all the time. Don't do that! Let them [the Orthodox] go to Hell! Don't let them know the truth! Let them see TV, let them play computer games! Let them die! They have to go to hell![20]

Paradoxically, by her blasphemies the possessed proved the truth of the Orthodox faith and personal holiness of Father Nikolay. And, as I mentioned already, the exorcism does not happen.

In the pilgrims' stories, miraculous changes occur not in the bodies of the narrators, for instance, a recovery from some illness, but in their personalities. These transformations, which I call 'small miracles', occur as a result of brief communication with the *starets* or merely through observing him. Some people say that they received consolation even without any contact with him, just by spending some time on the island. A pilgrim who suffered from deep personal discomfort and disorder received consolation and a feeling of harmony.

> Batiushka [the diminutive form of "father"] could see the future, but it was not the central point in his ministry. The central point was that he consoled everybody ... He just anointed us with holy oil from a test tube using a paperclip, but what a consolation was coming into the soul after that! Although he did not

[18] See for example: Christine D. Worobec, *Possessed: Women, Witches, and Demons in Imperial Russia* (DeKalb: Northern Illinois University Press, 2001).

[19] For a detailed history of discourses and practices of exorcism see, E. Mel'nikova, 'Otchityvanie besnovatykh: practiki i diskursy' ['Exorcism: Practices and Discourses]', *Antropologichesky forum*, 4 (2006), pp. 220–263.

[20] A. Alexandrov, *Pochemu my pravoslavnye?* [*Why Are We Orthodox?*], documentary (Moscow: Radonezh, 1998).

speak much, and it seemed that he addressed the same words to different people, having *received consolation* in their different personal circumstances.[21]

The famous ophthalmologist Vladimir Nepomnyashvchikh, who used to visit Gurianov in the 1990s, stressed his feeling of purification as a result of communication with him:

> Every time after my meeting with Father Nikolay tens of questions and problems just disappeared. As a result of the prayers of the *batiushka*, mind and heart cleared ... The soul calmed down, got ready for confession; offences vanished. This *inner purification* happens also when one visits other saints and holy places.[22]

Here, another visitor to the *starets* describes the experience of spiritual and probably even physical regeneration:

> After conversing with him I left his house with a feeling that *I became an absolutely different person*. I felt relief. What joy! It seemed to me that life was different, I got firm confidence in the future ... always after meeting with *starets* Nikolay my thoughts and feelings were put in order, sorrow vanished, the aim of life had become clear for the short-term future.[23]

Anthropologists who study pilgrimage have already pointed out that at the sacred place a pilgrim expects to have an experience of transformation of his or her personality as if he or she were going through the *rite de passage*, where travel to the sacred place has features of the liminal period.[24] Accordingly, communication with the *starets* is represented in the narratives of pilgrims as a rebirth of the person.

Meanwhile the local people's narratives about the *starets* are quite different from the two mentioned above. They do not agree with pilgrims and newcomers to the island from the cities that Father Nikolay, who served on the island of Zalita for more than 40 years, was a holy person. In their view, he was a good priest and at the end of his life, an elderly member of the village community

---

[21]   L. Iliunina, *Starets Nikolay Gurianov. Liubov', ko Gospodu Vedushchaya* [*The Elder Nikolay Gurianov: Love that Leads to the Lord*] (St Petersburg: Pravoslavny St Petersburg, 2007), p. 27.

[22]   *Vospominaniya o startse Nikolae Gurianove* [*Memoirs of the Elder Nikolay Gurianov*], ed. Galina Chinyakova (Moscow: Kovcheg, 2009), p. 102.

[23]   *Vospominaniya o startse Nikolae Gurianove*, p. 28.

[24]   See E. Turner and V. Turner, *Image and Pilgrimage in Christian Culture* (New York: Columbia University Press, 1978).

taken care of by the village. The newcomers complain of the 'locals' blindness': they could not see the obvious fact that they had been privileged to live side by side with the living saint. The newcomers and pilgrims refer to the spiritual ignorance of the local people as 'simplicity', the quality which they share with Father Nikolay. However, 'simplicity' in this case is not entirely a compliment; it means stupidity too. But of course it also means a kind of 'natural authenticity', or even 'inborn Russianness'.

Orthodox Christianity is understood by many Russians in a rather primordial way, as something naturally inherent in the national landscape and in people's minds and bodies. According to this popular argument, the degree of 'authenticity' of the place is closely connected with its remoteness. In the imagined geography of visitors to the island of Zalita, this place is located in the far periphery not only because it is an island, a piece of land isolated from the mainland, but also because of its closeness to the state border. The border (this border at least – the island is located less than 50 km from the Russian–Estonian border) is seen as the end of the Russian world, the edge of the Russian Orthodox world.

The locals, on the other hand, see the newcomers and visitors as religious fanatics who dedicate their whole life to religion. For the locals, typical 'miraculous stories' about Father Nikolay are dream narratives, just common local folk narrative genre. Father Nikolay appears to the islanders in their dreams as an ordinary person who speaks about their everyday needs and gives practical advice, just as their deceased relatives and neighbours would do. For example, the head of the village administration told us about a dream he had in which Father Nikolay ordered him not to drink water from the lake and stop taking a particular medicine which he used to take to cure his headaches. He followed his instructions and has felt better ever since.

Stylistic of Sanctity: Debates

His life itself is a great miracle. The sanctity of Father Nikolay is so obvious that it does not need any special justification, including invented miracles. His humility did not need any laudation when he was alive; similarly, there is no need for it now, after his death, because it contradicts the level of spiritual perfection he has achieved. Batiushka used to recite: "there are hundreds of Angels, where the simplicity is ..."[25] He was looking for simplicity, he has achieved it; it is impossible to enclose his sanctity in the construction of fantasy and ecstatic visions.[26]

This text, written by Igor Izbortsev, an Orthodox writer and journalist from Pskov, represents one opinion about Nikolay Gurianov's kind of saintness. That was a reflection of a heated debate which flared up after the death of the *starets* in 2002, between representatives of the right-wing fundamentalist Orthodox group led by his *keleinitsa* Tatiana Groyan and the rest of the believers. The fundamentalists appeared on the island at the end of the 1990s and started their struggle with the official Church for control over the *starets* Nikolay and his legacy. After his death, they bought his house, where they set up a museum, free of charge for all visitors. They did their best to establish control of the memory of Father Nikolay including such private details as his attachment to his cat, while they made attempts to promote their own image of this proposed saint via the Internet, newspapers and other media. These believers belong to a group of Orthodox people who were not satisfied with the canonization of Tsar Nikolas II as a passion-bearer (*strastoterpets*). Instead, they insisted on canonizing him as a Martyr and even as a co-redeemer, who suffered for the whole Russian nation, whilst promoting the canonization of such an ambiguous historical figure as Grigori Rasputin. The *keleinitsa* Tatiana Groyan, a linguistics graduate from Moscow State University, actively participates in polemics about the *starets* and has published a hagiographical book about Grigori Novy (Rasputin).[27] She claimed that Nikolay Gurianov venerated Rasputin and gave her his blessing for the canonization of this person.

Starets is not an official position within the Church; it is a reputation. The elders are not included in the official Church hierarchy and represent, in the eyes of many anticlerical believers, a kind of alternative religious authority. In contrast to the official Church hierarchs who are blamed for corruption and too close collaboration with the state, elders such as Nikolay Gurianov are believed to live ascetic lives in monasteries or poor remote parishes beyond political intrigues and economic interests. There are those who managed to

---

[25] This saying is ascribed to a famous monk of the nineteenth century, *starets* Amvrosy who lived in the Optina monastery. The full version of the saying is 'there are hundreds of Angels, where the simplicity is while there is no angel where sophistication is'.

[26] I. Izbortsev, 'Ya pomolius' za vas'. O zalitskom startse o. Nikolae Gurianove' ['"I Will Pray for You": About the Elder from the Island of Zalita Father Nikolay Gurianov'], *Proza.ru [Prose. ru]* (3 June 2003), at http://proza.ru/2003/03/07-70-1 (accessed 18 June 2011).

[27] T. Groyan, *Muchenik za Khrista I za tsarya Grigory Novy [Martyr Suffered for Christ and for Tsar Grigori the New]* (Moscow: Entsiklpedia Russkoi Tsivilizatsii, 2001).

preserve an ancient Russian Orthodox tradition uncorrupted. Paradoxically, the exceptional authority of *startsy* was officially acknowledged and artfully used during the campaign of the Patriarchate of ROC (Russian Orthodox Church) against the 'INN (individual tax numbers) jihad' organized by groups of Orthodox fundamentalists and nationalists.[28] In 2001, Tikhon Shevkunov interviewed four famous *startsy*, including Nikolay Gurianov, about their stance on the introduction of individual tax numbers. All of them – as represented in the Church mass-media – confirmed that there was no Satanic number (666) encoded in individual tax numbers and gave their blessing to believers to accept individual tax numbers.[29] Their position, transmitted via various media, played an important role in changing public opinion about INN among Orthodox people and, according to some analysts, helped to avoid a split in the ROC.

However, Tatiana Groyan and other Orthodox fundamentalists are not satisfied with the status given by reputation; they prefer to transform the symbolic capital obtained by the *starets* as a result of his personal charisma into a position in the Church hierarchy. Groyan claims that Father Nikolay was a hidden *episcope* who was secretly consecrated during the Second World War.[30] There are two possible explanations for why he did not reveal his high position to anybody except his closest friends, including Groyan. The first reason, as believers themselves would explain it, is his deep personal modesty, a quality that amazed almost everybody who visited him – or at least who published their memories about these visits. The other explanation is connected with the specific worldview of this group of believers, who are obsessed with conspiracy theories in their explanations of Russian history as well as current affairs. At the same time, these people reproduce the conspiracy model of the world but with themselves in the role of those with the power to create the conspiracy. In particular, they are sure that everything which is real (authentic, not fake) must be hidden and only a limited number of people should have access to this knowledge. Limitation of access to knowledge or other resources, for example

---

[28] See: A. Verkhovsky, *Politicheskoe pravoslavie. Russkie pravoslavnye natsionalisty i fundamentalisty, 1995–2001* [*Political Orthodoxy, Russian Orthodox Nationalists and Fundamentalists, 1995–2001*] (Moscow: Tsentr 'Sova', 2003), pp. 73–94.

[29] Interviews with three of these elders, including Nikolay Gurianov, are published in a book by a popular speaker of the ROC: A. Kuraev, *Segodnya li dayut 'pechat' Antikhrista'? Russkaya pravoslavnaya tserkov' ob INN* [*Is it Today when the 'Stamp of Antichrist' will be Given? Russian Orthodox Church on the Individual Tax Number*] (Moscow: Troitskoe slovo, 2001).

[30] T. Groyan, 'Nebesny angel. Plamenny molitvennik zemli russkoy za ves' mir' ['Heavenly Angel: The Flaming Russian Man of Prayer for the Whole of the World'] (Place of publication not indicated: Russky vestnik, 2002).

to the particular source of sanctity, provides it, and the privileged few and gatekeepers, with a desired halo of elitism.

This is why the celibate village priest Nikolay Gurianov was declared to be a hidden monk and *schema-episcope*. In 2000 or 2001, Tatiana Groyan, together with other *keleinitsa*, claimed to be a nun. Tatiana became Nikolaya, obviously in honour of the elder. It is not clear where they took the veil, but they definitely did so without the permission of the ruling archbishop Evsevii.[31] This way of taking the veil is perhaps a simulation of the phenomenon of secret nuns and monks in the Soviet period. An eparchial meeting in Pskov agreed that this rite was illegal and hence the women were not nuns. However, this decision had no effect; Tatiana Groyan, who moved to Moscow after the death of the elder, now calls herself 'schema-nun Nikolaya' and continues to wear a black nun's habit, at least in public.

Not only does the Life of Nikolay Gurianov in Groyan's version differ radically from other variants of his biography, she also ascribes fascinating miracles to him. Her memories about the *starets* contain impressive miracles which probably provoked the passionate response of Izbortsev detailed above. One of these narratives describes an episode when, shortly before his death, Father Nikolay was taken up to heaven:

> As Father himself witnessed, he came into the spiritual world of silence, dazzling light and wide open space. He was out of his body and enjoyed the divine delights of the Communion.[32]

Confrontations between fundamentalist believers who appropriated the house, archives and, to some extent, the grave of *starets* Nikolay, and their opponents, take the form of a sort of 'discourse war'. Each group is producing its own variant of hagiography, for example, the biography and miracles of the proposed saint. In some fundamentalist congregations, Father Nikolay has already been venerated as a saint, together with such ambiguous historical figures as Grigori Rasputin and Ivan the Terrible.[33] Interestingly, in their attempts to appropriate Father Nikolay, the people of the Groyan circle produce an icon which combines both 'private' and 'political' symbols of his sanctity. The icon portrays Father Nikolay as a monk standing with the icon of Grigori Rasputin

---

[31]   I. Izbortsev, 'Ne umolchim o vazhnom' ['Let's Not Keep Silence About Important Things'], *Blagodatny ogon'*, 11 (2004).

[32]   Groyan, 'Nebesny angel', p. 13.

[33]   One of these congregations is led by Father Alexander Sukhov (Leningrad oblast), who was excommunicated by the ROC in 2007.

and Prince Alexii in his hands, a little cat on his right side and a couple of birds on his left. Probably the birds appear on the icon not only because he liked to feed them, which must seem a strange habit from the villagers' point of view as to feed wild birds is an urban idea, but also because of one more story about his cat Lipa. The story says that once when Lipa was a little kitten he caught and ate a bird. Father Nikolay reproved him for his misbehaviour and the cat was so ashamed that he never again caught a bird for the rest of his life. The schematic, though recognizable, landscape of the island of Zalita depicted in the icon behind Father Nikolay possibly expresses the idea of his locality and authenticity.

For a while, it looked as if the mainstream Church had lost its struggle for this *starets*. However, recently, in 2009, 2010 and 2011, several large volumes of carefully edited memories about Father Nikolay have been published by respected Church publishing houses, and this is probably a sign that the ROC is still interested in promoting its own variant of this popular saint's portrait. The official Church media tend to present Nikolay Gurianov as an ideal parish priest. In the contemporary setting, where anticlerical moods are so widespread among believers and the wider public, the ROC urgently requires a positive image of a popular pastor, a role which fits Father Nikolay perfectly. It is no coincidence that the portrait of Father Nikolay, familiar to many believers, was put on the cover of the booklet for those believers who are still learning how to live a proper religious life within the church walls. This small book provides teachings about the regular sacrament of confession and the role of the priest in this Christian ritual and does not say a word about Father Nikolay.[34]

Conclusion

> Living saints pose considerable problems for a centralized, bureaucratic religious institution like the Catholic Church, for they obviate altogether the need for priestly intermediaries. The personification of the sacred center is a movement to the limits of ecclesiastical control, a control which begins to be regained only with the death of the saint and his or her transformation into a mute, hieratic, domesticated shrine.

---

[34] *O chem govorit' na ispovedi sviashchenniku* [*What to Tell a Priest in Confession*] (Moscow: Kovcheg, 2010).

When writing this, John Eade and Michael Sallnow had in mind the case of Padre Pio, analysed by Christopher McKevitt in their edited volume.[35] However, this observation can be extended to the Orthodox Church too. The charismatic authority of living saints, *startsy*, poses a challenge to the official Church, whose legitimacy is based, using Max Weber's classical typology, on the legal-rational type of authority. At the same time, the Church tends to represent itself as a traditional pre-modern (and even anti-modern) institution in order to stress its role as a vehicle for transmitting national traditions throughout the troubles that affected Russia in the twentieth century. This dissonance between real practices and their discursive representations leads to the credibility gap faced by the Russian Orthodox Church. This is probably one of the reasons why many people prefer to practise religion outside the church walls, without being controlled by a parish priest or a congregation. Very different in their political orientations and regularity of their religious life, all these people can accept an intimate and to some extent folkloric image of a saint who was attached to his cat and knew the future.

---

[35]   C. McKevitt, 'San Giovanni Rotondo and the shrine of Padre Pio', in Eade and Sallnow, *Contesting the Sacred*, pp. 77–97.

Chapter 8

Walking to Mother Teresa's Grave

Brian Kolodiejchuk, MC

... it is pilgrims we are, wayfarers on a journey, and not pigs, nor angels.

Walker Percy, *Love in the Ruins*[1]

'Pilgrimage, it seems, is written into our DNA', says Don Belt in *National Geographic*'s recent special edition on Sacred Journeys.[2] According to a Catholic Church document for the Jubilee Year 2000, 'pilgrimages symbolize the experience of the *homo viator* who sets out, as soon as he leaves the maternal womb, on his journey through the time and space of his existence'.[3] Indeed, throughout history 'human beings have always walked in search of new goals, investigating earthly horizons and tending toward the infinite'.[4] Pilgrimage, it may be said, 'is a global enterprise of deep antiquity and powerful psychological appeal'.[5] Not surprisingly, then, today as in the past, millions of people – around 300 million, according to *National Geographic* – go on pilgrimage every year. Among Christians, too, pilgrimages hold – and, it seems, increasingly so – an important place in the practice of their faith. Such sacred locations include churches, sites of apparitions, shrines honouring a saint or saints, birth places of the saints, the sites of their activities or of their martyrdom, or their tombs.

This chapter presents pilgrimage to the tomb of Blessed Mother Teresa of Kolkata (as Calcutta is now called) as an example of a contemporary, popular phenomenon that exhibits both traditional and contemporary aspects of pilgrimage.

---

[1]   Quoted in N. Shrady, *Sacred Roads: Adventures from the Pilgrimage Trail* (San Francisco: Harper San Francisco, 1999), p. i.

[2]   D. Belt, 'Sacred Journeys', *National Geographic Magazine*, Special Edition (2010), p. 24.

[3]   Pontifical Council for the Pastoral Care of Migrants and Itinerant People, *The Pilgrimage in the Great Jubilee* (Vatican City, 1998), 43.

[4]   *The Pilgrimage in the Great Jubilee*, 1.

[5]   E. Munro, *On Glory Roads: A Pilgrim's Book about Pilgrimage* (New York: Thames and Hudson, 1987), p. xi.

Early Life Pilgrimages: A Pilgrim Herself

Mother Teresa was very familiar with the religious notion of pilgrimage from her early childhood; indeed, pilgrimages were an important part of her faith and religious practice. With others, she visited Catholic shrines as an expression of her love and devotion and, no doubt, with the hope of deepening her religious experience. We could say, then, that Mother Teresa herself was a pilgrim before she became an object of pilgrimage.

In her childhood, Mother Teresa joined the groups that went every year to pray at the shrine of Our Lady of Letnice – a town some 50 kms north-west of her native Skopje. An atmosphere of prayer, singing and silent walking permeated these journeys with a religious spirit, but they were also, in a sense, a time of recreation and holidays. These pilgrimages, in fact, had a great influence on her vocation to be a missionary.

In 1928 Mother Teresa left for India and worked as a missionary teaching sister of the Loreto order for nearly 20 years. After she had founded the Missionaries of Charity dedicated to the service of the poorest of the poor, she continued to visit pilgrimage sites whenever the occasion presented itself. She was able to visit Fatima, Paray le Monial, Lisieux, Taizé and Our Lady of Guadalupe in Mexico, to name only the best known of these. In Kolkata, a sister describes trips to the nearby shrine of Bandel during Christmas week in this way:

> On any possible day Mother would arrange a bus or two according to the number of Novices and Professed and take us all to the Shrine of our Lady at Bandel for a pilgrimage-cum-picnic. We would always begin with the Rosary climbing the steps on our knees all the way up to where the Statue was. Then we were free to enjoy the food and drink, organize games, and Mother would watch us with so much joy and laughter.[6]

Pilgrim to Suffering Humanity

However, perhaps we can say that Mother Teresa became a pilgrim in another sense. With the firm conviction that Jesus is present in the poor and suffering, she went in search of the needy in those places where human beings were suffering. We might say that for Mother Teresa these were also in a sense places of pilgrimage. She took Jesus at his word when he said, 'Truly I tell you, just

---

[6]   Interview with a Missionary of Charity Sister, 11 February 2000.

as you did it to one of the least of these my brothers and sisters, you did it to me' (Mt. 25:40). With this vision of faith, she would go in haste to the places of natural disasters, of conflict or war or other events that were the cause of much suffering, offering immediate and effective help. Encounters with the poor were encounters with God himself and in this sense Mother Teresa herself was on a constant pilgrimage – she was a pilgrim to broken humanity.

Recognition During Her Lifetime: A Living Saint

Mother Teresa gave her whole heart and soul, the most precious potentialities of her person, to the service of the most abandoned, neglected and marginalized members of human society – in a word, she gave her best to the poorest of the poor. Though she herself did not seek attention or recognition,[7] Mother Teresa's love and compassion, translated into a tireless effort to alleviate the sufferings of the poor and needy, did not pass unnoticed. She received more than 700 awards and honours during her lifetime. But even more, it was the so-called common people who recognized her charity as the fruit of her closeness to God and called her a living saint.

It could be said, in fact, that even before her death, people made pilgrimages to Kolkata to meet Mother Teresa. She demonstrated heroic availability and patience in face of the continuous visits of people wishing to greet her and if possible speak with her privately. As one Kolkata priest testified:

> the daily pilgrimage of the people started whenever she happened to be in Calcutta ... My parishioner friends, some religious people, also non-Christians, asked me to accompany them to see Mother, to ask her blessing. It seems that the Gospel stories were re-enacted in those memorable days. The visitors met her on the corridor, touching her feet, receiving blessings from Mother and accepting medals and holy pictures. They felt so uplifted. The streams of people were on the increase, but she never showed impatience or tiredness. For her, all were [children] in need of some consolation, or other ... Her hospitality and availability were heroic.

---

[7]   Indeed, as she frequently stated, the constant media attention was one of her most intense sufferings.

Mother Teresa's Death and State Funeral

On 5 September 1997, Mother Teresa died at the Motherhouse of the Missionaries of Charity in Kolkata at the age of 87. The city whose name had become so closely linked with hers, hosted numerous dignitaries from around the world, including many heads of state. They came to pay tribute to this humble woman, whom they had esteemed for the difference that her 'drop' had made in the ocean of their world. Many of them had met her personally and were touched by her deep faith, selfless love and authentic living of the Gospel. Yet it was ordinary people, especially the poor, who paid her the greatest tribute. During the week of mourning, many thousands of people, walking hours to reach St Thomas Church where her body was exposed, came to bid farewell to the one who had been a spark of light, a sign of God's presence and love.

In her lifetime Mother Teresa had been a bridge between the rich and the poor. At the time of her death she became strikingly even more so, as a witness to the scene in front of St Thomas Church testified:

> The crowd on both sides was so huge, coming to see a lady who in the world's eye is nothing, but yet had the love of all those people because she radiated Jesus Christ ... I sort of looked down, and here was God's grace and mercy. It raised my spirits ... There was a beggar with his hands wrapped up; he visibly had leprosy and you couldn't see whether it was medicine or pus that oozed out ... Well, for over two and half hours, here is this beggar with leprosy, hands bandaged, hobbling along. Just behind him was a very rich Marwari[8] gentleman in a designer suit and a nice big gold bracelet on his hand and probably he had designer perfume. But here was this blazing contrast – a man of the gutter whom the world did not want to be around; on the other side, this very rich Marwari. The issue is that here was this contrast, rich and poor ... Knowing the Indian mind-set and culture, I don't know very, very rich Marwaris who would like to be pressed up against a man with leprosy, smelling, for two and half hours. But here, because of Mother Teresa, his status was gone, his position was gone. Both of them were sharing the grief with tears in their eyes, because they had lost someone whom they called "Mother". Probably both of them were not even Catholics, but here they were standing in the line, waiting to come inside.[9]

---

[8]   Marwaris are an elite group of people from the Marwar region of Rajasthan in India.

[9]   Interview with a close collaborator of Mother Teresa, 8 October 1999.

On 13 September, the government of India granted its distinguished citizen the exceptional honour of a state funeral. The prime minister of India at the time, Mr I.K. Gujral, spoke of the significance Mother Teresa held for the people of India. He said: 'I have come on a pilgrimage to pay homage to Mother on behalf of a country in grief. Mother has been a beacon of hope to millions of poor all over the world ... she was the solace of the rejected ones in this world.'[10] Pope John Paul II, as a sign of his personal affection and the deep appreciation of the Catholic Church, sent his secretary of state, Cardinal Angelo Sodano, to preside over the ceremony. She was buried on the ground floor of the Motherhouse of the Missionaries of Charity in Kolkata.

Her Tomb: Pilgrim Site

Immediately after the burial Mother Teresa's tomb became a place of pilgrimage for the many people who still continue to draw inspiration from her life and work. A report prepared in 1998 by the Motherhouse of the Missionaries of Charity summarizes the regular influx of pilgrims to Mother Teresa's tomb:

> The daily visitors include all kinds of people – rich and poor, young and old – of various nationalities and religions. All approach the tomb with reverence. Most of them spend at least a little while in prayer. Many sit for a time of quiet prayer and some spend long hours in prayer ... Masses are celebrated in the room by visiting bishops and priests and the faithful who accompany them – from all over India and from other countries. For the week from the anniversary of Mother's death to her burial (5 September–13 September) there are Masses celebrated or hours of Eucharistic adoration conducted throughout the day by groups of the [Missionaries of Charity] Sisters and groups from various Kolkata parishes.

Sister Nirmala Joshi, MC, Mother Teresa's successor as head of the Missionaries of Charity Sisters, comments: 'At the front gate of Mother House, Mother's nameplate is there. When Mother was on this earth it would show Mother Teresa, M.C. "IN" or "OUT", according to where Mother would be. But now it shows permanently "IN", for Mother is in to welcome everyone, available to everyone and for as long as each one wishes.'[11] Sister Nirmala further reflects on the many pilgrims making their way to the tomb:

---

[10]   Quoted in a letter from Fr. Christian Mignon, S.J., 12 April 1999.
[11]   Interview with Sr. Nirmala Joshi, MC, 1 November 1999.

The tomb of Mother has become a very important part not only of our Mother House, but also of the whole of Calcutta. Daily we have people coming and praying at the tomb of Mother ... The rich and poor, young and old, spiritual leaders of all religions and cultures, dignitaries from India and abroad, all come to pay homage to Mother, to spend a little time in prayer, asking for favours ... This has become a place to find comfort, peace and inspiration.[12]

Another MC Sister, a close collaborator of Mother Teresa for decades, reports on the influx of visitors to Mother Teresa's tomb:

There has been since the day of her burial, and continues to be, a constant flow of people coming to Mother's grave to pay respects and to ask for graces. They come individually and in groups, people from every country, religion and walk of life. They come on their own, they come on organized pilgrimages, and many groups bring a priest to offer Holy Mass on the altar near Mother's tomb. The number of visitors to Mother's tomb is constantly increasing, though the numbers vary from day to day depending on the liberty of the people. Public holidays and festivals, as well as Sundays, see a greater number of people coming than other days because the people are free from work and school obligations.[13]

A long-time assistant to Mother Teresa at the Motherhouse reflects on how people are drawn to God through the powerful example of Mother Teresa:

Mother said: "People are hungry for God and young people want to SEE God's love in action". The number of volunteers and visitors from all over the world that continued to come when Mother was alive and even now after her death is proof enough that material riches do not satisfy the heart's longings. Leaving aside the tourists, there have been thousands of persons who have come to Mother's tomb just to pray, or perhaps ask for a favour. Silence prevails and there is a feeling of being on pilgrimage rather than a tourist attraction centre.[14]

Prominent visitors to Mother Teresa's tomb have included: former presidents from Albania and the United States; government officials from all over India as well as from many parts of the world (for example, from Armenia, the Czech Republic, Croatia, Columbia, El Salvador, France, Germany, Great Britain,

[12]   Interview with Sr. Nirmala Joshi, MC, 1 November 1999.
[13]   Interview with a Missionary of Charity Sister, 22 February 2000.
[14]   Interview with a Missionary of Charity Sister, 11 February 2000.

Iran, Israel, Italy, Japan, Macedonia, Norway, Singapore, South Africa, Thailand, the United States, Zambia, Albania, Vietnam, Canada, Switzerland, Mexico, Australia, Tibet and Bangladesh); public figures and famous sports personalities also make visits to the tomb. Singers, writers, film makers, artists and scientists also come to pay their respects or to draw inspiration from her life and work.

Many distinguished religious leaders have visited the tomb, including Catholic cardinals, archbishops and bishops, and leaders of other Christian denominations such as the Dean of Westminster. Leaders of other religious beliefs, for example, the head of the Jewish World Congress and the Dalai Lama, have also visited Mother Teresa's tomb.

But the vast majority of visitors are the 'ordinary' people who felt that Mother Teresa was their advocate and friend, indeed their 'mother'. On average, the number of visitors to the tomb is more than 107,000 per year. On Good Friday; on Christmas Day; on 26 August (Mother Teresa's birthday); on 5 September (the anniversary of her death); and on 2 November ('All Souls') local people flock in the thousands. The pilgrims come on their own or in organized groups from parishes, prayer groups, movements, companies, universities, schools or agencies. They come to ask Mother Teresa's intercession for their needs, praying for healing, for light in difficult life situations, for success in careers or in school examinations; newlywed couples come to the tomb straight after the wedding in the church to seek Mother Teresa's blessing. The average number of Masses celebrated at the tomb in a year is 400–500. Sometimes priests come in large numbers to offer Mass. There is a weekly Mass on Fridays, offered especially for all the intentions written and left at the tomb. Even non-Christians come to receive the blessing with Mother Teresa's relic at this Friday Mass. Pilgrims bring rosaries, medals, statues and place them on the tomb to then take for their families and friends. Many people (especially Hindus) carry home flowers from the tomb as a blessing. No one goes away empty-handed; they always receive medals and pamphlets after their visit.

As Mother Teresa's tomb is situated in the Motherhouse, visitors can also see Mother Teresa's room as it was when she died. It has become a popular attraction. Recently the High Commissioner of Zambia saw the room and was both surprised and impressed; he remarked to a Missionary of Charity Sister who was guiding him through the premises, 'The greatest person in the world stayed in this simple room!'. In a small museum adjacent to the tomb, the pilgrims can see relics/artefacts that Mother Teresa used and learn more about her life, spirituality and message by means of a photo exhibition, books and other published materials, her inspirational words and even hear her recorded voice. Mother Teresa's tomb, as well as her room and the small simple museum/ exhibition, make a deep impact on visitors. To take just several examples from the visitors' book:

It has been incredibly powerful to be here and kneel at Mother's tomb.

I was deeply moved, and I felt a new intimacy with Mother (whom I knew and met often) and I experience a new or renewed desire to give myself totally to God.

I wanted to come and see her while Mother Teresa was alive but I just could not make it. But my heart is filled with joy that I was able to come and see her eternal light burning here, which would definitely change many people.

Came with a heavy heart but feel wonderful now after coming to you.

What a peaceful place. After seeing the Mother's room and the exhibition, a feeling came to my mind that she is somewhere here watching us and praying for us.

En tu casa he aprendido que Dios me ama, y ya no me siento sola. Gracias, Madre.

I found peace in this house.

This has been one enlightening experience.

I felt the presence of God.

I've learned what true love is and how to be and how to live before the Lord through Mother Teresa.

The legacy of serving the poorest of the poor and the message of 'love one another' will linger on down through the portals of history ... Today, Mother Teresa seems to be as loving and fresh as yesterday as I walked through this sacred place.

Proof to all generations that one soul can make a big difference to humanity. Thank you.

Mother Teresa is not history. My visit here has moved me and has challenged me for my future ministry.

I now feel and long for a strong desire to serve the poor in the spirit of Mother Teresa!

In addition, a number of other special visitors come to the Motherhouse and Mother Teresa's tomb. Among them are: consul generals, commissioners, members of the Legislative Assembly of India, military officials, international delegates of education and medical conferences held in Kolkata, study tours of businessmen, university students, schools and colleges, delegates from other faith conferences and Christian denominations, pilgrimages by religious communities and formation groups, superior generals, provincials, cardinals and bishops, sports personalities and celebrities like Brian Lara, and so on. There are also requests to dedicate a day of recollections by religious communities and individuals.

Following Her Footsteps in Kolkata

In Kolkata there is also a large group of volunteers who help the sisters daily in one of several centres for the poor in the city. These (mostly) young people come from a wide variety of backgrounds and religious persuasions. Some spend a day or two and others come for months at a time. But whatever the time spent, they leave enriched by their time of service and prayer. As one of their activities they make a pilgrimage on foot to several of the historical sites of the city connected to Mother Teresa, such as the Loreto Convent and St Mary's School where Mother Teresa was principal before she began the Missionaries of Charity; 14 Creek Lane, the top floor of a three-story building where the first group of sisters lived from 1949 until 1953; and Motijeel school – the site where Mother began her first slum school, writing with a stick on the ground under the tree. Perhaps this form of pilgrimage will be made by more visitors in the future and not only by the volunteers.

Other Faiths

As during her lifetime, so also now, Mother Teresa continues to attract people of other faiths. Not only Catholics or Christians visit her tomb; a good number of Hindus, Muslims, Buddhists, Jains, Zoroastrians, Sikhs, Brahma Kumaris, Bhahai and members of other religions, as well as those without any religion, come and are able to relate to her in some way, even considering her as a mother. A Muslim girl who had lost her mother came to the tomb to share her pain as she felt Mother Teresa is her own mother. A Muslim engineer came to clean Mother Teresa's statue and polish it because he loves her and wanted to show that in action.

Every year on 10 or 13 September an interfaith prayer service is held at Mother Teresa's tomb. Christians, Hindus, Muslims, Buddhists and members of other religions share their reflections on Mother Teresa, read from the Bible, Koran, Bhagavad Gita, chant prayers or sing classical devotional songs. Their reflections are focused on Mother's holiness, union with God, service to humanity and peace. To give an example, the general secretary of the Indian Sufi Society, Mir Rahman, explained his presence in this way: 'We celebrate Mother's birthday every year for the late nun was a saint for all religions.'[15] A local newspaper ran a picture of people at the tomb with the following caption: 'Visitors 5 September included the elderly, young, blind and lame people. Hindus, Muslims and Christians prayed at the tomb for peace and harmony in their own way and read from their respective Scriptures.'[16] After visiting the tomb, P.T. Vishwanath Sharma, India's ex-Minister of Religion (a Hindu), said: 'The real spirit of religion is service to mankind which Mother knew well. God bless her.'[17]

Process of Beatification and Canonization

Because of Mother Teresa's widespread and solid reputation of holiness and the many favours being reported through her intercession, Pope John Paul II permitted the opening of her cause of canonization in 1998. The formal investigation of Mother Teresa's life and holiness, the process of canonization proper, was the Church's discernment and, in her case, confirmation of the reputation for sanctity already established among the people of God. In the process there were three main phases:

---

[15] 'Prayerful India Celebrates Mother's 89th Anniversary of Her Birth', *Indian Currents* (6 September 1999), p. 61.
[16] 'Hundreds Pay Homage to Mother Teresa on Death Anniversary', *The Herald* (5 September 2000), p. 8.
[17] Visitors' book in Motherhouse, entry on 3 June 2006.

1. the inquiry or gathering of data (testimony and documents) in the Archdiocese of Calcutta where Mother Teresa died. Once the process began on 12 June 1999, she was called a Servant of God;
2. the study of this material resulting in a *Positio*, the detailed presentation of the life, virtues and reputation for sanctity; and
3. the evaluation of this study by a commission of nine theologians and then by another commission of cardinals and bishops.

The conclusions and recommendations resulting from all of this work were, lastly, presented to the pope for his final judgment. If the pope's judgment is affirmative and the person is deemed to have lived an heroic Christian life, then the candidate is known as Venerable. Mother Teresa's decree of heroic virtue was promulgated by John Paul II on 21 December 2002. From that date until her beatification she was known as the Venerable Servant of God, Mother Teresa of Calcutta.

The next phase of Mother Teresa's cause was the confirmation of a miracle that occurred through her intercession. A miracle in a cause of canonization serves as a sign of God's confirmation of the discernment of the Church. If there is some unknown reason that should disqualify someone from beatification or canonization, God would not answer someone's petition made to a candidate for beatification with a miracle. A miracle, then, is taken as God's confirmation of the positive judgment by the pope, based on the formal work of the cause in the diocese and in the Congregation for the Causes of Saints, of the widespread sense among the faithful that, in this case, Mother Teresa truly lived an exemplary Christian life. In fact, two miracles are required: one occurring after her death for beatification, and another occurring after beatification for her canonization. The cure of Monica Besra on 5 September 1998 was judged to be a miracle and paved the way for Mother Teresa's beatification which took place before an estimated crowd of 300,000 at St Peter's Square in Rome on 19 October 2003.

Besides being a formal requirement for beatification and canonization, the cause proved a unique and excellent opportunity to acquire as much information on Mother Teresa as possible. As the years pass, it would have become increasingly more difficult to obtain first- or second-hand information – especially to gather the personal testimonies of those who knew her. This task was both easy and difficult: easy because people readily cooperated by providing their testimony and documents, and difficult because there were so many leads to follow – literally from all around the world. Fortunately, after two years of diligent effort by a good number of people, the Congregation for the Causes of

Saints was presented with 83 volumes of testimony and documents, comprising approximately 35,000 pages.

Utilizing this abundant and rich material, I supervised the preparation of a *Positio* of about 5,000 pages showing with examples and facts how Mother Teresa lived the Christian (theological) virtues of faith, hope and charity, and the human (moral) virtues of prudence, justice (towards God and neighbour), courage (or fortitude) and self-control (or temperance). There were further chapters on humility, the virtues of the three vows of her religious life (chastity, poverty and obedience), and special gifts, with an emphasis on the phenomenon of 'darkness', as Mother Teresa called it.

Mother Teresa Center

One of the important projects that the Postulation of the Cause of Canonization of Mother Teresa began several years ago is the Mother Teresa Center. The Center (MTC) is a non-profit organization created to be a centralized and authoritative source of information on Mother Teresa. Its aim is to promote genuine devotion to Blessed Teresa and authentic knowledge of her life, work, holiness, spirituality and message through the preparation and publication of her authentic writings, preparation and distribution of devotional materials (booklets, pamphlets, prayer cards, medals) in various languages, handling permissions for the use of her words and image, collecting, preserving and exhibiting Mother's genuine relics and articles of historical importance and maintaining an official informational website: www.motherteresa.org.

At present, the Center maintains a museum next to the chapel in which Mother Teresa's tomb is situated. The Center also prepared a major exhibition on Mother Teresa's life, work and spirituality that has been travelling in various countries. It has about 80 panels plus various artefacts/relics such as a sari, copies of Mother Teresa's hand-written letters, sandals, and her prayer book. In the future, the Center will establish other public spaces (for example, in Rome) where pilgrims can 'encounter' Mother Teresa (for example, exhibition, video presentations and relics).

The hundredth anniversary of Mother Teresa's birth fell on 26 August 2010. There was wide interest in the centenary around the world and numerous expressions of appreciation, love and devotion shown for her. Many events were organized by both secular institutions and the Church: symposia, film festivals, cultural programmes, art and music programmes, photo exhibitions, novenas and special Masses. The largest celebrations were held in India, Italy, Albania and Macedonia, but almost every country has had some form of tribute to Mother Teresa. For example, in Beirut there was the unveiling of a three-metre commemorative bronze statue of Mother Teresa on a base two-metres high, in gratitude for 'her brave deeds during the Lebanese wars'. UNESCO held an exhibition on Mother Teresa's life as part of their programme in Delhi and Paris. Other government and civil institutions honoured her in various ways – from postage stamps and commemorative coins, to the naming of a train, the 'Mother Express', in India, which hosts a travelling exhibition on her life and work. The 'Mother Express' will have visited almost all of the big cities in India over a period of about six months, with many thousands of people having the opportunity to view the exhibition.

As can be gleaned from the above description, pilgrimages to Mother Teresa's tomb, as well as visits to her room, a museum and other sites directly associated with her life, exhibit elements both old and new. On the one hand, pilgrims arrive for one or even many of the classical reasons for a pilgrimage: to see a place where something happened, to draw near to something sacred, to seek pardon from God (in some cases by making the pilgrimage as a penance), to hope and ask for a miracle, to express thanks and/or love of God, to answer the sense of an inner call to go, to satisfy their curiosity (concerning what others have experienced), to break the routine of ordinary life with the hope that something new may happen, to reclaim lost or abandoned or forgotten parts of oneself, to make a vacation more interesting, to honour a vow made in response to an extreme circumstance, to prepare for death, to do something because an acquaintance did it and one desires to be among the privileged.[18] On the other hand, there are some non-traditional or very contemporary features demonstrated by pilgrims to Mother Teresa's tomb. For example, many pilgrims are non-Catholics and even non-Christians; faithful of many religious creeds come to visit and/or pray. There are also ecumenical and interfaith prayer services throughout the year. Another characteristic of many pilgrims is their desire to participate in the service to the poor of the Sisters and Brothers.

It should also be noted that Mother Teresa's tomb is on the tourist map of Kolkata. Thus many tourists come, some of whom at least, we may surmise, do not enter with a religious motive; what happens during their visit is known only to God and themselves. As a result, 'the boundaries between pilgrimage and

[18]   See J.D. Clift and W.B. Clift, *The Archetype of Pilgrimage: Outer Action with Inner Meaning* (Mahwah: Paulist Press, 1996), pp. 42–62.

tourism become blurred' in many instances.[19] My own experience and anecdotal testimony indicates that most people come with a variety of motives, including a combination of both religious and non-religious motivations.[20]

Conclusion

Perhaps no Christian since St Francis of Assisi has had such an influence on so many people of diverse backgrounds as Mother Teresa has had in our times. People of faith or of none, as well as tourists to Kolkata, take the opportunity to visit Mother Teresa's tomb. The plaque resting on the tomb has the words taken from the Gospel of St John: 'Love one another as I have loved you' (John 15:12). Every visitor to the tomb is able to read – and hopefully take to heart – these words. Mother Teresa herself would be very pleased if she and her work continue to help people draw closer to God and/or increase their concrete service to the poor, their 'love in living action', as she liked to call it.

Given the multi-cultural and multi-religious backgrounds of the pilgrims to Mother Teresa's tomb, it can rightly be said that the

> peaceful and harmonious mixture of peoples from all classes, ethnicities and races which gather together at the pilgrimage site can certainly be an image and foretaste of the ideal humanity of the future, one which is already beginning, but usually in much turmoil, conflict, resistance and even bloodshed: the multi-racial and multi-cultural reality of today's world.[21]

As has been noted, 'A visitor passes through a place, the place passes through the pilgrim'.[22] In various ways, a visit to Mother Teresa's tomb (as to other pilgrimage sites) to some degree at least transforms the pilgrim[23] and helps meet 'the basic human need to make a *connection* with something outside themselves,

---

[19]   S. Coleman and J. Elsner, *Pilgrimage: Past and Present in the World Religions* (Cambridge, MA: Harvard University Press, 1995), p. 214.

[20]   On this question see for example, E. Cohen, 'Pilgrimage and Tourism: Convergence and Divergence', in A. Morinis (ed.), foreword by V. Turner, *Sacred Journeys: The Anthropology of Pilgrimage* (Westport: Greenwood Press, 1992), pp. 47–61.

[21]   V. Elizondo, 'Introduction', in V. Elizondo and S. Freyne (eds), *Pilgrimage* (Maryknoll: Orbis Books, 1996), p. viii.

[22]   Cynthia Ozick, quoted in Shrady, *Sacred Roads*, p. 4.

[23]   According to Coleman and Elsner, the 'theme of motion signifying transformation is implicit' in the act of pilgrimage (*Pilgrimage*, p. 211).

some holiness or value which helps ground the pilgrim in a new being, in a new lease on life, in something which gives meaning and direction and which is frequently experienced as healing'.[24]

Pope Benedict XVI has pointed out that the 'lives of the saints are not limited to their earthly biographies but also include their being and working in God after death'.[25] Thus, it is not only her example that Mother Teresa leaves as a legacy. For people of so many different backgrounds and beliefs, her spiritual presence, intercession and guidance will continue to enrich their lives and a pilgrimage to her beloved Kolkata and the Motherhouse will be a privileged place of encounter, prayer and inspiration.

---

[24] Clift and Clift, *The Archetype of Pilgrimage*, p. 152.
[25] Benedict XVI, *Deus Caritas est*, n. 42.

Chapter 9

Reformulations of the Pilgrimages to Santiago de Compostela

Linda Kay Davidson

Introduction

The Compostela pilgrimage – in its development, configuration and resulting reconfigurations – has had both to depend on and to endure the ministrations of a variety of institutions, individuals and historical events. During the last nine centuries its popularity and importance have grown, ebbed and, once again, surged. And through this tumultuous development, the stresses of both outside and inside supports, in a kind of yin-yang of both collaboration and opposition, have created a unique phenomenon, which has borne fruit of international importance.

This pilgrimage has grown with such great abandon that it has been staked to hold it and hemmed in both to confine it and simultaneously to permit it to flourish, much like the garden tomato plant. The typical tomato plant support has a series of small metal horizontal hoops that grow larger in diameter toward the top, all held together with three vertical metal poles anchored in the ground. The metal piece shelters and shapes the plant when it is young, small and vulnerable. It supports the plant as it grows with three stakes that splay outward and upward.

The Compostela pilgrimage resembles the tomato plant and its support. Each leafy branch of the plant represents the unique pilgrimage journeys that ultimately bear the fruit of the individuals' endeavours. The stakes are the institutions that protect and support, and each – in its own way – tries to mould the pilgrimage. The first stake is the Church, which – through the Archbishop of Compostela and the Archconfraternity, for example – promotes, protects and interprets the spiritual aspects of pilgrimage. The second stake is the local, regional and national governments that are responsible for providing and maintaining infrastructure such as roads and security. The third stake is the local citizenry, individuals and groups that help sustain pilgrimage by devoting time, energy and money. In pilgrimage terms, the three fundamental stakes, acting in consort or in competition, hold the framework solid to give the pilgrimage within aid, protection and freedom to develop.

In this chapter I will first summarize the formulation of the pilgrimage and then turn to concentrate on the stakes of the frame and how, over the centuries, the buttressing of the pilgrimage has reformulated it. In doing so, I will also look briefly at external forces that potentially could have destroyed the pilgrimage. Then I will to turn to pilgrims themselves to see how they have modified the pilgrimage for their own purposes over the centuries. In doing so, I think we can discern seven reformulations of the Compostela pilgrimage within this paradigm, one of the reformulations resulting from external forces, a handful of others on the part of Church and State, and two on the part of the pilgrims themselves.

Medieval Formulation

To understand the process of reformulation, a brief review of the formulation of the pilgrimage will be helpful. The origin of the Compostela pilgrimage lies in ninth-century Iberia. From the tomb's discovery (Santiago Peregrino), to the Saint's appearance in the Battle of Clavijo (Santiago Matamoros), to the recognition of the Compostela pilgrimage as universally important – took less than two centuries. By the late tenth century Compostela and the pilgrimage, supported by the efforts of Church and State, were universally recognized as important, such that in 997 Muslim warrior Almanzor sacked the city. The eleventh-century Muslim historian Ibn Hayyan confirmed Compostela's importance: 'Santiago is ... one of the sanctuaries most frequented, not only by the Christians of Andalus, but by the inhabitants of the neighboring continent who regard its church with veneration equal to that which the Muslims entertain for the Kaba at Mecca.'[1]

Two of the stakes, Church and monarchy, collaborated closely during the medieval formulative period of the Compostela pilgrimage, among them King Alfonso II of Asturias who financed the construction of a church on the site.[2] Sometime after 1150 and the death of Gelmírez, the so-called *Voto de Santiago*,

---

[1]   Cited in J. O'Callaghan, *History of Medieval Spain* (Ithaca: Cornell University Press, 1983), p. 105.

[2]   For more on this, see S. Moralejo, 'The *Codex Calixtinus* as an Art-Historical Source', in J. Williams and A. Stones (eds), *The* Codex Calixtinus *and the Shrine of St. James* (Tübingen: Gunter Naar Verlag, 1992), pp. 211–12.

an annual tribute to the Saint via the Compostela church in the form of harvest bounty and booty, was brought about.[3] For the next five centuries, religious and secular authorities, keeping in mind the pilgrimage's ability to buttress faith and attract trade, collaborated in its support. Their main focus was physical infrastructure to support the pilgrims.

Both lay and religious people helped develop the routes. The twelfth-century pilgrimage 'Guide' in the *Liber Sancti Jacobi* names and praises seven laymen for their work in clearing the roads.[4] Domingo de la Calzada's and Juan de Ortega's road-building efforts in the twelfth century promoted them to sainthood. In the eleventh century, a queen of Navarra had a bridge built over the river Arga – to help pilgrims avoid price overcharging by local ferrymen.[5]

The routes' security lay in the hands of certain religious orders that patrolled portions of the Road. Local authorities and municipal groups, sometimes called *hermandades*, took a major part. In 1318 Estella's civil authorities spent weeks chasing down John of London who had robbed pilgrims sleeping in an inn.[6]

Churches and monasteries offered food and lodging, a tradition of charity that has continued through the centuries. When pilgrim numbers increased, there was a boom in building hospices, primarily under the aegis of the Church. The Cluny enterprise founded several in the Iberian Peninsula and throughout Europe for Santiago pilgrims. Monarchs and nobles founded hospices. Local confraternities dedicated to Santiago concerned themselves with charity for pilgrims.[7] Churches and confraternities also took care of dead pilgrims. Roncesvalles, León and Oviedo designated specific burial grounds for Santiago

---

[3]   In a later fabrication, King Ramiro I of Asturias is credited with having initiated the *Voto de Santiago*.

[4]   W. Melczer, *The Pilgrim's Guide to Santiago de Compostela* (New York: Italica Press, 1993), p. 88.

[5]   Mayor of Sancho III or Estefania of Garcia el de Nájera.

[6]   J. Sumption, *Pilgrimage: An Image of Mediaeval Religion* (Totowa: Rowman and Littlefield, 1975), p. 255.

[7]   Some of the earliest documents attesting to this are either undated or, perhaps, forged. Early writings have given the Cluniac monastic system much of the credit for the development of lodging along the Road, even on the Iberian Peninsula. This is not completely the case, as John Williams points out. More recent writings attribute the growth of the *caritas* system to the entrepreneurship of Iberian leaders. See J. Williams, 'Cluny and Spain', *Gesta*, 27/1–2 (1988), pp. 93–102. See also L. Vázquez de Parga J.M. Lacarra and J. Uría Ríu, *Las peregrinaciones a Santiago de Compostela* (3 vols, Madrid: CSIC, 1948), vol. 1, p. 331, for more information.

pilgrims. In 1128 Archbishop Diego Gelmírez of Compostela donated land to the pilgrim hospice for a pilgrim burial ground.[8]

Yet the fragile collaboration was fraught with tensions. The problem was to define the boundaries between what was ecclesiastical and what was secular. Sometimes Church and State worked together, as during the late fifteenth-century civil wars, when the archbishop of Compostela supported Isabel and Fernando. In turn, the monarchs later reconfirmed the *Voto de Santiago* and pledged funds for the Hospital Real.[9] Other times the princes of the Church and the princes of the palace were at odds. The story of the volatile political alliance between Archbishop Diego Gelmírez, Queen Urraca and her son Alfonso VII is one instance. Urraca and Gelmírez squared off, battling each other in a saga of double-dealing, on-again-off-again alliances, sieges and comic-opera escapes. This raw power struggle was fuelled on both sides, in part, by dreams of controlling the wealth and prestige generated from the Compostela pilgrimage. In another example, in 1366 King Pedro of Castilla had Compostela's Archbishop Suero Gómez and the Cathedral Dean Pedro Álvarez murdered because the king thought they supported Henry of Trastámara in the fight for the Castilian throne.[10]

During much of the Middle Ages regional princes competed, not as their modern counterparts do with powerful football teams and lavish stadia, but with lavish churches and powerful relics. This is the background of Alfonso X of Castilla and León's patronage of the church at Villalcázar de Sirga in the second half of the thirteenth century. In a clear case of relic envy, *Cantiga* 218 in his *Poems to the Virgin Mary* promotes a miracle cure at the expense of Compostela's

---

[8]   D. Webb, *Pilgrims and Pilgrimage in the Medieval West* (London: I.B. Tauris, 1999), p. 88. Also Vázquez de Parga et al., *Las peregrinaciones*, vol. 1, p. 360.

[9]   For more on this, see T.D. Kendrick, *St James in Spain* (London: Methuen, 1960), pp. 34–60.

[10]   D.M. Gitlitz and L.K. Davidson, *The Pilgrimage Road to Santiago: The Complete Cultural Handbook* (New York: St. Martin's Press, 2000), p. 349. In the 1460s, during the reign of King Enrique IV, Bernardo Yáñez de Moscoso, called by a contemporary historian the 'tyrant of Compostela', had already taken physical control of several Galician villages that were part of the Cathedral's ecclesiastical jurisdiction. Yáñez tried to get the Archbishop, Alonso II de Fonseca y Acevedo, to cede the villages. When he did not, Yáñez kidnapped the Archbishop and held him prisoner for two years. During that time, Yáñez also set siege to the Cathedral. His family tried to ransom him out of gaol, using Cathedral treasures, which provoked a bloody battle. A. de Palencia, *Gesta hispaniensia. Ex Annalibus suorum dierum collecta*, ed. R.B. Tate and J. Lawrance (2 vols, Madrid: Real Academia de la Historia, 1999), vol. 2, pp. 229, 231.

Apostle: a crippled, blind German pilgrim could find no cure in Compostela, but was cured in Villasirga on his return trip.[11]

In the eleventh century the Church orchestrated incentives for pilgrims, issuing indulgences for pilgrims to the Holy Land and to Compostela. Papal delegation to the Cathedral of Compostela of the power to grant plenary indulgence could date as early as 1122, but it is more likely a much later development.[12] The Church also encouraged recording and publicizing the miracles worked at Christian shrines. This is the context of the 22 miracles of Book II of the *Liber Sancti Jacobi* and of the '*Veneranda dies*' sermon for the Saint's day: 'The sick ... are cured, the blind are given sight, the lame are lifted up, the mute speak ... and ... the prayers of the faithful are heard, and ... the bonds of sins are loosed.'[13]

Thus, by the end of the twelfth century the Church offered transcendental rewards for making the trek: absolution, indulgences and hope for miracles. The monarchies were both supportive of the Compostela pilgrimage and envious of its renown, prominence and riches. Local resources helped develop security and amenities and in doing so contributed greatly to the prosperity of towns along the Road. The three stakes of the framework had held together and had forged a union to allow the pilgrimage to form and thrive, which it did through the fifteenth century.

Reformation, Counter-Reformation, Enlightenment and Pilgrimage

External pressures on the pilgrimage also affected its growth. Beginning in the sixteenth century, local and pan-European events bore down on the Compostela pilgrimage. In 1589 fear of Dutch and English pirates along the coast was so great that the Saint's bones were hidden away, and ultimately the hiding place was forgotten – something to which I will return later. On the larger canvas and with very broad strokes: north of the Pyrenees, the Reformation/Counter-

---

[11]   Alfonso X el Sabio, 'Esta é como Santa Maria guareceu en Vila-Sirga un ome bõo d'Alemanna que era contreito' (Cantiga 218), ed. W. Mettmann, *Cantigas de Santa Maria* (2 vols, Vigo: Edicións Xerais de Galicia, 1981), vol. 1, p. 682.

[12]   It is more likely that this did not happen at least until the mid-thirteenth century. Fernando López Alsina attributes it to the fifteenth century: F. López Alsina, 'El cartulario medieval como fuente histórica: el Tumbo A de la Catedral de Santiago de Compostela', *Pistoia e il Cammino di Santiago* (Perugia: Edizione scientifiche italiane, 1984), pp. 93–118.

[13]   'Veneranda dies' and 'De miraculis sancti Jacobi', in *Liber Sancti Jacobi. Codex Calixtinus de la Catedral de Santiago de Compostela* ([Madrid]: Kaydeda, 1993).

Reformation spawned a kind of schizophrenic relationship to pilgrimage. On the one hand, the Reformation called the thriving pilgrimage industry into question as it effectively debased the pilgrimage currency of indulgences. Whether these certificates were ridiculed (Wyclif in the fourteenth century; Hus in the fifteenth) or decried as nothing more than a Church income source (Luther in the 1520s), the international aspect of the Compostela pilgrimage was undercut – a kind of reformulation by disparagement, which in turn accounted for the first large drop in numbers of Compostela pilgrims, which reformulated the pilgrimage from one of the top three medieval pilgrimages to just another Catholic pilgrimage.

On the other hand, Counter-Reformation Europe supported pilgrimage. Confraternities in Catholic Europe promoted and sustained it. For example, in the 1590s the Chalon-sur-Saône (France) confraternity grew from 50 to 91 members, all of them pilgrims.[14]

United Spain defined itself as exclusively Catholic and Fernando and Isabel designed the final push against Granada as a religious war. The Inquisition, created for other purposes, soon became an effective means both of suppressing the reformist Protestant currents that were entering Iberia from the north and of censoring heterodox intellectuals. For most of the period between 1502 and 1974 Spain was officially a one-religion state, in which the Catholic faith was fundamental to national identity. The Church supported the monarchy and the monarchy supported the Church, and thus the Compostela pilgrimage would benefit by their mutual interests.

In this environment, Counter-Reformation Compostela pushed to extend its wealth and power. One target was to expand the collection area of the *Voto de Santiago* tribute from Galicia and some southern Spanish provinces to include León and the Castillas. This proposal was met with such hostility that it was not resolved for decades. While the 1612 decision was pro Compostela, the prolonged court battles had called into question two core elements of the Santiago canon: Santiago's appearance at the Battle of Clavijo and Santiago's having preached on the Peninsula.[15]

Additionally, by the early seventeenth century the Reconquest war was history. The need to rely on warrior Saint Matamoros was waning. Many believed that for the new age an intellectual saint, a poet and mystic, would be

---

[14]   Among the 91 members were 14 women. *Women on Pilgrimage*, trans. Christiane Buuck, at http://webcache.googleusercontent.com/search?q=cache:DDtXWWYG4qcJ:www.saint-jac ques.info/women.htm+santiago+confraternities+%2216th+century%22&cd=6&hl=en&ct=cl nk&gl=us (accessed 15 September 2010).

[15]   See Kendrick, *St James*, for a detailed study of the legal suits and counter-suits.

an appropriate patron and Santa Teresa de Avila was proposed as co-patron of Spain. Even though Santiago emerged victorious, the mere suggestion of another patron saint for Spain indicates an internal weakening of the pre-eminence of the cult of the Apostle James.[16]

Paradoxically the patronage conflict did not undermine the Compostela pilgrimage and the glory of the city. National Counter-Reformation ideology favoured continual investment in the pilgrimage's infrastructure. The Hospital Real was under construction in the 1520s. The Cathedral added cloisters, a sacristy and several chapels. In 1643, as part of the patronage conflict outcome, the Crown of Castilla paid 1,000 gold *escudos* to the Cathedral, which allowed for finishing the Capilla Mayor in 1672.[17] Carlos II (1665–1700) re-secured the *Voto de Santiago*, now termed the *Ofrenda nacional*, which helped pay for additional construction.[18]

At the same time, the economic chaos of the times widened the gap between the rich and the poor, creating a migrant underclass of beggars and thieves who plied the Road as false pilgrims. This provoked attempts to control them in Navarra (1520) and Compostela (1532).[19] In 1590 Spain's Felipe II forbade the wearing of pilgrimage attire and required would-be pilgrims to carry official documentation. Carlos III published a similar decree in 1778.[20] The threat of the Inquisition also diminished pilgrimage from north of the Pyrenees. When German Protestant Bartholomäus Khevennhüller visited Compostela in the last decade of the sixteenth century, he was arrested for not kneeling at the

---

[16]   King Felipe named her co-patron in 1618; Pope Urban VIII agreed in 1627, but by 1630 recanted and Santiago was once again the sole Spanish patron saint. The Cortes de Cádiz named her co-patron in 1812. For more, see K. Rowe, 'St Teresa and Olivares: Patron Sainthood, Royal Favorites, and the Politics of Plurality in Seventeenth Century Spain', *Sixteenth Century Journal*, 37/3 (2006), pp. 721–73. Kendrick's *St James* is invaluable in sorting out this process.

[17]   M. Chamoso Lamas, 'El pórtico real de la Quintana de la catedral de Santiago', *Cuadernos de Estudios Gallegos*, 1/1 (1944), pp. 44–58.

[18]   It kept the Cathedral Chapter 'wealthy and powerful and ambitious' (Kendrick, *St James*, p. 147). The bell tower was constructed from 1738 to 1750. Both it and the Obradoiro façade were designed by Fernando Casas y Novoa.

[19]   In 1520 King Enrique II of Navarra restricted pilgrimages, based on a fear of epidemics. A Bern, Switzerland, regulation in 1523 decreed that no Santiago pilgrims, travelling salesmen, and beggars could be allowed in anyone's homes. A similar edict was issued in Compostela in 1532. R. Plotz, 'Peregrinatio ad limina Beati Jacobi', in P. Caucci von Saucken (ed.), *Santiago. La Europa del peregrinaje* (Barcelona: Lunwerg, 1993), pp. 17–37.

[20]   Vázquez de Parga et al., *Las peregrinaciones*, vol. 1, pp. 278–9.

Apostle's Tomb.[21] In united Catholic Europe the pilgrimage had always been *de facto* Catholic; in divided Europe it was to be *de jure* exclusively Catholic. This tightening of the rules was the second of the reformulations: the goal was to make the pilgrimage into one carried out by only the right kind of people, those accepted by the authorities.

The late eighteenth-century Enlightenment, coupled with economic depression, war and political chaos, had by the early nineteenth century substantially diminished pilgrimage to Compostela. Carmen Pugliese half-jokingly remarks that Bonaparte's troops were the only people on the Road to Santiago in the first decade of the nineteenth century.[22] In Spain, divisive Carlist Wars saw a swinging between ideological extremes, involving, among other things, the proper relationship between government and Church. Was the State to be secular or mono-confessional? Was its role to embody and support the Catholic Church, or merely coexist with it? The importance of Santiago and of Compostela was again a bone of contention. In 1812 the liberal Cortes de Cádiz named Santa Teresa de Ávila co-patron of Spain. The *Voto de Santiago/ Ofrenda nacional* was abolished in 1812, reinstated a few years later by King Fernando VII, and abolished once more in 1834, as part of the *desamortización*, the expropriation of Church property. The loss of the *Ofrenda* income had wide-ranging repercussions on the Cathedral. Government financial aid and governmental help plummeted. An 1840 budget report of the Compostela Hospital Real asserted that without continuing funds it would have to close.[23]

Data about pilgrimages during the sixteenth, seventeenth, eighteenth and nineteenth centuries is scarce and contradictory (detailed numbers can be found in Appendix II).[24] That said, recorded numbers in the nineteenth century lead to estimates of between 90 and 150 pilgrims annually, and some Holy Years as many as 600 pilgrims. By the end of the eighteenth century, reports indicate that only two or three dozen pilgrims trekked to Compostela annually, with never more than 800 in any year. During the years 1802 to 1884 the number

---

21   V. Hantzsch, *Deutsche Reisende des XVI. Johrhunderts* (Leipzig: Dunker & Humblot, 1895), pp. 90–94.

22   C. Pugliese, *El Camino de Santiago en el siglo XIX* (Compostela: Xunta de Galicia, 1998), pp. 27–8. Her detailed study of nineteenth-century pilgrimage data is vital for the understanding of this century.

23   *Manifiesto sobre gastos del Hospital de Santiago* (Santiago: Imprenta de Campaña, 1841), at http://www.galiciana.bibliotecadegalicia.xunta.es/gl/catalogo_imagenes/grupo.cmd?p ath=100139 (accessed 1 September 2010).

24   The most reliable numbers are found in the Hospital Real's records, but the Hospital took in only sick pilgrims and only pilgrims from outside Galicia. Cathedral records are incomplete.

of pilgrims was reduced even further. In general, pilgrims numbered only in the dozens, with Holy Years counting perhaps 500 pilgrims.[25] Yet at the same time Compostela Cathedral officials noted special crowds in holy years:

> 1617: Day of the opening of the Puerta Santa: overcrowding of the Cathedral.

> 1628: The procession through the Cathedral was suspended: no one could move because of the crowds.[26]

> 1794: Architect Miguel Ferro Caaveiro made a note on one of his blueprints: so many people on holy days that only two-thirds of the people fit in the Cathedral.

The anecdotal evidence indicates that there were times when the Cathedral was completely overflowing. The records indicate a paucity of pilgrims. This evidence is not contradictory, but complementary. Cathedral officials had begun to use the term *pilgrimage* to include trips by local and regional people who came a short distance for a short time. The Church had effectively redefined pilgrimage in the direction of *romería*, local pilgrimage. This is the third major reformulation of *pilgrimage*, meant to put on the best face for the Compostela pilgrimage and Cathedral in those times of prolonged low numbers of long-distance pilgrims. In our tomato cage metaphor, the Church stake was propping up the pilgrimage in its weakened state.

Rediscovery of the Bones of Santiago

The mid-nineteenth century, seemingly the nadir of the Compostela pilgrimage, was also a time of important archaeological excavations. The 1878–9 work resulted in the discovery of bones thought to be those of Santiago (remember that they had been lost after the 1590s). A mere five years later Pope Leo XIII affirmed their authenticity (with the Papal Bull 'Deus Omnipotens'), and declared a special Holy Year in 1886. Shortly thereafter, in 1889, the archbishop reconstituted the long-dormant Apostolic Archconfraternity.

---

[25]   Pugliese, *El Camino*. The monarchs came – when they were in power: Isabel II in 1858 and King Alfonso XII in 1877. When King Alfonso XIII came to give the *Ofrenda nacional* in 1904, dressed as the Grand Master of the military Order de Santiago, his invocation emphasized the familiar Santiago-and-Spain-together theme.

[26]   M. Vidal Rodríguez, *La tumba del Apóstol Santiago* (Santiago: Seminario C. Central, 1924), p. 147.

The rediscovery of the bones was fortunate, one that the Church seized in response to its critical loss of revenue and the decrease in pilgrim traffic. As one of its strategies to attract more pilgrims, the Cathedral began to offer public lectures on aspects of the cult of Santiago, the discovery of the bones, and the Cathedral's architecture.[27] Along with the Cathedral's efforts, over the next decades there was a more concerted effort by civic groups to attract pilgrims. For example, Compostela's mayor secured half-price train fares for pilgrims and luggage fees were waived.[28]

For the Holy Years after the discovery of the Saint's bones, the Cathedral began a more concerted effort to have pilgrims register.

Table 9.1   Registered pilgrims to Santiago (1897–1920)

Year	Registered pilgrims
1897	965
1909	140,000
1915	97,825
1920	110,834

The numbers seem impressive, so let us look at some details. In 1897, 965 *registered* pilgrims. That same year, the newspaper *El Eco de Santiago* reported that by 24 July, 3,000 pilgrims had already arrived, some of whom had travelled on foot a distance between 16 and 72 kilometres. The 1909 number includes the first organized British pilgrimage since the Middle Ages. They travelled by boat, train and bus, walking only a short processional distance from the Plaza to the Cathedral. In 1915 and 1920, more than 90 per cent of the tallied pilgrims came from the Archdiocese of Compostela. The data demonstrates that in the early twentieth century the definition of pilgrimage continued its reformulation. The journey had been devalued. Pilgrimage now encompassed any visit to the Compostela Cathedral. In addition, the city had begun promoting non-religious attractions, such as, 'Galician-themed cultural events ... a soccer tournament,

---

[27]   The lectures were presented by Fidel Fita, one of the experts whose research and writings helped convince the Pope of the authenticity of the 1879 discovery.

[28]   S.D. Pack, 'Revival of the Pilgrimage to Santiago de Compostela: The Politics of Religious, National, and European Patrimony, 1879–1988', *The Journal of Modern History*, 82 (2010), p. 349, from *Archivo Histórico Diocesano de Santiago de Compostela (AHDSC)*, Fondo General, 1.33/490.

and beginning in 1916, a bullfight series'.[29] Pilgrimage could now be fun. The recent reformulation has been further reformulated to include entertainment and cultural events, a new dimension to a once religious-centred activity. It was becoming tourism. This enhancement of the pilgrimage experience in the holy city with entertainment and cultural events has continued to the present day.

Franco-Era Pilgrimages

Francisco Franco labelled his rebellion as a crusade, evoking Spain's history of Church and State united against evil. Newspapers were using the phrase 'National Catholicism'. Franco would rescue the Church–State from the godless leftists. The iconography of those years could not have been more blatant, as seen in Arturo Reque Meruvia's 1949 painting, which recalls Vigarny's sculpture of Queen Isabel la Católica in Granada. Sasha Pack noted that in 1938, 'Nationalist propagandists exploited [the Santiago pilgrimage] to the fullest extent possible. Buses shuttled tourists to shrines along the pilgrimage route as docents narrated stories of divinely inspired nationalist victories'.[30] In power, Franco supported the cult of Santiago and the Compostela pilgrimage. He reinstated the national *Ofrenda* in 1937.[31] He promoted group pilgrimages by the Falange, the military and youth groups. In the 1943 Holy Year there was a special chartered train pilgrimage from various cities to Compostela. The *Voz de Galicia* newspaper called the 1948 Holy Year celebration a 'harmonic synthesis of the military and the religious'.[32] That year an estimated 140,000 pilgrims arrived in Compostela, and, as the reformulated tradition allowed, most came by bus or train. One sponsored pilgrimage that year went back to the tradition of the long-distance, non-mechanized journey. According to Sasha Pack:

---

[29]   Pack, 'Revival', p. 349; from *Archivo Histórico Universitario de Santiago de Compostela* (AHUSC), Fondo Municipal, 1341, 1347, 1348.

[30]   Pack, 'Revival', p. 352.

[31]   His special envoy that year, General Fidel Dávila, presented the *Ofrenda* in Compostela with these words: 'Receive this tribute from a people ... bravely fighting to continue the *Camino* [Road] that you blazed. When the religious traditions and ... ties weakened ... Spain ... fell victim ... [to] ... secular atheism ... But faith could not disappear in the people so loved by the Apostle. For its defence Falangists formed legions and regiments of crusaders ... who proclaim you for their Patron and Guide'. G. Redondo, *Historia de la iglesia en España, 1931–1939* (Madrid: Rialp, 1996), p. 322. Translation mine.

[32]   *La Voz de Galicia* (12 June 1948), as cited in Pack, 'Revival', p. 352.

About one hundred Spanish youth – clad in Falangist blue rather than the traditional pilgrim's outfit – would walk the medieval route from Roncesvalles over thirty-three days carrying tents and supplies on their backs. In addition, 288 members of the Spanish army's mounted cavalry undertook a twenty-day march to Santiago de Compostela, stopping en route at Clavijo.[33]

By the 1950s an economically faltering Spain began to exploit its tourist potential as a way of revving up its economy, even though the desired influx of foreign visitors would inevitably introduce currents of liberal thought and behaviours that clashed with the Francoist ideology. Franco's government was aware of the potentially compatible relationship between tourism and pilgrimage, especially international pilgrimage, which could bring in more foreign moneys. By the 1960s the game plan focused on preservation and reconstruction of monuments along the Road as part of the initiative to encourage international tourists to explore Spain beyond the beaches. A huge advertising campaign attracted over 100,000 pilgrims for the 1965 Holy Year. The pilgrim-tourist reformulation still held: a Ministry of Information and Tourism representative reported in July 1965 that 5,000 pilgrims reached Compostela daily. Most brought their own food and left the city in the afternoon.

A fundamental conflict lay at the heart of these efforts and their results. Was the journey to Compostela meant to be a traditional religious pilgrimage or a form of tourism? Both the Church and the State struggled to have it both ways. Both sides were aware of the value of high numbers and both seemed willing to consider anyone who visited Compostela a pilgrim. The three stakes – Church, State and individuals – seemed willing to tolerate ambiguity to continue the pilgrimage's growth. I have found only one example of dissent about the new reformulation of pilgrimage: in 1937 the *Eco franciscano* contrasted pilgrims 'who made their pilgrimage with the fervour of sincere, old-fashioned Christians: 25, 40, 70, 100 kilometres on foot, some barefoot, with only bread and water', and 'the pilgrims – as we will call them out of habit – who have made their journey in high comfort, as tourists'.[34]

---

[33] Pack, 'Revival', p. 354.
[34] *El Eco franciscano*, 54 (1937), p. 364.

After Franco: The Road Connects Spain and Europe

After Franco's death, the *destape* was like opening the lid of a suitcase holding far too many clothes: they spilled out in every direction. Spain's traditional national Catholic sense of identity began to come into question. Spain saw itself as a confederation of ancient tribal cultures each with its own language and ways of doing things, and, paradoxically, as part of a modern Europe.

Spain received fewer than a million tourists in 1950, but the number rose steadily, reaching more than 34 million in 1973, and 60 million in 2007.[35] And Compostela? Both the national government and the Xunta of the Autonomía of Galicia collaborated in a consistent, ongoing and effective strategy to present Santiago de Compostela as an exceptionally important aspect of European culture. Not Spanish, European. Compostela received the following designations:

Table 9.2   Compostela's prizes and designations

Year	Organization	Recipient	Title
1984	Unesco	Compostela	Patrimony for Humanity
1985	Unesco	Compostela	World Heritage site
1987	Council of Europe	Pilgrimage	First European Cultural Route
1993	Unesco	Pilgrimage	World Heritage: Patrimony for Humanity
2000	European Union	Compostela	European Capital of Culture
2004	Príncipe de Asturias	Pilgrimage	Concord Prize

Results? Galician tourism has grown over the last two decades, by a factor of 150 per cent since 1990. Of the 5.7 million tourists who visited Galicia in 2007, 85 per cent entered Compostela.[36]

---

[35] For the 2007 data, 'Spain Attracts Near 60 mln Tourists in 2007-group', *Reuters UK*, News and Business Section (14 January 2008), at http://uk.reuters.com/article/idUK L1431282220080114 (accessed 6 October 2010).

[36] 'Galicia recibió un 8% más de turistas durante el 2007', *La Voz de Galicia* (1 January 2008), at http://www.lavozdegalicia.es/galicia/2008/01/02/0003119927729213484 4326.html (accessed 6 October 2010). In 2002, there were 4.4 million tourists in Galicia, at http://colindavies.net/Galicia.htm (accessed 1 October 2010). See also P. Ordoñez, J. Parreño and R. Piño, 'Rural Tourism in Spain: Natural Resources as Sources of Competitive Advantage', *World Review of Entrepreneurship, Management and Sust. Development*, 1/1 (2005), pp. 45–56,

The State marketed the Camino as a cultural treasure, a World Heritage site, and had no compunction about downplaying the religious aspects. State-sponsored secularization can be seen in promotional material such as the adoption of a 'Pelegrin' as the 1993 Holy Year mascot. The image was ubiquitous: on phone booths, in newspapers, on postage stamps, in advertising, on civic banners – and devoid of religious symbolism.

The government effort would not have been so effective were it not for the labour of a number of individuals, both clerical and lay, who had become energized by the Camino and had devoted their efforts to documenting its history, restoring its ambience and providing logistical support to its users. Priests like scholar-anthropologist and innkeeper Elías Valiñas in O Cebreiro; Padre Javier in Roncesvalles, who painted markers along the Navarran route each spring; Padre José María Alonso Marroquín in San Juan de Ortega, who served homemade garlic soup to passing pilgrims; the schoolteachers who opened unused classrooms to us in the 1970s for temporary hospices; the people in each village who took pride in hosting the few pilgrims who came by.

The informal support structures worked well for small numbers of pilgrims, but when the tide began to rise, it demanded more, and offered opportunities to the government, Church and commercial entities who appreciated the value of investment in infrastructure for attracting more affluent pilgrims. Franco had begun it in 1953 with the transformation of the Hospital Real to the Hostal de los Reyes Católicos, part of the luxurious Parador system. León's medieval pilgrim hospice (later headquarters for the Orden de Santiago) became the Parador Hostal San Marcos in 1964. The twelfth-century pilgrims' hospice in Santo Domingo de la Calzada was converted to a Parador circa 1993.

More modest pilgrims' lodging became available nearly everywhere, much of it as a result of finely coordinated efforts of the Autonomías, various villages' own groups, the Scouts, the local religious infrastructure, and newly-formed Spanish- and foreign-based confraternities. Tent cities, especially during holy years, were set up in various places along the Road, as in Castrojeriz. In 1974 in O Cebreiro we slept on straw in a drafty barn. Now the heated Refugio there houses 80. The change from dilapidated or simply non-existent pilgrim lodging to nearly luxury accommodation occurred rapidly. Take, for example, our experiences in Hornillos. In 1979 we slept on the church porch in the open air; the bathroom was wheat stubble in a nearby field. In 1983 we cohabited with a million flies on the floor of a half-ruined house over a sheepfold. On the site of that later

at http://www.environmental-expert.com/Files/6471/articles/6551/f471039122118516.pdf (accessed 21 October 2010).

demolished house stands today's pilgrim hospice with a kitchen, hot water, a lounge, and comfortable beds. All along the Road enterprising residents catered to pilgrims' needs, marketing food, lodging and paraphernalia.

The boom had begun, spurred both by State and Church. In 1982 Pope John Paul II declared: 'From Santiago, I launch an appeal ... to you, old Europe: discover yourself. Be yourself. Find your origins. Live once more those values that made your history glorious.'[37] But the aims of Church and State, while compatible, were quite different. The governments yearned for more tourism, financial gain, and unity with a secular Europe. The Pope was pleading for re-Christianization of a secular Europe. By the early 1990s, while the State pushed for higher numbers, the Church was pushing for more authentic Christian content of the pilgrimage. Its main tool was limiting the conferral of the *Compostelana* to only those pilgrims who had walked a minimum of 100 kilometres. To prove their legitimacy, pilgrims presented a credential with official dated stamps from each community along the Road. Since 1993, two stamps per town were required in a Church-authorized passport. Today, the dated, stamped passport is not in itself sufficient proof. In the Oficina de Acogida staffers now quiz pilgrims about their motives. If 'spirituality' does not rank high, the pilgrim receives only a certificate of completion of the trek. This emphasis is clear on the Acogida and Cathedral websites: '[The *Compostelana*] is only for pilgrims who [come] on foot, by bicycle or horse, who wish to do the pilgrimage in a Christian sense ... motivated by devotion, a vow, or piety.'[38]

In the 2010 Holy Year the Church tried to raise the value of the spiritual definition of the pilgrimage by requiring entering pilgrims to show their *Compostelana* in order to have access to certain portions of the Cathedral. Professor Steven Raulston observed: 'In May [2010], the line was long, but anyone with patience could enter through the Puerta Santa and follow a circuit that was limited to the *girola*, the chamber behind the bust over the high altar,

---

[37] *Acto europeo en Santiago de Compostela. Discurso del Papa Juan Pablo II* (paragraph 4), 9 de noviembre de 1982, at http://www.vatican.va/holy_father/john_paul_ii/speeches/1982/november/documents/hf_jp-ii_spe_19821109_atto-europeistico_sp.html (accessed 25 November 2010). Translation mine.

[38] 'Esta credencial es sólo para los peregrinos a pie, bicicleta o a caballo, que desean hacer la peregrinación con sentido cristiano, aunque sólo sea en actitud de búsqueda ... La "Compostela" se concede solo a quien hace la peregrinación con sentido cristiano: devotionis affectu, voti vel pietatis causa (motivada por la devoción, el voto o la piedad)', at http://peregrinossantiago.es/esp/preparacion/la-credencial/ (accessed 7 October 2010). Translation mine.

and the crypt. The alternative was to enter through Platerías ... to visit the nave and the Pórtico de la Gloria, but not the *girola*, bust or crypt.'[39]

While in the early twentieth century the Church labelled as a pilgrim anyone who visited Compostela, it has now rescinded that broad definition, reformulating again the pilgrimage to refocus on Christian spirituality. Local and national governments have learned the advantages of advertising the pilgrimage to the tourist world and they continue to bring international popular performers to hype the Holy Years. This is another instance when two stakes of the pilgrimage framework are at odds. How this dichotomy of aims will resolve itself lies in the future.

Pilgrimages to Compostela

In 1998, father and daughter Donald and Maria Schell made a pilgrimage on foot together to Compostela. Afterwards, they published portions of their personal diaries in a book entitled *My Father, My Daughter*. One day, Donald and Maria were overtaken by a French pilgrim. Donald wrote the following: 'We were moving faster as we walked with him. It felt good ... The simplicity of his conversation carried us along like his practiced, effortless stride.'

Maria's entry is this:

> The wind blew cold on our backs as we walked up the ridge. I had been feeling
> lonely and abandoned by Dad in his conversation with the Frenchman. I wondered
> if he had noticed how he had walked ahead of me to keep up with the man's pace,
> or how much they had spoken in French, a language I don't understand.[40]

Donald and Maria Schell were pilgrims together, but had different thoughts and different reactions. Individual and idiosyncratic variations in and insights into pilgrimage make for pilgrimages to Compostela. Plural. We must always bear in mind that each pilgrim and thus each pilgrimage is unique. As the metal tomato frame holds the plant so that it can grow, developing various leaves, branches and, finally, fruit, the support structure of the pilgrimage supports, but cannot mandate exactly how the particular pilgrimages will evolve.

---

[39] Email correspondence with Professor Steven Raulston, University of the South, Sewanee, TN, 7 November 2010.

[40] M. Schell and D. Schell, *My Father, My Daughter: Pilgrims on the Road to Santiago* (New York: Church Publishing, 2001), pp. 49, 52.

The stereotype of a Compostela pilgrim, the baseline against which we measure reformulations, was formed in the Middle Ages, when huge numbers of pilgrims arrived in Compostela – on foot, by horseback, in carriages, from pious monarchs to the truly penitent.

So said Margery Kempe in 1417: 'And so we abided ... 14 days in that land and we had such great cheer, high devotion ... and tears of compassion.'[41] And Domenico Laffi in the 1670s: 'Had not the glorious St James saved us by a miracle, we should certainly have been lost. So, we emerged from danger, having looked death in the face with pounding hearts.'[42] So said Nicolà Albani in 1745, reaching the outskirts of Compostela: 'I threw myself down on my knees and kissed the ground ... Singing ... I headed barefoot for the sacred city.'[43]

This combination – arduous journey, heightened spirituality – the ideal of the Church, is found in some pilgrims today. 1979: a 70-year-old man who limps slowly up a hill some 10 kilometres outside Nájera and gets into a car, helped by his wife. They spend the night in a nearby hotel. The next day, he returns to the same spot and walks 10 kilometres further, repeating the same activities as before. He does what he can because, he tells us, 'I am determined to fulfill the vow I made to Santiago when I was nearly killed in WW II'.

2010. A wheelchair-bound woman boots up her computer and accesses the Virtual Pilgrimage to Santiago de Compostela. She spends several days on the site, often reading in her Bible. Sometimes she prays.[44]

In a kind of parallel secularization of the pilgrimage milieu, there were those who went on judicial pilgrimages, having been condemned by civil or religious authorities. Others went for vocation, not avocation. The twelfth-century author of the 'Veneranda dies' sermon warns against fakes: guards, money changers, pardoners and beggars.[45] In Holy Year 1319 Roger de Bonito was sentenced to pilgrimage to Rome, Santiago and Jerusalem for murdering a bishop.[46] In 1188

---

[41]   'And so thei abedyn ther xiiii days in that lond, and ther had sche gret cher, bothyn bodily and gostly, hy devocyon, and many gret cryes in the mend of owr Lordys Passion, with plentyvows terys of compassion'. M. Kempe, *The Book of Margery Kempe. Annotated Edition*, ed. B. Windeatt (Cambridge: D.S. Brewer, 2004), pp. 227, ll. 3645–54. Modernization mine.

[42]   D. Laffi, *A Journey to the West: The Diary of a Seventeenth-Century Pilgrim from Bologna to Santiago de Compostela*, trans. and intro. J. Hall (Leiden: Primavera Pers, 1997), p. 46.

[43]   N. Albani, *Viaje de Nápoles a Santiago de Galicia [Verídica storia de Nicola Albani]* (Madrid: Consorcio de Santiago, 1993), pp. 225–6. Adaptation and translation mine.

[44]   'The Future? New Google Service Allows Virtual Pilgrimages to Santiago', *Latin American Herald Tribune* (8 September 2010).

[45]   'Veneranda dies', *Liber Sancti Jacobi*, fols. 85r–85v, p. 36.

[46]   http://www.internationalschooltoulouse.net/vs/pilgrims/motive.htm (accessed 1 October 2010). On 5 April 1445, Saint-Trond's (Belgium) magistrate sentenced Peter Tutelers to

kidnappers seized two knights of the household of the King of England who were making the pilgrimage and held them for ransom.[47] Modern corollaries abound – 1987: two Belgian youths, one sporting a hypodermic needle hanging around his neck, find themselves walking the Road to Compostela instead of being in a Belgian prison.[48] 1990: posters along the Road warn against false priests. 2010: two young men jump on their bicycles at St-Jean-Pied-de-Port and ride for a few hours. They check into a pilgrim hospice, nap a while, and then spend the rest of the night drinking in a town bar. They do this for 15 days. In Compostela, they go to confession, attend mass, receive the *Compostelana*, and head home.

Many pre-modern pilgrims engrossed in their spirituality also marvelled at the architecture, sculpture and art that they saw along the Road. Travel educated them. Like the noble sons of sixteenth-century Europe making the obligatory visit to the centres of the Italian Renaissance, or the Romantics' celebration of the Grand Tour, some pilgrims also combined their spirituality with tourism. The cleric Domenico Laffi in the late seventeenth century visited Compostela, Madrid, Granada and Cordoba, as well as Jerusalem. His contemporary, the Italian Zani Ercole, swung through Poland, Denmark, Italy, Portugal and Spain, including Compostela. Occasionally, in fact, the educational aspects of pilgrimage tourism predominated. In 1748 young Jean Bonnecaze told his parents he wanted to make the pilgrimage to Compostela as a subterfuge for his real desire: to go to Spain to study. They thought he was out of his mind.[49]

Confessions like this one indicate the beginning of a shift to what David Gitlitz calls the 'New Pilgrimages', in which pilgrims define for themselves what experiences their pilgrimage will include and what meanings it will have. Education is surely one of these meanings. The earliest study-tour recorded at the Cathedral may be this entry, dated 26 October 1916: 'On a study trip from the University of Granada, [we are] full of wonder and veneration in this

---

two pilgrimages, one to Rome, another to Compostela. His crime? Blasphemy, doubly bad because he committed it during Holy Week [E. Van Cauwenbergh, *Les Pèlerinages expiatoires et judiciaires dans le droit communal de la Belgique au moyen âge* (Louvain: Bureaux du Recueil, 1922), p. 35].

47 Webb, *Pilgrims*, p. 97.

48 From the personal diary of 1987 pilgrim Deborah M. Gitlitz. Used with permission. See also A. Bell, 'New Departures', *New Statesman & Society*, 3/82 (1990), p. 28.

49 In 1789 Jean Pierre-Racq trekked from Brussels to Compostela. Although there were nights that he had to sleep outdoors, he managed to stay in more than a dozen hospitals, convents or hermitages, including Roncesvalles, Villafranca, León, Sarria, Mellid and San Juan de Ortega. J. Bonnecaze and J.P. Racq, *Voyage de deux pèlerins à Compostelle au XVIIIe siècle* (Pau: Cairn Éditions, 1998), pp. 21, 35–40.

church of apostolic magnificence and ... faith.' It was signed by one professor and five students.[50]

The newly formalized structure that uses the Camino as a classroom is perhaps its most unusual reformulation (number six, if you're counting). An academic pilgrimage can focus on many subject areas because the Road is imminently flexible and infinitely rich. Since 1974, when David Gitlitz, I, and six others made the trek as a credit-bearing academic programme, other colleges and universities have been sponsoring educational pilgrimage programmes. On the whole, evaluations have noted the pedagogical success, and sometimes the life-changing effects, of these programmes. 1985: A German student made a bicycle pilgrimage for 'cultural and historical reasons'. He later returned to university and finished a PhD.[51] 2000s: Holly Alspaugh: 'I ... challenged myself ... going on a six-day, sixty-mile pilgrimage to Santiago. Study abroad was one of the best decisions I have ever made, because I have come back to the United States more confident in myself, as well as in Spanish.'[52]

Pre-modern pilgrimage was an arduous spiritual journey to a holy place. Its arduous nature made it a sacrifice. And for many it still is, but with a shift of emphasis that is the final major reformulation. In the 1980s and 1990s many pilgrims began to identify the pilgrimage as 'suffering', and measured the success of the pilgrimage on a scale of pain. In one example, a pilgrim's severe foot problems caused such agony 'that ... he sat down at the side of the road and began to cry, believing that his journey was over'. This pilgrim, however, got medical help and continued the pilgrimage, content that he could do so.[53]

Today's pilgrims have turned the concept on its head. For pre-modern pilgrims, suffering was an offering. For the new pilgrims, it is largely ego gratification. Pre-modern pilgrims had little choice in the matter. Today's walking pilgrim chooses to spend his vacation time on the Road. This has been made possible both by rising income levels and longer vacation time, between 30 and 40 days annually in Europe. As Gitlitz pointed out, for new pilgrims the emphasis is often the Road. For them it is not the Compostela pilgrimage any longer. It is the pilgrimage *to* Compostela. It is the going, not the getting there.

---

[50]   'En excursión de estudio de la Universidad de Granada, llenos de asombro y veneración en esta Iglesia de suntuosidad apostólica y de fe de cimientos españoles'. One of the students was Federico García Lorca. The registry volume is opened to this page in the Cathedral Museum Library.

[51]   Information from N. Frey, *Pilgrim Stories: On and Off the Road to Santiago* (Berkeley: University of California Press, 1998), p. 130.

[52]   http://www.ship.edu/Modern_Languages/Student_s_Adventures/ (accessed 4 September 2011).

[53]   Frey, *Pilgrim Stories*, p. 109.

Moreover, modern walking pilgrims do not have to begin at their homes; they can start anywhere they like. The Church, indeed, hoping to preserve some element of sacrifice and suffering, mandated the 100-kilometre-minimum for the *Compostelana*. But the further refinement in this shift from the day-tripper to the long-term trekker comes from the new walking pilgrims themselves. Those who walk more than the required 100 kilometres often see themselves as being more of a pilgrim. And while they suffer blisters, they also discuss them with pride as if they were a source of merit. Some walking pilgrims cannot – or choose not to – carry their own backpacks as they walk and hire someone to take them to the day's endpoint. Those who lug their belongings with them term those who walk unencumbered, *turigrinos*, a new composite which shows their disdain for those who would take the pilgrimage lightly.[54]

Conclusion

The tomato cage. Three support pillars: Church, State and the individuals whose efforts and diverse motives have sustained the Santiago pilgrimage during its centuries of development, a development characterized by diverse interests, sometimes competing, sometimes in tandem, and sometimes mutually supporting. Sometimes these interests have flip-flopped, as when the Church redefined pilgrim as any Christian who showed up in Compostela, and later required the pilgrim to have walked a certain distance.

The pilgrims themselves have not been shy at reformulating pilgrimage. Remembering that each pilgrimage is a unique journey with unique responses, all pilgrimages – from pious to capricious, from avocational to educational – are variations on a tradition formulated in the Middle Ages and reformulated over and over again to meet current conditions and the varied needs of the participants. The ninth-century pilgrimage seedling, carefully nurtured, contained, and supported in its frame, in its maturity has borne multiple fruits, tens of thousands of individual pilgrim experiences that in the aggregate today we call the Pilgrimage to Santiago de Compostela.

---

[54] Conversation with Dr Lynn K. Talbot, pilgrim to Compostela in 1974 and nearly annually since 2006 (8 November 2010).

Appendix I: Vocabulary for the Purposes of this Chapter

Albergue	Pilgrim lodging
Archicofradía	Archconfraternity, housed in the Compostela Cathedral
Cofradía	Confraternity
Compostela	City in Galicia
Compostelana	Official credential offered to the pilgrim at the end of the journey
Credential	A kind of passport for which pilgrims obtain stamps in each of the cities they pass through
Holy Year	When the Saint's day (25 July) falls on a Sunday: [every 6, 5, 6, 11 years] 1909, 1915, 1920, 1926, 1937, 1943, 1948, 1954, 1965, 1971, 1976, 1982, 1993, 1999, 2004, 2010, 2021
Hospice, Hospital	Medieval pilgrim lodging
Ofrenda nacional	Renaming of the *Voto de Santiago*, when it was renewed in 1643 by Felipe IV
Santiago	St James the Greater, one of the 12 disciples
Voto de Santiago	Term given to the annual donation to the Compostela Church, supposedly originated as a result of Santiago's appearance at the ninth-century Battle of Clavijo (see *Ofrenda nacional*)

Appendix II: Pilgrim Statistics

Seventeenth Century

Table 9.3   Pilgrims in the three decades 1630–1660[55]

Spanish [not Galician]	859	± 24%
Portuguese	191	± 5,3%
French	2,046	± 56%

---

[55]   Data adapted from E. Portela Silva, Historia de la Ciudad de Santiago (Compostela: Universidad de Compostela, 2003), especially pp. 256–9. See also M.T. García Campello, 'Enfermos y peregrinos en el Hospital Real de Santiago durante el siglo XVII (de 1630 a 1660 – Libros de ingreso de enfermos)', *Compostellanum*, 18/1–4 (1973), pp. 5–40.

Eighteenth Century

The Cathedral's *Actas Capitulares* of 1705 to 1777 recorded giving alms to 229 people, most of them priests and clerics. Only 29 of the recipients are clearly designated as pilgrims.[56]

Nineteenth Century and Early Twentieth Century

Between 1802 and 1884 11,608 pilgrims registered, an average of 140 annually. Of the total, 71 per cent were from Spain: 8,225 Spaniards, 3,383 foreigners. The vast majority of the foreign pilgrims were Portuguese, followed by French. Among the Spaniards, pilgrims came predominantly from León, Castilla, Navarra and Asturias. Galicians accounted for about 13 per cent of the registered pilgrims.

Table 9.4   Registered pilgrims (1804–36)

1836	Hospital Real	37 pilgrims	Hospital total: 3,286
1840	Hospital Real	25 pilgrims	Hospital total: 2,656
1804	Rabanal Hospice	32 pilgrims	Total pilgrims: 738
1832	Rabanal Hospice	119 pilgrims	Total pilgrims: 268

From 1884 through 1905, 4,910 pilgrims arrived in Compostela, 66 per cent of them Spaniards. Of the Spaniards, Galicians accounted for about 38 per cent. Seventy-eight per cent of the foreign pilgrims (nearly 1,300) were Portuguese.

Table 9.5   Holy Years: Numbers of registered pilgrims

1897	965
1909	140,000
1915	97,825
1920	110,834

[56] Data extracted from A. López Ferreiro, *Historia de la SAM Iglesia de Santiago* (12 vols, Santiago de Compostela: Seminario Conciliar Central, 1908), vol. 10, doc. 29, pp. 127–37, curiously, only five of the years between 1705 and 1777 record alms-giving for the month of July.

Appendix III: Vacation and Holidays, 1900–2000[57]

Table 9.6   Days of vacation and holidays in diverse countries (1900–2000)

Country	1900	1980	2000
France	23	30	36
Germany	18	29	42.5
Italy	24	35	41.5
Netherlands	5	33	37.5
Spain	31	30	36
Sweden	13	30	38
Switzerland	18	28	33
United Kingdom	20	28	32.5
United States	*5*	*22*	*20*

[57]   M. Huberman and C. Minns, 'The Times They Are Not Changin': Days and Hours of Work in Old and New Worlds, 1870–2000', *ScienceDirect: Explorations in Economic History*, 44 (2007), pp. 538–67, at http://www.sciencedirect.com (accessed 2 August 2010). I've altered the chart by taking out several years and countries.

Index